D1522155

The Lovemap Guidebook

Authored or coauthored by John Money

Hermaphroditism: Inquiry into the Nature of a Human Paradox, 1952
The Psychologic Study of Man, 1957
A Standardized Road-Map Test of Direction Sense, 1965
Sex Errors of the Body and Related Syndromes, 1968/1994
Man and Woman, Boy and Girl, 1972/1996
Sexual Signatures, 1975
Love and Love Sickness, 1980
The Destroying Angel, 1985
Lovemaps, 1986
Venuses Penuses: Sexology, Sexosophy, and Exigency Theory, 1986
Gay, Straight, and In-Between, 1988
Vandalized Lovemaps, 1989
Biographies of Gender and Hermaphroditism, 1991
The Breathless Orgasm, 1991
The Kaspar Hauser Syndrome of "Psychosocial Dwarfism", 1992
The Adam Principle: Genes, Genitals, Hormones, and Gender, 1993
The Armed Robbery Orgasm, 1993
Reinterpreting the Unspeakable, 1994
Gendermaps, 1995
Principles of Developmental Sexology, 1997

Edited or coedited by John Money

Reading Disability: Progress and Research Needs in Dyslexia, 1962
Sex Research: New Developments, 1965
The Disabled Reader: Education of the Dyslexic Child, 1966
Transsexualism and Sex Reassignment, 1969
Contemporary Sexual Behavior: Critical Issues in the 1970s, 1973
Developmental Human Behavior Genetics, 1975
Handbook of Sexology, Volumes 1-7, 1977-1990
Traumatic Abuse and Neglect of Children at Home, 1980
Handbook of Human Sexuality, 1980
Handbook of Forensic Sexology, 1994

The Lovemap Guidebook

A Definitive Statement

JOHN MONEY

CONTINUUM • NEW YORK

1999
The Continuum Publishing Company
370 Lexington Avenue
New York, NY 10017

Printed in the United States of America

Library of Congress Cataloging-in-Publication Data

Money, John, 1921–
    The lovemap guidebook: A definitive statement / John Money.
        p.   cm.
    Includes bibliographical references and index.
    ISBN 0-8264-1203-3 (hc. : alk. paper)
    1. Sexual attraction. 2. Sexology.   I. Title.
BF692.M57 1999
306. 7–dc21
                                                                        99-28248
                                                                            CIP

For the new Hopkins generation:
Jennifer, Geoffrey, and Michael

Acknowledgments

The National Institute of Child Health and Human Development, Department of Health and Human Services, United States Public Health Service has supported the author in psychohormonal research for forty-two consecutive years, currently under Grant number R25 HD-00325-42.

The American Foundation for Gender and Genital Medicine and Science contributed toward the cost of publication.

Christine Leov Lealand and Gregory K. Lehne have given permission to use excerpts from their writings and discussions.

A word of special thanks to Craig Dethloff of the Department of Classics at Johns Hopkins University for his help in locating Greek etymologies for the paraphilias subsumed under protectorship and rescue.

Thanks go to Sally A. Hopkins and William P. Wang for their meticulously industrious work on this book.

JOHN MONEY, PH.D.
Professor Emeritus
of Medical Psychology and Pediatrics
The Johns Hopkins University and Hospital
Baltimore, Maryland

Contents

Introduction

In the contemporary age of astronomy, the Johns Hopkins University houses the planetary headquarters of the Hubble Space Telescope. This remarkable eye in the sky relays pictures of the firmament that used to be unknowable — far beyond the farthest beyond. By contrast, it is truly remarkable that the Johns Hopkins University houses no department or division of sexology and sexological medicine.

As if to underscore this omission, the oldest book in the library of the Johns Hopkins Institute of the History of Medicine is a sexological work. It is a 1480 copy of the 1466 first edition, published in Cologne by Johann Guldenschaft, of *De Pollutione Nocturna* (Nocturnal Emissions). The author is Jean Gerson (1363–1429), Chancellor of the University of Paris and Dean of the Cathedral of Notre Dame. The content of Gerson's book is an examination of the spiritual competence of a priest to celebrate the Mass after having had a wet dream (oneirogmus) the previous night. The impurity of the dream lay not so much in the loss of semen as in the erotic ideation and imagery that accompanied the loss.

The ideation and imagery of the wet dream is one of the manifest forms of what, in this *Guidebook,* I have called the lovemap. The lovemap may manifest itself also in masturbation fantasies or in daydreams and reveries with or without culminating in orgasm. It may also be enacted in practice with a partner.

Lovemaps exist synchronously in the mind and the brain (the mind-brain). They may or may not be orthodox and in conformity with a preordained dictate. Some are malignantly pathological, as is the case in assaultive rape, erotic self-asphyxiation, and serial lust murder. They may be associated with diagnosable brain pathology, though on the basis of today's sexological technology this association is commonly not recognized. Whether conventional or pathological, a lovemap is typically resistant to change, with or without intervention. Medications have proved beneficial, however, in bringing severely pathological lovemaps under some degree of control and in preventing relapse.

In Gerson's day, even the conventional lovemap of man-woman eroticism in the wet dream of a priest was considered to be a temptation of the devil. The priestly ideal was chastity and abstinence. He should resist temptation with righteousness. Righteousness required confession, remorse, prayer, and penalty. Penalties included fasting, renunciation of other carnal comforts, and self-flagellation. In those cases in which the tortures of the Inquisition forced a false confession of a copulatory pact with the devil and his demons, the punishment was death by burning in order to save the soul from the damnation of the flesh. A confession of a sexual pact with the devil was proof of heresy and witchcraft, for which reason Christian women by the hundreds of thousands were burned alive. Gerson directed the heresy trial of John Huss (1369–1415) and voted to have him burned at the stake.

Should Jean Gerson happen to find himself reincarnated as a juror in an American courtroom of the present day, he would not be confronted by serious culture shock, despite the passage of six centuries. The explanation lies in the similarity between the theological sexology of Gerson's era and the legal sexology of a sex offender trial today. At both extremes of the six centuries, the expression of sexuality is, by fiat, declared to be voluntarily motivated and its control a personal responsibility. If sexuality is not monogamous and procreative, it requires confession, repentance, and remorse as a sin or a crime, and it is subject to chastisement and punishment. Simply to be accused of sexual misconduct is tantamount to being convicted and condemned.

The lovemap predicament of a sex offender could be handled differently. Sex offending could be used as a call to arms to leave the sexology of the fifteenth century and to embark on a scientific and medical sexology for the third millennium, up front and out in the open. This is the way that will lead to an understanding of the development of the human lovemap, how it goes awry, and how it can be prevented from going awry. Prevention is a public health issue and is the key. Otherwise, pathological lovemaps spread from each generation to the next like an exponentially expanding epidemic, at terrible cost to the individual and to the society.

Maybe the era of the ending of the second millennium has a chance to leave its positive mark on history by becoming known as the era that spawned a National Sexological Institute as a new branch of the National Institutes of Health. This volume, *The Lovemap Guidebook*, is well suited to be its blueprint. The American citizenry has shown its readiness to advance. Let it be hoped that our leaders will hear us.

The Lovemap Guidebook sums up twenty years of work in the science and theory of lovemaps. *Lovemap* is a term that first appeared in print in the proceedings of an Australian national conference in 1981. I had coined the term earlier for use in human sexology lectures at The Johns Hopkins University and School of Medicine. I needed a word for the entity, whatever it may eventually be proved to be, that directs and sometimes misdirects the affairs of Eros and of lust in the mind and brain (the mindbrain).

This book is written so as to appeal to the reader with a personal curiosity about lovemaps in everyday life and relationships, as well as to the professional and academic reader. It is a scientific book but, unlike many textbooks, is not overloaded with bibliographic documentation that interrupts the flow of the meaning. As well as being scientific, the book is humanistic. It uses historical and transcultural data as well as laboratory and clinical data, and it looks at historical, ethical, legal, and religious issues as well as issues that are biomedical and evolutionary. It is mostly about the human species, but does not neglect relevant evidence from other species.

The second part of the book delves more deeply than the first half into abnormal lovemaps. In the lingo of "Personals" advertisements in the print media and on the Internet, lovemap anomalies are often known as fetishes or kinks. In colloquial and legal language, they are named deviancies or perversions. Biomedically, they are classified as paraphilias. It is a special feature of the book that the origin of the paraphilias is examined phylogenetically as well as ontogenetically — in other words, from the point of view of paraphilias in the evolution of the human species and of paraphilias in the development of particular individuals.

The epistemic postulate on which this book is based is scientific impartiality and nonjudgmentalism. That is the only way to obtain data that are potentially self-incriminating and subject to social condemnation. For the same reason, the concepts of personal motivation and moral blameworthiness are not used as causal explanations of the paraphilias. A genuinely causal explanation still requires political commitment and funding if it is eventually to be found. Then prevention should be possible and cure effective rather than palliative.

With the help of a detailed index, the reader is able to locate information in response to the following questions:

- How do lovemaps develop from conception to maturity?
- How much of lovemap development is phylogenetic, i.e., preordained by our being members of our species?
- Is there a connection between the evolution of lovemaps and the evolution of language?
- How much of lovemap development is ontogenetic, i.e., determined by our individual development?
- How similar and how different are the lovemaps of boys and girls, men and women?
- How much is known about the multiple and sequential determinants of lovemaps, e.g., genetic, hormonal, and social determinants?
- What makes some lovemaps sexually underpowered and others over-powered?
- What makes some lovemaps kinky or paraphilic?
- What are the religious and legal histories of lovemaps?
- What are the transcultural similarities and differences between lovemaps?
- Can lovemaps be controlled voluntarily?
- Do punishment and imprisonment cure lovemap maladies, e.g., paraphilias?
- What are the most egregious myths about lovemaps?
- What can be learned from other species?
- What are the evolutionary precursors of the paraphilias?
- Biomedically, what are the treatments for paraphilias?
- Who draws the dividing line between normal and abnormal lovemaps, and what are the criteria?

The book contains an extensive definition of terms; it is virtually a dictionary of the paraphilias. There are forty or more named paraphilias, many of which are not listed in standard dictionaries, textbooks, or diagnostic manuals, including *DSM-IV.*

The societal and economic cost of lovemaps gone awry is incalculable. Their political consequences may be enormous, especially if paraphilic lovemaps are dealt with only as moral and legal improprieties or as crimes that lack a scientific explanation or the research needed to find one. *The Lovemap Guidebook* is, therefore, a timely book.

JOHN MONEY, PH.D.
January 29, 1999

1

Polarization: History and Doctrine

Biology and Social Construction
Dualism: The Flesh and the Spirit
Voluntary Responsibility
Criterion Standard
Sex and Sexuality: Good and Bad
Proceptivity: Courtship
Ethology of Courtship
Proceptive Morbidity
Nose, Eyes, and Skin
Grooming
The Cerebral-Sacral Connection
Juvenile Sexuality

Biology and Social Construction

There is a no-man's land in today's sexology, with snipers on both sides. On one side are the forces of uncompromising biological determinism. On the other side are the forces of uncompromising social constructionism. Those who roam in the no-man's zone are attacked by biological determinists for veering toward social constructionism and by social constructionists for veering toward biological determinism. Among biological determinists, the extremists lay their bets on genetics and molecular biology as the sole determinants of some part or other of human sexual behavior, whereas the extremists of social constructionism lay their bets on social and political determinants, exclusively. They follow Michel Foucault (1978).

Both sides are caught in a Catch-22 on the issue of freely informed consent or voluntary choice. Biological determinists do not propose a biological determinant of voluntary choice which must, therefore, be construed as a nonbiological determinant of at least some part of human behavior. Likewise, social constructionists do not propose a socially constructed determinant of voluntary choice, from which one must construe conversely that some part of human behavior is not socially constructed.

There is no escape from the dilemma of voluntary choice except to allow that, as common sense dictates, it is both biologically and socially constructed. Together, both play a role in determining human behavior and, in addition, the ideation and the imagery that may precede or accompany behavior. One does not need to take sides in the biology/social-constructionism debate, nor in the nature/nurture debate to which it belongs. The truth is that nature needs nurture and vice versa. So also, biology needs social construction and vice versa.

In the rhetoric of social constructionism, the so-called medical model is one of the prime biological targets. There would be no psychological or psychosexual pathologies, according to the constructionist argument, if the medical model of pathology were abandoned. Instead, there would be only variations of normality. Carried to its logical extreme, this line of reasoning arrives at the conclusion that, in human sexuality, nothing between consenting adults is abnormal. To maintain this fiction, socially condemned sexual behavior is classified not as sexual at all, but as coercion or violence. Offenders are relegated to the criminal justice system.

Human sexuality is not bimodally distributed like two scoops of ice cream, one vanilla and the other chocolate, one good and the other bad, or one normal and the other abnormal. On the contrary, human sexuality is distributed on a series of continua, like spokes through the axle of a wheel, each ranging from recreational to pathological, with multiple gradations in between.

The difference between bimodal thinking and continuum thinking is especially significant with respect to the kinds of sexuality that are known popularly as kinky, legally as perverted, and biomedically as paraphilic. Paraphilic sexuality may be innocuously recreational at one end of the graded scale; whereas at the other end, it is morbidly pathological and perhaps criminal. Many people misprize this principle of degrees as, for example, in the case of recreational versus pathological sadomasochism (see chap. 2). Instead, they erroneously use the term *paraphilia* as always signifying pathology. The true mark of pathology in a paraphilia is the extent of its fixatedness, exclusivity, and compulsiveness. The principle that paraphilic sexuality of any type ranges, by definition, from the minor to the major ends of a graduated scale is so little understood among today's sexologists, as well as among the public at large, that it needs to be drawn to the reader's attention here at the outset of this book.

Dualism: The Flesh and the Spirit

THE DIVISION BETWEEN sexual practices that are societally tolerated and those that are not may very well have had its roots long before the dawn of recorded history, in a stone-aged religious doctrine of the dualism of opposites. In ancient Chinese wisdom, this dualism is formulated as the polarity of the yin and the yang. The yin is feminine, and the yang is masculine. The yin is cool, dark, weak, and passive. The yang is warm, bright, strong, and dynamic. The yin and the yang are not adversarial, but reciprocal halves of the same whole.

By contrast, the ancient lineage of the dualistic doctrine of two polarized halves at war with one another lies far from China, in the region to the north and east of the Mediterranean basin into which so-called Aryan tribal culture diffused in prehistoric times. Eventually, the Aryans spread their prototypic Indo-European language and their dualistic religious doctrine across India, Persia, Greece, and western and northern Europe.

Oral history, as compared with written documents, has a brief half life. The Vedic scriptures of Hindu India are among the oldest surviving accounts of the Aryan religious tradition of dualism. The gods of the Vedic pantheon are representative of the principle of destruction as well as the principle of preservation and protection. They are responsible for both the evil and the good that befalls humankind.

Under the tutelage of Plato in the fourth century B.C. and for centuries to come, prototypic Aryan dualism became transformed from mystical doctrine regarding the unfathomable dualism of the gods to rational doctrine regarding the metaphysical duality of ultimate reality versus reality that is knowable.

Platonic rational dualism encountered Persian mystical dualism after Alexander the Great's conquest of Persia in the second century B.C. Persian religious dualism was a centuries old legacy from Zoroaster, also known as Zarathustra. Zoroastrian dualism of good and evil, the deity and the devil, heaven and hell, angels and demons, eventually penetrated the Hellenistic philosophies of Gnosticism and Neo-Platonism from the second to the fourth centuries A.D. Syncretized with Old Testament theology, Hellenistic dualism thenceforth had a formative influence on the development of early Christian doctrine in Alexandria and other centers of scholarship in Asia Minor. The version of dualism in Neo-Platonism was that the soul descended into corporeality as a consequence of having been ensnared by its own concupiscence and desire. Hence, the injunction to abstain from, for example, flesh, wine, and sexual intercourse.

Hellenistic Gnosticism dualized a supreme being and a subordinate demiurge responsible for the existence of the world. Correspondingly, it dualized light and darkness, spiritual and material, and good and evil. Gnostics were subdivided into those who had received the divine spark of enlightenment and those who had not. Full enlightenment required a life of ascetic renunciation of sex, marriage, and procreation.

The dualism of secular Gnosticism became assimilated into the dualism of Hellenistic Christian Gnosticism. Although religious Gnosticism did not survive the adoption of Christianity as the state religion of Rome and Byzantium in the fourth century A.D., the Gnostic doctrine of dualism survived in Christian theology. The direct link between Gnostic and Christian dualism was by way of Manicheanism through the theology of Saint Augustine in the fifth century A.D.

The founder of Manicheanism was Mani (A.D. 215–76). Babylonian by birth, Mani was, by upbringing, a member of a Jewish Christian Baptist sect. He was also a spell-binding preacher and missionary. As in Gnosticism, in Manichean dualism redemption was not by the grace of God but by personal renunciation of the evils of the flesh. This was possible only for the enlightened, the *electi*.

Others, the *catechumeni*, were condemned to indulge in the material pleasures of the flesh.

As a religious cult, Manicheanism claimed the youthful Augustine (A.D. 354–430) as one of its scholars. After eight years, he converted to Christianity and left Milan to return to his homeland in north Africa. There he became Bishop of Hippo. According to his autobiographical *Confessions*, he struggled mightily with the ungodliness of concupiscent desire. In his writings, he locked the dualism of Manichean and Gnostic doctrine into Christian theology, to which he added the new doctrine of original sin. The curse of original sin was to have been born of woman as a product of carnal congress. The achievement of godliness required renunciation of carnality and other indulgences of the flesh. Christian doctrine and practice ever since have borne the mark of Augustinian dualism.

The dualism of the flesh and the spirit in Christian doctrine and its antecedents has permeated the secular doctrines of Christendom. For example, it separates the material sciences from the life sciences. In medicine, it separates organic from psychogenic etiology and, in sexology, biological from sociological explanations.

Voluntary Responsibility

LEGAL DOCTRINE IS premised on the dualism of guilty and not guilty. Guilty equates with evil, the devil, demons, and sin. Not guilty equates with righteousness, godliness, and redemption from sin. The law is judgmental. Legal judgmentalism is premised on the doctrine of universal free will and voluntary responsibility for all of one's own personal conduct. The one exception is that of the narrowly defined M'Naghten rule of legal insanity, which means being incapable of knowing right from wrong.

Forensic sexology is a junior offspring of forensic psychiatry and psychology. Like its parents, it came into existence as a captive slave of forensic judgmentalism. Within the judicial system, forensic sexology is discredited unless it subscribes to the legal fiction of personal moral responsibility for every manifestation, voluntary or otherwise, of one's own sexuality.

The legal doctrine of moral responsibility is tantamount to a doctrine of causality, namely that the cause of one's sexual behavior, as well as its control, is voluntarily motivated and determined. This is a judgmental explanation that dispenses with the nonjudgmental impartiality of scientific determinism. The philosophy of judgmental determinism is embedded not only in the law, but also in the idiom of the vernacular language where it is encoded into everyday moral philosophy. Judgmentalism is so pervasive that, although on trial for his life, a sex offender in most instances has no other idiom with which to explain himself/herself. Experts in sexology are likewise captives of the vernacular. It requires vigilant effort and special training to take even a routine sexological history without using expressions that imply judgmentalism and moral responsibility.

The philosophy of judgmentalism has had a stealthy effect on sexology by separating sexuality into two divisions: the one politically correct, good, and moral, and the other politically incorrect, bad, and immoral, if not downright criminal. To maintain the facade of scientific objectivity, moral and immoral are generally equated with normal and abnormal, respectively. Changing the terminology may conceal judgmentalism, but it does not get rid of it, for there are two meanings of normal, the one numerical and statistical and the other ideological and judgmental. In everyday usage, being sexually normal means being, if not ideal, then acceptable to those who exercise the power of enforcement. There is, however, no absolute criterion. What is normal and abnormal varies according to time and place, historically and transculturally.

Criterion Standard

LIKE ALL BRANCHES of knowledge, sexology is shaped by its time and place and, in turn, reshapes its time and place. At the end of the second millennium and in the realms of Christendom and Islam, sexology's position relative to established dogma is similar to that of astronomy in the sixteenth century before Copernicus ushered in the heliocentric era or of biology in the nineteenth century before Darwin ushered in the evolutionary era. Freud notwithstanding, sexology as a science has not yet found its Copernicus or its Darwin. Consequently, sexology is still a protoscience, held captive by a dualistic doctrine of sexuality that is either good or bad, virtuous or sinful. Good sexuality belongs academically to sex education, therapy and research, whereas bad sexuality is relegated to criminology and misdemeanor. It is relabeled as violence, aggression, and the abuse of power. Some bad sexuality is relegated also to infectious disease or to the recently named "epidemic" of teenaged pregnancy.

It goes without saying that there is no absolute and universal criterion that separates normal from abnormal sexuality, so also good from bad sexuality. The line of demarcation is a matter of the politics of power, not of the rationality of science. To illustrate, it was political clout, not reason, that condemned to failure the legitimation of the sexuality of gays and lesbians in the military, as promised by Presidential candidate Bill Clinton. The political compromise of "don't ask, don't tell" notwithstanding, the military continues to maintain the juridical and religious dualism according to which homosexuality is classified as bad.

The politics of bad sexuality are also the politics of forbidden sexuality. The politics of the forbidden restrict the content of the curriculum in sex education, the procedures for treating sexological maladies, and the scope of what gets approved, funded, and published in sexological research. Restrictions on research apply especially to childhood sexuality and, hence, to the beginnings of both good and bad sexuality in the early years of life, prior to the advent of adolescence and young adulthood. It would be the kiss of death to submit a grant application for the developmental investigation of childhood sexual rehearsal play or the developmental content of juvenile sexual ideation and imagery. The applicant's own institution as well as extramural private or public funding institutions would all respect the fiction that equates childhood sexuality with innocence, except for sexual molestation and abuse. The concept of developmental sexological health and well being in childhood is widely rejected.

The sexual ideation and imagery of adolescence and maturity are the outcome of both proximate and distal determinants or causes. The more distal determinants may reach back in time beyond childhood and infancy to the unborn months in the womb and beyond that to the formation of the genome when egg and sperm unite. By contrast, the proximate determinants are the most recent ones. It is only by having access to all the links in a developmental chain of the determinants of sexual ideation and imagery that one will arrive at a causal explanation which is intellectually satisfying as well as pragmatically useful for both the individual and society. In the absence of such an explanation, the maladies of sexual ideation and imagery will appear to be haphazardly determined, and sexology will continue to be the protoscience which it presently is.

Sexology will not be able to graduate from protoscience to full science unless the maladies of sexual ideation and imagery in adolescence or earlier and in adulthood or senescence are investigated with scientific impartiality and nonjudgmentalism. Criminalization, punishment, and the death penalty do not lead to causal explanation and effective prevention. Effective prevention is absolutely essential if society is to be enabled to protect itself from those children in each new generation who grow up with aberrations of sexual ideation and imagery such as those which underlie the practices of, among others, sadistic serial sex murdering and violent rape.

Sex and Sexuality: Good and Bad

TO KEEP UP with political correctness, sex education is nowadays called sexuality education. Sexual is the adjective. Sexuality, the noun formed from it, means the state or condition of being sexual. Although sexuality is not a legitimate new adjective, its adjectival usage is currently politically correct. So also is the plural noun, sexualities. The most likely explanation of this new sexuality vogue is that it preempts sexuality for the social sciences and leaves sex for biology. Sex, it is said, is what you're born with, and sexuality is what you are molded into by upbringing. Historically, sex also is of the flesh, whereas sexuality is of the spirit: sex is more physical and animalistic, whereas sexuality is more sensuous and sacramental. Sex is for procreation, while sexuality is for relationship, even without procreation. There is even a hidden implication that sex is more masculine and untamed, whereas sexuality is more feminine and morally constrained.

Sexuality is the new dictionary way of reviving the age-old religious separation of carnal knowledge from sanctified desire. There is something more respectable and sublime about sexuality as compared with sex, for it is possible to talk and write about sexuality while avoiding mention of actual sexual practices like masturbation, oral or anal sex, and even copulation and orgasm. Sexuality is a cleaned up version of sex. It is an existential state of being, not a schedule of performance.

Regardless of nomenclature, the polarization of either sexuality or sex into good and bad is no way to advance the science of sexology. Polarization, sectarian dogma, and polemics belong together, which is the state of affairs in sexology today. Thus, there are books about good sex, as in achieving bigger and better orgasms and a more sublime partnership; and there are books about bad sex, as in suffering from memories, either historically recalled or therapeutically contrived, of sexual molestation and trauma. One outcome is that sexological research into the causality of either good or bad sexuality makes little progress. Sex offenses, for example, being classified as bad, are prosecuted criminologically instead of being investigated as sexological maladies that constitute an epidemiological problem in public health and well being, generation by generation.

Sexological maladies are simultaneously maladies of both sex and eroticism, a combination for which there is no ready-made term in English—hence the somewhat clumsy combination *sexuoerotic.* Sexuoerotic conjoins what is happening between the thighs with what is happening between the ears. Erotosexual does the same, but with the emphasis on Eros.

Proceptivity: Courtship

SYSTEMATIC SEXOLOGY RECOGNIZES three successive stages or phases of an encounter, namely, proceptivity, acceptivity, and conceptivity. Conceptivity deals with fertility, sterility, conception, and gestation, which qualifies it as being sexual but not erotic. It is a specialty of obstetrics and gynecology for women and of urology and andrology for men.

In animal husbandry and laboratory research, it is more common to use the term *receptive* than *acceptive* and to apply it only to females in heat or estrus. The male was ostensibly always ready to be lured by an estrous female. That paradigm is too simple for primates, amongst whom the male may need a female's invitational prompting. Also, the female's readiness may not necessarily be restricted to the period of estrus, which is the case in the bonobo (Kano 1992; Waal 1996) formerly known as the pygmy chimpanzee. In human primates, the woman does not have a period of estrus, and there is no established correlation between copulatory readiness and the phase of the menstrual cycle. In human sexology, it is more accurate to speak not of female receptivity but of mutual male and female acceptivity. The male accepts the female and the female accepts the male, whatever the sexual practices in which they reciprocally and uncoercively engage.

The maladies of acceptivity are comprised of failure or partial failure of the genital organs to perform reciprocally in a sexual relationship with a partner, irrespective of the etiology of the failure. In men, failure includes insertion phobia, erectile failure or impotence, premature ejaculation, ejaculatory failure, genital numbness, and copulatory pain (dyspareunia). In women, failure includes penetration phobia, insufficient vaginal lubrication, vaginal muscle spasm and closure (vaginismus), anorgasmia, genital numbness, and copulatory pain.

According to conventional wisdom, the maladies of acceptivity are subdivisible into those that are organic in origin and prognosis and those that are psychogenic. There is no hard and fast dividing line between the two, however. For example, it formerly was claimed that up to 85 percent of cases of impotence were psychogenic. That was in the era before the first discovery, early in the 1980s, of the arterial and venous pharmacodynamics of the blood flow of erection. Nowadays, the treatment of impotence is predominantly with injectables, for example, papaverine hydrochloride, phentolamine mesylate, and prostaglandin E1, to regulate bloodflow in and out of the corpora cavernosa. As of 1998, there is also the oral medication, much hyped in the media, sildenafil (Viagra). Pharmacologic treatment does not rule out supplemental couple counseling, which may be necessary if their reciprocal relationship is an adversarial one such as, for example, when erectile failure in the man meets vaginal penetration phobia in the woman.

The imagery, ideation, and practices of proceptivity precede acceptivity and may feed into the maladies of acceptivity. Proceptivity itself was long overlooked in animal sexology until Frank Beach in 1976 published a paper under the title of "Sexual Attractivity, Proceptivity, and Receptivity in Female Mammals." To attract a partner, Beach pointed out, a female must not only be estrual but also must participate with the partner in a species specific courtship ritual or mating dance which leads into copulation. Without the ritual, neither partner is prepared to accept copulation.

The courtship ritual in four-legged mammals is species stereotyped, as if performed by a preprogrammed biorobot, with little or no variation between individuals or between separate performances. Among primates, the great apes are less biorobotic than other species, but it is among human primates that there is greatest flexibility of the length and diversification of the courtship ritual. The abridged version of the ritual goes by the name of foreplay. Foreplay takes over where getting acquainted and flirting leave off and the likelihood of genital contact is already presumed. Foreplay may be a brief perfunctory fondling and kissing or a slowly erotic stimulation of all the senses and all of the body.

Ethology of Courtship

THE UNABRIDGED VERSION of the courtship ritual can be observed when two strangers attract one another's romantic attention. Despite individual variations, the underlying design is the same and is species specific. In human beings, the design begins with establishing eye contact and holding the gaze, while at the same time perhaps becoming flushed or blushing. Then one of the pair tests the other by demurely drooping the eyelids and averting the gaze so as to see, upon returning the gaze shyly with a squint, smile, or flutter of the eyelashes, whether the other person has continued to look. This maneuver may be repeated as a prelude to moving closer together. The opening gambit in conversation may be banal, but it is the vocal intonation and animation, not the content that counts. The flow of speech becomes accelerated, more breathy, and louder. Banality is outweighed by the vocal enthusiasm of simply being heard. Laughter, even if the humor is contrived, invites the couple to rotate, so that, facing one another, they can share it and bring themselves closer and closer. The tongue emerges, wetting the lips. Clothing is casually adjusted or shed, fortuitously revealing a little more bare skin at least around the wrists, ankles, or neck. Arms and legs change positions, and gesturing brings them, as if inadvertently, in contact with the other person, sending a frisson running up and down his or her spine. If there is no recoil, then there is closer touching, patting, or holding, and the two people, before they know what they are doing, begin mirroring each other's gestures, and synchronizing their bodily movements as if in preliminary rehearsal for copulatory synchrony. Meanwhile, in addition to the observable cues of body language and vocal communication, there are the autonomic nervous system signs of increased heart and breathing rate, dry throat, goose bumps, sweatiness, and maybe butterflies in the stomach, and genital arousal. If the female vulva is not vasocongested and wet from vaginal lubrication and if the male penis is not erect from vasocongestion and damp from urethral glandular ooze, then these signs of genital arousal will appear in the ensuing segment of the proceptive phase, namely, foreplay.

Proceptive Morbidity

THE HUMAN COURTSHIP ritual is variable not only individually but also idiosyncratically. The evidence of idiosyncrasy may be manifested in actual practices or in self-reports of sexuoerotic ideation and imagery in fantasy, dreams, and daydreams. Proceptive idiosyncrasies, as already mentioned, go by the name of *kinky sex* or *fetishes* in the vernacular. In the law, in older medical writings, and in contemporary psychoanalysis, kinky sex is named *perversion*. More recently, Freund has suggested that some of the perversions should be called *courtship disorders* (Freund et al. 1983, 1984).

The contemporary biomedical and nonjudgmental name is *paraphilia*. The advantage of the biomedical term is its impartiality. Etymologically, it means beyond or altered (Greek, *para*) and love (Greek, *philia*). Some sexologists (see p. 19) mistakenly equate the term *paraphilia* with deviancy and legal condemnation. They fail to allow for the quantitative stretch between paraphilias that are playful (ludic) and harmless at one extreme and those that are pathologically morbid at the other. Serial lust murdering is one example of a pathologically morbid paraphilia, whereas optional viewing of lascivious videotapes for sexual arousal is not. The ludic-morbidity scale applies to paraphilic rehearsal in ideation and imagery as well as to its implementation in actual practice.

Nose, Eyes, and Skin

PROCEPTIVE SIGNALS ARE transmitted to and received through the nose, the eyes, or the skin of the recipient. Among mammals, the four legged subprimate species are those in which the vomeronasal organ in the nose of the male is the organ of proceptive arousal. It picks up the scent of a secretion, a pheromone, synthesized in the vagina of the female only when she is in heat and ovulating. Pheromones are sexual attractants in various other species also, including reptiles and insects. Pheromonal sexual attraction among primate males is evident in the male's sniffing, nuzzling, and poking of the nether parts of the estrous female.

In the human species, oral sex is perhaps an evolutionary residual of pheromonal attraction: some, though not all, men are intensely turned on by performing oral sex on a female (cunnilingus); and most women, it would appear, not so intensely by performing it on a male (fellatio). The receptor cells for pheromones are located in the vomeronasal organ inside the nose near the nasal septum. It is possible for human beings to respond to a pheromone without being aware of the stimulus, as when women who share group living quarters synchronize their menstrual cycles in response to a pheromone secreted in underarm perspiration (McClintock 1971). They do not, through the senses, recognize the presence of the pheromone. If there is a pheromone that acts as a human sexual attractant, it might do so biorobotically without presenting itself to conscious awareness—a curious possibility.

In evolutionary terms, among primate species, where the nose leaves off, the eyes take over. This takeover is visibly evident in those species of primates in which the hind parts of the female in estrus become swollen and changed in color. In human females, there is no periodic swelling or coloration of the genitalia, but the shapeliness of the buttocks is, nonetheless, a visual turn on.

Although the evidence is cumulatively anecdotal rather than systematically statistical, it would appear that males more than females of the human species are dependent on the sense of sight for sexuo-erotic turn on, whereas females more than males are dependent on the contrectative or skin senses. The difference is proportionate, not absolute. Males more than females are programmed to be aroused by closeup depictions of the genitalia. Females are responsive less to the genital anatomy than to the whole body morphology. Whether this difference in programming is innate or culturally acquired or a combination of both remains to be ascertained.

Grooming

IN HUMAN BEINGS, well groomed means being neat, tidy, and of smart appearance. A horse is well groomed when its coat has been well brushed. A monkey or ape grooms a friend by finger combing its fur and removing detritus, a procedure that corresponds to massage in humans. Statistics are missing, so no one knows the ratio of men to women who either give or receive massage, nor the amount of time doing it, nor the ratio of those for whom massage produces a state of bliss versus those who can't tolerate body massage, nor the peak age of massage and body fondling. What is known, and has been demonstrated in newborn rat pups, is that a deficiency of maternal lick-grooming leads to a failure to thrive and possibly to premature death. Without the skin stimulation of grooming, the pituitary gland fails to secrete growth hormone, not only in rats but also in human babies. Premature babies that receive a full quota of rubbing, patting, cuddling, and fondling thrive and leave the newborn nursery sooner than do those who are grooming deprived (Money 1992; Field 1995, 1998).

Good mother/infant grooming in infancy and early childhood makes for good proceptive, lover/lover grooming in adolescence and adulthood. Grooming is accompanied by a release from the pituitary gland of the hormone oxytocin. Oxytocin promotes mother/infant pairbonding. It also regulates milk flow from the breast of the feeding mother and plays a role in labor and childbirth. It has been said to be a bonding hormone (Carter et al. 1997).

The Cerebral-Sacral Connection

IN CASES OF accidental injury with complete severance of the spinal cord, the brain is disconnected from the organs and parts of the body below the level of the injury (Kreuter et al. 1996; Charlifue et al. 1992; Smith and Bodner 1993). Sexologically, the outcome is that no messages are transmitted to the brain from the genitalia nor from the genitalia to the brain via the neural pathways of the lower, sacral end of the spinal cord. Erotosexual ideation and imagery fail to stir the genitalia. Correspondingly, stimulation of the peripheral genitalia, even though it may evoke a local reflex reaction, fails to register erotic sensation, including genital orgasmic sensation, in the mind. The exception, recently discovered in women, is that those with spinal cord injury may experience a blunted or protopathic sensation of a sexual nature. It is conveyed directly to the brain, outside of the spinal cord, by the way of the vagus nerve of the autonomic nervous system (Komisaruk et al. 1997).

The vagus nerve notwithstanding, the chief sexological lesson of spinal cord deconnection is that pelvic and cerebral sexuality are both mutually interactive and quasi-autonomous. The maladies of sexual ideation and imagery have their etiology within the cerebrum rather than in the sexual anatomy of the crotch and the pelvis. Thus, it is possible for a man or woman with total severance of the spinal cord to have a dream that culminates in an as-if orgasm which is, in fact, a phantom orgasm existing in the imagery of the dream but not in the functioning of the peripheral genitalia (Money 1960; Comarr et al. 1983).

Juvenile Sexuality

EVER SINCE JEAN Gerson was Chancellor of the University of Paris in the fourteenth century (see also pp. 11, 225, 226), the era when the great plague, the Black Death, killed off up to three quarters of the people in some parts of Europe, there have been two antithetical visions of the sexuality of childhood: the one, a vision of childhood innocence, and the other of childhood corruptibility. These two visions have been in part reconciled by the doctrine that corruption of childhood sexual innocence is brought about by exposure to corrupting influences, including, today, explicit sex education, depictions of pornography, the corrupt practices of those whose innocence has already been lost, and the approaches of sexual victimizers.

In the history of sexology in Christendom, the earliest references to childhood sexuality are preserved in the penitential handbooks of the sixth century and later, written for the guidance of priests hearing confessions and prescribing penances. For example, the penitential of the Synod of North Britain (dated around A.D. 520) required an adult masturbator to do penance for a year, whereas for a boy of twelve, forty days sufficed (quoted in Bullough 1976, 368).

Gerson (1363–1429), who was also a Dean of the Cathedral of Notre Dame of Paris, wrote *De confessione mollicei* (Children's Confessions) as a penitential guide for confessors, so that they might better arouse a sense of guilt in juvenile penitents. As quoted by Ariès (1962, 107–8), Gerson considered childhood masturbation a serious matter: even though not accompanied by ejaculatory pollution because of age, masturbation would take away a child's virginity more than if he had gone with a woman. Moreover, masturbation borders on sodomy. To save themselves from sin, Gerson advised that children at play should not be allowed to kiss, to touch one another with bare hands, or to gaze at one another indecorously. So as to guard against promiscuity, children should not share a bed with either adults or other children. The child who failed to prevent any of the foregoing sins was required to report each instance in confession, and likewise, the sins of any of his classmates at Gerson's school of Notre Dame. Gerson attributed the sins of childhood sexuality to natural corruption (original sin) independently of an acquired sense of guilt.

By declaring all expressions of childhood sexuality as corrupt and sinful, Gerson left no place for the concept of the developmental progress of sexuality from infancy through prepuberty and adolescence to adulthood. Childhood sexuality became an offense to be confessed and brought under control by means of penance, punishment, being spied on, and becoming secretly an informant on one's classmates and friends.

Gerson's concern with semen loss had its origin in the pre–Christian doctrine of semen depletion as a deprivation of the body's supply of vital spirit and as a cause of illness and maybe death (Money 1991b, 1997b).

Semen depletion theory was taken up and medicalized by the Swiss physician Simon André Tissot in the mid-eighteenth century. His *Treatise on the Diseases Produced by Onanism* was first published in Latin in 1758, since which time it has been translated and revised in many editions in Europe and America (Tissot 1832/1974). It fueled the antisexualism of Victorian medicine, exacerbated the furor over masturbation, and universalized neonatal circumcision in the United States as a putative preventive of masturbatory wastage of the seed in adolescence.

From Gerson in the fourteenth and fifteenth centuries until the onset of the twenty-first century, semen depletion/conservation theory has held sexology hostage and, in labyrinthine ways, continues to do so. It endangers the practice of sexological research, especially research into the ideation and imagery of the maladies of sexuality in childhood and adolescence, for it may lead to false accusations of pedophilic or ephebophilic sexual abuse, and freezes research funding.

2

Love and Lust

Power and Taboo

The word *taboo*, from the Polynesian *tapu* or *tabu*, entered the English language in the late eighteenth century. It filled a gap in the dictionary and gave a name to conduct forbidden to certain individuals or social classes, under threat of physical or spiritual reprisal or social exile. Polynesian taboo applies chiefly to the desecration of the dead and their burial places, inadvertently or otherwise, and to disrespect of royal or priestly authority. Elsewhere on the planet, taboos apply to restrictions on eating, fasting, and food preparation; on vocabulary relative to age and sex of speaker and listener; on activities relative to menstruation and childbirth; and on sexual practices, partners, and frequencies. In general, a taboo is defined as a sacred interdiction imposed upon the use of things or words or the performance of certain actions, commonly imposed by chiefs and priests, and empowered by the force of custom.

A taboo restricts something that the human species would ordinarily do or engage in during the course of development, but on an irregular schedule, not a biorobotically fixed one. To illustrate: a taboo on the speed of breathing would be too easily overridden by the biological clock of the lungs to be effective. Similarly, a taboo on seminal emission could be too easily overridden in sleep to be effective, whereas taboo on all methods of masturbation or on the frequency of sexual intercourse is a possibility, at least for some people.

The function of a taboo is to give power to those who impose it over those upon whom it is imposed. The younger the age at which the taboo is first imposed, the greater the likelihood that it will be obeyed for a lifetime, eventually by self-policing alone. Then, as priests and politicians well know, the merest suggestion of imposing sanctions on the taboo breaker elicits obedient conformity. It is this principle of elementary behavior modification that underwrites the transmission of the centuries' old sex taboo to today's generation of children.

Complete ecclesiastic enforcement of the sex taboo in some religions requires celibacy and renunciation of marriage as well as chastity, abstention, or at least a vow of abstention, from sexuoerotic practices or their ideation and imagery. Early in the history of Christendom, failure of abstinence, as for example in wet dreams, called for denial of the flesh by way of extreme fasting, flagellation, and related practices from which a state of ecstatic masochistic bliss may ensue.

If all the members of a society were able to maintain celibacy and abstinence for a lifetime, the species would become extinct. That being highly unlikely, the vow of celibacy and abstinence is taken only by a religious elite. Dualism comes to the rescue of the remainder of the population by way of the polarization of love and lust. Love is above the waist, clean, pure, and sacramental. Lust is below the waist, dirty, impure, and diabolical.

Romantic Love

IN DIFFERENT TIMES and places, as in India today, marriages have been arranged according to family traditions so as to match political power, religion, social status, spoken language, land ownership, and wealth. The major requirement of the arranged marriage is the production of progeny, irrespective of love. Romantic love was revived in the courts of European nobility, from the end of the 11th century onward, in the love songs and poems of the troubadours (Capellanus 1957; Money 1985). Theirs was an elegiac romantic love for it was about love unrequited. The fair lady for whom the young knight would forfeit his life was either already married or betrothed to someone else. If they consummated their passion, then it was considered to be not love but lust that impelled them, and the ending was homicide, suicide, or both. The infatuation of love was considered too disruptive to be the basis of a marriage, though not on the dramatic stage. Shakespeare used the formula in Romeo and Juliet, as did the great composers of nineteenth-century grand opera, in which love was equated with death.

Like today's popular performers, the troubadours sang of love to an already converted audience when they sang to the peasantry and townspeople of Europe. Long before the spread of the Imperial Roman system of arranged marriage, the common people had followed the betrothal system of romantic affiliation (Wikman 1937) still extant in contemporary Iceland. In Denmark, the betrothal system was known as night courting (Hertoft 1977), and in Finland, as taking your night legs for a walk. Transplanted to New England, it was known as bundling (Stiles undated). In Scandinavia, at the end of the winter, country people no longer needed the warmth of a log fire in the farm kitchen to protect them from freezing to death. The girls moved to the top floor of the small barn with an upper floor that served as the unmarried girls' house. They climbed up through a trap door and closed it. The roving bands of boys who serenaded them on weekends had access only if the girls lowered a rope ladder from the upper window. Eventually, if it became evident that a boy and a girl were romantically attracted, then their friends would arrange to leave them alone on subsequent visits. Next, the protocol was in three stages: first the boy slept clothed above the covers, then clothed below the covers, then both together, undressed. Thereupon, they announced and celebrated their betrothal. Formal marriage followed, only if they proved fertility by creating a pregnancy. Love merged into lust in this betrothal system, instead of each being dissociated from the other.

The troubadour revival of romantic love in medieval Europe had two sequelae. One was to react against it and against the fatal attraction of women by branding them as witches and lighting the fires of the witch-hunting Inquisition of the late medieval and early Renaissance period. These fires burned hundreds of thousands of women at the stake as witches and heretics with unnatural powers of seduction who, while asleep, cohabited with Satan or his demons. Thereby, they made their men impotent and sterile and their animals and fields unproductive.

The second sequela was to liberate the romantic love affair, even among the nobility, to be a legitimate precursor of a family approved marriage. Nowadays, falling in love is widely regarded as a touchstone for each new sexual relationship, regardless of the suffering brought on each disbanded partner and family. In addition, falling in love is so important a touchstone that it may have to be confabulated so as to justify engaging in a lust affair. Marriages based on romantic love and those that are family arranged are neither superior nor inferior to one another in potential quality or durability.

Limerence and Bonding

MOST PEOPLE WILL not need a dictionary to define love and lovesickness, and they know that lovesickness may be serious enough to terminate in suicide, homicide, or both. Until recently, however, there was no word in scientific English to encompass what in the vernacular is known as being in love, falling in love, being love-smitten, love-stricken, or being lovesick as an outcome of love unrequited. *Limerence* is the new word that fills the scientific gap. It was coined in 1979 by Dorothy Tennov. Sexology has deferred to the arts and literature and has been skittish about accepting love and lover/lover bonding as suitable topics for scientific study.

Limerence is one of a trio of potential human reactions that share certain features in common. The other two are acute grief and divine bliss. Acute grief may be triggered by the unexpected experience or announcement of sudden death. Divine revelation or born-again salvation both may trigger divine bliss. All three may be precipitated suddenly and unpredictably, though they may be cumulative in onset. Although their duration is variable, they may persist for a long time. There is no sure-fire method of intervention that will ameliorate their intensity or bring them to a close, except the passage of time. Being able to talk to an empathic listener also may be beneficial.

Limerence has no limit to the age of onset. It has been known to occur during the prepubertal years (Money 1980, 148) and in the geriatric years, but onset during the years of adolescence predominates. It is possible for juvenile limerence to continue into adolescence and adulthood and to be restricted to only one partner in a lifetime. It is also possible to have a string of limerent affairs or, more rarely, two or more overlapping affairs. Preoccupation with the limerent partner is so obsessively pervasive, however, that it usually brooks no competition, and all the more so if there is uncertainty as to whether one's own limerence is trustworthily reciprocated.

Whether or not reciprocated, limerence interferes with the functioning of the autonomic nervous system. It upsets the alimentary canal. Bowel movements are subject to irregularity. Palpitations and the butterflies of anxiety lurk in the stomach in anticipation of the next encounter with the lover. The hands go clammy with perspiration. The biological clock of sleeping and waking is thrown off kilter. Obsession with the lover is revealed in dreams and waking ruminations in which the next meeting with the lover is rehearsed over and over again. The imagery of erotic fondling, hugging and kissing, foreplay and copulation becomes vivid and is more or less worrisome relative to the individual's degree of sexual emancipation.

Although limerent attraction may occur despite even a large age discrepancy, more often than not the two partners are of the same generation. By societal custom, age discrepancy is tolerated provided the female is of childbearing age, even if the male is older or younger.

Limerent attraction is predominantly between male and female. Same sex limerence, when it occurs, does not differ from limerence between male and female.

From the viewpoint of evolutionary sexology, it may be surmised that, like grief and divine bliss, limerent bliss is one of those phenomena of human apperception and behavioral response that belonged in the protohuman brain before the advent of verbal language representation in the brain. Hence by its very nature, the experience of being lovesmitten is inarticulate. Love is proverbially blind, irrational, and mad. It is cut from the same cloth as music, rhythm, and dance where it still belongs, especially in teenagers (Money 1998b). For uncounted millennia, it has been a call to mating. It has ensured the continuance of the species.

Except for the age of puberty with its surge of sex hormones and its prevalence of first limerence, there is no yet known hormonal or other neurochemical accompaniement of limerence, which is not surprising as there has been no search for a correlation. The pituitary hormone, oxytocin (see chap. 1), with its reputation as a mother/infant bonding hormone would be worthy of investigation as a limerence hormone (Carter et al. 1997).

There is no fixed time limit to the duration of limerence. Exact figures are lacking, but it is known that limerence may persist for a lifetime. More likely, it persists at high intensity long enough to overlap with the conception and birth of a child, after which it becomes transformed from a two-way into a three-way bondship. If the baby does not become bonded, then its survival is in jeopardy from neglect and abuse. For some couples, the transition to a three-way bondship is imperfect. Then, without limerence, the parents may become unbonded, perhaps irreparably. There is no guaranteed method of rebonding, psychotherapy or counseling notwithstanding. That leaves only three alternatives: tolerance of the status quo, dissolution of the relationship, or escalation of unbondedness with, in the worst scenario, homicide, suicide, or both. Such is the human condition, in the present state of knowledge.

Bonding and Autism

IN EVOLUTIONARY SEXOLOGY, the concept that lover/lover pairbondship may have its own coding in the human brain, most probably in the paleocortical limbic system, was first brought to my attention in the case of a young woman with a double diagnosis of Turner syndrome and autism (Money 1983). The autistic mode of thinking and speech made it impossible for her to engage in logical explanations.

Thus, she had no logical explanation for outrageously demanding that her teenaged sister was never to wear nylon hose. Since the sister wore nylons when she dressed up to go on a date with her boyfriend, it was not too difficult to deduce that the patient was envious of the sister's having family permission to have a boyfriend and go out on dates. Although older, the patient herself was sequestered at home, deprived of sex education, and of assistance to establish a dating relationship with any of the boys she met at her special school for the learning handicapped and academically retarded.

Comparatively, there was no ready explanation of the patient's disruptive outbursts against her thirteen-year-old brother. She demanded that he never be seen in athletic or bathing shorts, nor dressed without socks on. It required more than two years of weekly sessions of combined remedial teaching and sex therapy with an unusually gifted therapist before an explanation was forthcoming. The patient's own words were to the effect that if it were her brother's bare legs and bare feet now, what would it be next. She had accused him of improper advances, thus jeopardizing his future. The parents thought of their daughter as being an infant, not an autistic young adult, and so were disposed to blame the brother, despite his denials. The patient's dilemma was that her brother was the only young male she saw consistently at close range; and that toward him, she did have romantic and lustful longings. The mechanism of pairbondship in the limbic brain was presumably intact. By contrast, the mechanism for troopbondship was presumably autistically defective, thus rendering the patient incompetent at establishing ordinary social and dating friendships.

It is possible to construe autism as predominantly a syndrome of defective troopbondship that originates innately. Turner syndrome is not only innate but also genetic in origin, insofar as there is only one sex chromosome, an X, with a total of forty-five, not forty-six chromosomes per cell. The phenotype is female, except for short stature and agenesis of the ovaries. Without ovaries, the ovarian hormones of puberty are not produced.

Selectively, there is a range of various possible congenital defects in Turner syndrome, e.g., of the heart. Autism might conceivably be one such associated defect. If so, the association is rare; but it does lend credence to the idea that autism has a genomic origin. It also lends credence to the hypothesis that the pairbondship of love and

lust, on the one hand, is distinct from the troopbondship of social interaction with friends, family acquaintances, and peers, on the other
hand, both being governed in the limbic pathways of the brain.

A less than autistic degree of impaired troopbondship manifests
itself as social shyness and awkwardness which, by limiting the circle
of friends and acquaintances, limits also the chances of matching
with a partner in a pairbondship in which there is an intimately reciprocal convergence of love and lust (Gilmartin 1987).

Hypophilia

WHENEVER, OR FOR whatever reason, there is a reciprocally incomplete
convergence of pairbonded lust and love, then logically there is either
too much or too little of either the one or the other or each becomes altered. Too little lust is hypophilia, too much is hyperphilia, and too altered is paraphilia. The Greek derivations are *hypo*, too little; *hyper*,
too much; *para*, beyond or altered; and *philia*, love. In this nomenclature, *philia* is customarily used as being synonymous with the less frequently used *lagnia*, lust. Terminologically, however, *hypolagnia,*
hyperlagnia, and *paralagnia* are not currently in familiar usage.

When Masters and Johnson (1970) published their volume on the
hypophilias, its title was *Human Sexual Inadequacy*. Inadequacy sig-
nified failure to measure up to the criterion standards set forth in the
prior book, *Human Sexual Response* (1966). In the Masters and
Johnson scheme of classification, sexual inadequacies are manifested
as disorders of acceptivity/receptivity (see p. 25). In males, they include inter alia, deficiency of erection or timing of ejaculation, and in
women, deficiency of lubrication or of reaching orgasm. The defining
feature of each of the sexual inadequacies is an insufficiency, incom-
pleteness, or diminution in the performance of the organs of coition
or in the timing of its sequential phases. Hence, the classification of
inadequacies as hypophilias.

Phobic avoidance is a specific manifestation of hypophilia that is
commonly overlooked. Among Oriental and southern Asian peoples,
there is a widespread cultural phobia against kissing. Deep tongue
kissing, although a staple of love scenes in American cinema, is cen-
sored from movies and television in countries where kissing is phobi-
cally avoided as obscene.

In the culture of the West, a socially prescribed avoidancy of male-male kissing is widely pervasive, perhaps more in today's older than younger generation. Among men with a bisexual or homosexual history, there are some who have a male-male kissing phobia. Whatever the genital intimacies in which they may participate, provided the intimacy of kissing is avoided, they are enabled to maintain a self-definition as heterosexual, irrespective of engaging in otherwise homosexual acts.

In North America, there is officially a phobic avoidancy and censorship of penial vaginal penetration in live shows, movies, videos, and print media, and on television and the Internet. This cultural phobia spills over into the private lives of some individuals. In both males and females, it takes the form of the hypophilic syndrome of penetration phobia. If severe, penetration phobia interdicts copulatory penetration and prevents pregnancy.

An additional syndrome of hypophilia is one that Masters and Johnson did not account for: sexuoerotic apathy, inertia, or avoidance, also known as anhedonia (Money 1980, 77–80). This syndrome represents not a failure of functional completeness but a failure even to get started.

The psychoanalyst and sex-therapist, Helen Singer Kaplan, popularized this failure by renaming it lack of sexual desire. The appeal of her book (Kaplan 1979), according to some sex therapists, was that it provided an alibi for their clinical failure rate, namely, that they had cured all the easy cases with the Masters and Johnson method of couple therapy and, henceforth, were confronted with a more challenging diagnosis.

Sexological anhedonia is in some instances secondary to and symptomatic of another syndrome. Depressive illness is a common example. The incidence of anhedonia is elevated also in men with Klinefelter syndrome in which the basic defect is an extra X chromosome, making a total of 47, XXY, instead of 46, XY. In men and women with a history of hypopituitarism, regardless of etiology, there is an elevated incidence not only of anhedonia but also of absence of the experience of falling in love.

In both the 47, XXY, syndrome and in hypopituitarism, there is no consistent correlation between the degree of sexual anhedonia and the circulating blood levels of sex hormones, with or without hormonal replacement treatment. There are, however, some male cases in which the degree of apathy/inertia is ameliorated by high dosage treatment with the testicular hormone, testosterone. Testosterone replacement treatment is more effective in cases in which there is a deficiency in the blood level of the hormone. If the deficiency is in the intracellular hormonal uptake and usage, even very high dosage treatment is likely to be ineffectual, irrespective of etiology and diagnosis.

Testosterone has very limited applicability for females, as it produces unwanted bodily masculinizing effects. There is no evidence that the blood level of ovarian hormones, estrogen and progesterone, directly affect anhedonia in the lovemap of females. In males, by contrast, these hormones suppress the body's synthesis of male hormone, and so they have a generalized antiandrogenic effect that resembles the effect of surgical castration.

Overall, sex hormones do not constitute a panacea for the manifold syndromes and symptoms of hypophilic lovemaps, but when properly matched with an etiology and diagnosis of hormonal insufficiency, they work very well.

Hyperphilia

IN HYPOPHILIC DISORDERS, love and lust are deconnected at the expense of lust which, to a variable degree, becomes dormant and anhedonic. With lust off stage, love and devotion may, apart from being erotically neutered, persist more or less unchanged. In a marriage or other long term relationship, the lovemap often becomes transformed in this way. By contrast, in hyperphilia, the transformation is reversed; lust is spared from extinction, but its convergence with love is in eclipse. Some loveless marital or cohabitational bonds persist in this way, with one partner, male or female, relating to the other as if to an animated toy for expediting orgasm.

Unlike hypophilia, hyperphilia has received scant medical attention. For both males and females, it has sometimes been named *hypersexuality* but more frequently as *nymphomania* in females and *satyromania* (or *satyriasis*) in males. For males, *womanizer* is a less stigmatizing term as is *Don Juanism,* which may even be tinged with a touch of envy. For females, there is no corresponding term, hypersexuality in women having traditionally been morally stigmatized as harlotry and promiscuity unsuited to the dignity of sexually genteel ladies. Respectable women seeking a consultation for hypersexuality have been known to have met with snide and unseemly remarks. They are wrongly assumed to be voluntarily in control of sexual self-constraint and are chastened for not exercising enough of it.

The ideals that people are supposed to live up to, and the laws designed to enforce them to do so, vary according to place and time. For example, in most Islamic states a male, though not a female, is permitted to support four partners in legal marriage. In Christendom, although marriage is by law restricted to only one partner, a man with sufficient political power might have other partners without being exposed by the press or the sex police. This was so in the case of presidents of the United States until, in the late twentieth century, the Clinton presidency.

Complaints of being oversexed by reason of wanting sex too often or too promiscuously do not routinely have equivalent sexological significance. A complaint needs to be responded to at face value and then placed in context. For example, the context may be that a couple had no mutual complaints regarding sexual frequency while they lived together, unmarried. Becoming married changed the legal power each held over the other. It changed also the sexuality of cohabitation to the sexuality of husband/wife and of parenthood. Under the new rules, the prior sexuality of the pair may appear oversexed to the one partner and undersexed to the other. Being unmarried is the time for sowing wild oats. Being married is the time for settling down. For some couples, a parallel change accompanies the menopause.

In Hindu and related cultures, even hypophilia may be misconstrued as oversexed hyperphilia, so great and obsessive is the fear of the dire health consequences of the depletion of semen, the most precious concentrate of the vital spirit, *sukra* (Joshi and Money 1995).

Semen depletion theory, and its converse semen conservation, are most anciently attributed to the writings of traditional Indian Ayurvedic medicine, in the first or second centuries A.D. (Basham 1959) but preserved orally from a much earlier date. The theory took a new lease on life in Christendom under Jean Gerson in France (see chap. 1) in the fourteenth century, and was medicalized by Simon André Tissot (1758/1974) in the eighteenth century. Tissot associated excessive semen depletion with promiscuity and prostitution (the social vice) and also with masturbation (the secret vice) as the cause of the symptoms of, in particular, syphilis and gonorrhea, which were considered a single disease before germ theory was formulated in the 1870s.

Tissot's theorizing diffused widely. It still influences the taboo on masturbation. By contrast, its opposite was confined to tribal New Guinea and parts of Melanesia (Herdt 1981, 1984, 1987). This is the folk theory of semen transfusion (see Money 1997b), according to which prepubertal boys need men's milk sucked from the penises of postpubertal boys in order to enter puberty and to become fertile husbands and fathers.

Erotomania

IN ADDITION TO signifying an elevated frequency of sexual performance or an insatiable search for new sexual partners, hyperphilia may signify also a monomania—a fatal attraction to someone who is unresponsive and unavailable as a sexual partner. The type of monomania has been known as erotomania. The more frequent diagnosis is Clérambault-Kandinsky syndrome (CKS). In 1981, a nationally famous instance of fatal attraction was that of John Hinckley Jr. for the young actress Jodie Foster (Clarke 1990). Repeated importunation having met with no success, Hinckley declared the immensity of his desperation by attempting to assassinate President Reagan and sacrifice his own life. Only hours before the assassination attempt, he addressed a farewell note to Jodie Foster: "Goodbye! I love you six trillion times. Don't you like me just a little bit? (You must admit I am different). It would make all of this worthwhile, of course" (Money 1986, 127).

By definition, it is pathognomonic of fatal attraction in CKS that it is doomed to failure insofar as the object of attraction is remote and unobtainable by reason of social or legal status, wealth, fame, religion, occupation, age, consanguinity, or whatever. Initially, the two people may have known one another on an asexual basis, as student and teacher, priest and intern, et cetera. There is particular vulnerability in the doctor-patient relationship, which involves talking about sex if a sexual or reproductive problem exists and palpation of the body and exposure of the genitalia in even the routine physical examination.

CKS is not well recognized in the practice of medicine. Many medical students graduate without instruction in how to recognize it and deal with it. This was so in the case of a good looking young gynecologist who became the recipient of the infatuation of an out-of-state patient, herself a former nurse. He had assisted in surgical procedures that had enabled the patient to become pregnant. Her first correspondence was a thank you note and request for a follow-up appointment. Progressively, her notes became love letters. The gynecologist sought the advice of a woman psychologist. It was agreed that she would tell the patient that the gynecologist, having no further procedures to perform, would not reply to her letters. Instead, the patient might write to the psychologist. All to no avail. In a move of desperation, the patient addressed love letters to the gynecologist's home, with the intent of provoking his wife to seek a divorce on grounds of infidelity. As months passed into years without reply, the patient made the delusional discovery that she could decipher secret messages from the doctor concealed in song titles that he had ostensibly requested from the disc jockey of a local radio station. She construed them as her gynecologist's way of conveying his undying love for her, without risking retaliation from his wife. She was aware of becoming progressively disabled mentally. Her final communication reported hospitalization for manic depressive psychosis. It was not possible to get information directly from the patient's husband or family.

Stalking

AS WELL AS being associated with one-sided, unrequited limerence, the symptoms of CKS may be associated with a one-sided breakup of what was initially a reciprocal affair or marriage. In the media, there are frequent headlines of a jilted lover or spouse stalking and blackmailing the erstwhile partner, kidnapping the children, and terminating in murder/suicide. A nationally headlined case in 1992 was that of sixty-two-year-old Sol Wachtler, Chief Judge of the State of New York (Franks 1992; Henican 1992; Wachtler 1997; Caher 1998).

The story that eventually emerged in the print media was that the judge, a pillar of establishment respectability, had been having an adulterous affair with a woman whose stepfather was the judge's wife's paternal uncle. The two had first met at a family party when the girl was in early adolescence and the judge was around thirty and married. Eventually, she became the second woman in his life throughout her three marriages. For forty years, he had only one marriage with four children. Upon the death of his inamorata's stepfather, the judge became executor of his multimillion dollar estate. After her third divorce, she took up with a new paramour and terminated her sexual affair with the judge.

Thereupon, the judge's rationality became divided into total rationality in continuance of his professional duties and total irrationality in pursuit and harassment of his lost lover. As if a novice in the ways of the law and its intelligence agencies, he embarked on a cloak and dagger drama of threatening phone calls which could easily be traced to his car phone or to pay phones in various parts of the country where his work called him. On the phone, he used a voice-disguising electronic attachment. Naming himself David Purdy, he impersonated a hired investigator from Texas. Dressed in cowboy garb, he left blackmail notes at the desk of the woman's center city apartment house and threatened to release sexually explicit tapes and photos of her with her new paramour. With a condom attached, he sent a sexually insulting card to the woman's teenaged daughter. He threatened to abduct the girl unless he received a twenty-thousand-dollar ransom, a paltry sum between multimillionaires. The money in an envelope was to be left on the steps leading from the street to the basement door of a building adjacent to the woman's apartment house. Because of her high powered political connections, she was able to appeal first hand to the director of the FBI, who assigned upward of eighty agents to work on the case. They followed the judge's every move from Albany to the drop-off steps in New York City.

At this stage of the drama, the judge wavered and betrayed himself. He phoned his nearby hairdresser with a request to pickup the envelope containing the ransom money, paid a taxi driver to deliver a note to the doorman at his friend's city address, and tore up another note he had in his pocket. He put the torn pieces in a public trash receptacle from which the police easily retrieved them. Next, he drove off in the direction of his rural home on Long Island. On the way, the police closed in on his automobile and arrested him. He was prosecuted and sentenced to fifteen months in prison.

Eventually, the judge attributed his bizarre behavior to a grossly excessive mix of psychoactive medications which paved the way for manic hyperactivity and loss of judgment. He may have been correct; but CKS occurs also without pill taking.

When the pleas of a jilted lover or deserted spouse pass unheeded, then stalking may be the primary ensuing symptom of reprisal. Common sense says to call the police and obtain a restraining order against the stalker. That may be an unwise move, even a deadly one, if it exacerbates the stalker's limerent desperation into murder and/or suicide. Stalking shows the dark side of love and limerence. Once you become incorporated into the dreams and fantasies of another person's lovemap, there your image dwells entrapped within that other person's mind and brain, powerless and with no escape exit. This is the jeopardy of love unrequited. Too easily, it transforms the ecstasy of love into agony and grief, ending in a tragedy of hate and vengeance.

Infatuation

BY CONTRAST WITH hyperphilic syndromes characterized by excessive attachment to a particular partner is the syndrome characterized by multiple limerent affairs in sequence. The recipient of each new infatuation is the equivalent of what a fresh fix is for a drug addict. The syndrome has no formal name, but those affected by it have been referred to in slang as *love junkies* and also, inaccurately, as *love addicts* (Peele and Brodsky 1975). Liebowitz (1982) gave it the infelicitous name, *hysteroid dysphoria*. Men or women with this condition say that they feel mentally empty and unable to be productive in their careers, except when under the limerent spell of a new love affair. If the new affair carries the risk of being illicit, the gamble of avoiding discovery enhances its thrill. If it is discovered, it may bring social disgrace and career ruination. Undiscovered, it eventually loses its luminosity which gives way to depressive self-sabotage and abandonment of the relationship. Then the cycle is reset with the advent of a new infatuation. In childhood, there may have been a history of imposed and unpredicted separation and loss, possibly by death, of a closely bonded relative or friend, but the etiological significance of such a history remains unascertained.

In those cases in which a limerently infatuated lover wins the hand of the one he/she woos, the ensuing relationship is marked by pathological possessiveness and jealousy. The partner becomes a prisoner of love, in some cases literally housebound and not permitted in public unaccompanied. Even a passing glance from a potential rival is likely to evoke both verbal and physical abuse. There is no special name for this phenomenon of oppression, except *jealousy*.

Inability to bring a limerent affair to an end happens not only as a sequel to rejection by the partner but also as a sequel to the death of the partner. Then the bereaved survivor may meticulously preserve the deceased's personal effects, as if in readiness for his/her return. Similarly, the survivor may obsessionally set a place at the meal table for the deceased and continue to do so for years. Not a day passes without praying for the safety of the departed one, or actually conversing with him/her, planning to be reunited and to do things together.

The various syndromes of hyperphilia are neither gender nor age selective. There is no known systematic correlation with genetics, hormones, toxins, or other neurochemistries. Their neural pathways in the brain have not yet been ascertained. However, hyperphilia, usually under the name of *hypersexuality,* is known to be sporadically associated with some instances of traumatic brain injury and of geriatric brain degeneration, as in Huntington and Alzheimer disease (see also chap. 5). It may be one of the earliest signs of degenerative brain disease, in which case it may escape diagnosis and be characterized instead as indecent exposure, sexual harassment, invasion of privacy, child abuse, or masturbation. Regardless of etiology, there is, as yet, no definitive method of prevention, intervention, or reversal.

Sporadically and unsystematically, the lovemap symptoms of the various hyperphilic syndromes may show some degree of overlap with manic depressive bipolarity, with obsessional schizoid rumination, with delusional paranoia, with obsessive compulsive disorder (OCD), and with so called sexual addiction (Carnes 1983). Nonetheless, hyperphilic syndromes are sexological syndromes in their own right, not to be equated with any of these other entities.

Norms

HOW MUCH SEX is too much, and how little is too little? These questions belong to the larger question of what is normal and what is abnormal, for which the answer is that there are no absolute criterion standards. Moreover, there is no exact correspondence between the statistical norm of what people actually do, and the ideological norm of what they should do to conform to the ideals and demands of those who exercise power and authority over them. The principle of two norms, statistical and ideological, applies not only to how frequently people have sex but also to how they have it, alone or with a partner; to the variety of partners, either male, female, or both; and to the variety of sexual acts in which they might engage.

Oral sex and anal sex, since they preclude procreation, have long met with ecclesiastical condemnation. Nonetheless, the pursuit of oral and anal sex, as either the performer or the recipient or both, is in some people hyperphilic in intensity. If only one of two partners is either orally or anally hyperphilic and if the other partner is repulsed by oral or anal sex, then the partnership, whether gay or straight, is jeopardized. It is probable that more men are enthusiastic about giving oral sex than women are about receiving it, but certified statistics are lacking.

There are no tabulated norms, as there are for growth in height and weight, for frequency of having sex or frequency of achieving orgasm. If there were such tables, they would have to be not only age and male/female specific but specific also to the effect of being with or without a partner or partners, to the revival effect of having a fresh partner, to the constraining effect of lack of privacy, to the weariness effect of work and family care, and so on.

Overall, sexual frequency tables would be expected to show that coital and orgasmic frequency declines with age and familiarity, and that individual variation is extensive. For some established couples, coital frequency is no more than four times a year. Allowing for supplemental masturbating orgasms, the orgasmic frequency may be higher. For other couples, both coital and orgasmic frequency are several times a week over many years, gradually tapering off to a lesser frequency until age eighty or beyond.

At the upper end of the spectrum of orgasmic frequency, some males have reported having several orgasms, three or more, on a daily basis, each with ejaculation. One patient, a paraphilic sex offender, reported up to as many as ten orgasms daily during adolescence and young adulthood. Each sex offender's orgasm is accompanied by his own personalized sex-offending imagery. In the absence of a participating partner or if the partner is exhausted, the orgasm is achieved by means of masturbation.

Hyperorgasmia would appear to be more prevalent in the sex offending than in the general male population. However, it is not exclusive to sex offenders. It has been reliably self-reported by nonoffender males in association with either heterosexual or homosexual imagery while alone, masturbating, if the partner is worn out or with the partner.

Multiorgasmia with ejaculation in the absence of a refractory period is not unheard of in males, especially in youth. In older males, it is less frequently heard of, and there is usually a slight detumescent recovery period. The penis that maintains a rigid erection for hours is in a state of priapism, which is pathological. It may be brought on by a blockage of blood flow, which is, for instance, known as a side effect of the clumping of red blood cells in sickle cell anemia. Prolonged priapism becomes very painful and is not at all erotic. Temporary priapism may be a side effect of the new treatment of impotence with intracavernosal injections of papaverine hydrochloride, prostaglandin E1, or by mouth with tablets of Viagra. Being able to maintain a long-term erection with more than one orgasm is attractive to some men but not necessarily to their partners also.

Whereas most males have a refractory period between orgasms, nonrefractory multiorgasmia is well known as a female phenomenon, though its prevalence in the population at large has not been ascertained. Multiple orgasms occur in the context of a continuous session of sexual intercourse or masturbation and not necessarily on a daily schedule. Eventually, the point of satiation is reached, and sexual activity comes to an end.

Anecdotally and rarely, there have been claims of female multiorgasmia triggered by ideation and imagery alone in the absence of any contractative stimulation; but there has been no systematic investigation of this claim in either sex. Clinically, however, it is known that comprehensive investigation of such a claim may reveal it to be attributable to a neuroepileftiform type of sexological brain malfunction and to be responsive to antiepileptic medication.

There is, for instance, the case of a professional woman who experienced embarrassing attacks of impending orgasm that urgently interrupted her work with clients. Masturbation brought no relief. There was no alternative except to wait until the attack subsided, which it would do in as much as thirty minutes without an orgasmic climax. Gynecological findings were negative. Some examiners attributed the attacks to insatiable sexual desire, which the woman found humiliating. Eventually, she consulted a gynecologist who referred her to a female sexologist who took a detailed sexological history. That led to a neurological referral, which in turn led to a diagnosis of atypical orgasmic epilepsy, responsive to antiepileptic medication.

One of the strategies of the New Right's puritanism in sex therapy has been to set an arbitrary ideological norm for coital and orgasmic frequency. Frequency above the norm is defined as abnormal and is named *sexual addiction* (Carnes 1983), for which the treatment is based on the twelve step Alcoholics Anonymous program for the treatment of alcoholism.

It is not scientifically logical to say that a person is addicted to a bodily process. An alcoholic is not addicted to drinking or swallowing but to the substance, alcohol. Intake of the substance may be by mouth, or by an enema, rectally, or by injection intravenously. The repetition of its intake, not the route of its intake, is what qualifies alcoholism as an addiction. Thus, it does not make sense to say that someone is addicted to sex or to having sex. By comparison, it might make sense to argue that a man is addicted not to sex overall but, say, specifically to female garments. That would signify that cross dressing brings with it a sense of well-being and relief of tension; that after a binge of divesting himself of his female wardrobe, the cross dresser would undergo a withdrawal reaction; that withdrawal would be relieved by a binge of purchasing replacements; and that, in addition, cross dressing would be not only for display or entertainment, but as an essential adjunct to genital arousal and performance. *Fixation*, however, is a more correct term than *addiction*.

The man who has a fixation on female garments and whose sexual performance without them is inadequate is diagnosed in the official nosology as a fetishistic transvestite, which means a cross dresser with a fetish for female garments. Fetishistic transvestism belongs in the category of paraphilia. It is seldom, if ever, reported by a woman.

A person diagnosed as a fetishistic transvestite or as any other type of paraphile carries the stigma of being abnormal, which most people resent. One strategy by which to circumvent the stigma is to change the name of the diagnosis. This has happened in the case of transvestism. In the course of the last half dozen years, transvestites have become self-defined as being, together with transexuals, among the *transgendered;* witness the book title, *Current Concepts in Transgender Identity* (Denny 1998).

Another strategy by which to circumvent paraphilic stigmatization is to question the validity of its inclusion in the nosology of pathology in the first place. This is the strategy that was followed in the gay liberation movement, which, in 1974, brought about the declassification of homosexuality as a pathology and its exclusion from the American Psychiatric Association's nomenclature (Money 1995). Timing helped. The declassification of homosexuality took place in the historic era of liberation—colonial, black, women's, and gay liberation—known also for being the pre-HIV/AIDS era before the gates of the sexual revolution began to close. It helped also that, in the vernacular vocabulary, the homosexual community became self-identified as gay and lesbian. These words, with a more wholesome ring than any word contaminated by sex, continued to be politically prudent in the counterrevolutionary climate of the 1980s and 1990s. By then, in popular usage, sex had become increasingly disengaged from gender. At the same time, gender became neutered, while the criminalization of sexual lust proceeded apace (Money 1993, 355) as it continues to do at the close of the millennium.

Paraphilia

WHEREAS IN THE hypophilias love outperforms lust, and in the hyperphilias lust outperforms love, in the paraphilias love and lust are deconnected (dissociated), each to perform independently of the other.

Deconnection is exemplified in the person of a serial lust murderer, usually a male. Not only is he a serial lust murderer but also the neighbor who lives next door. He is a family provider and a lay preacher. He is bonded in love to his wife, though without lust for her. Lust belongs to the actuality and imagery of lust murder, replayable mentally. The neighbors are astonished when he is arrested as a lust murderer. So also is he, to a certain extent, for while lust murdering, he has undergone an altered state of consciousness, or fugue state.

The most frequently diagnosed of the forty-odd paraphilias are those which are legally sex offending. Those that are legal mostly go undiagnosed or misdiagnosed. This is what had happened to a woman requesting treatment for what she self-diagnosed as nymphomania. Her history was that every weekend she lost a subjectively internal battle to stay at home setting a good example for her pubertally aged daughter. Instead, after the child was asleep, the mother would take on her harlot personality and take off for a classy hotel bar and restaurant in the neighborhood. There, it was predictable that she would pick up a sexy male to provide drinks and dinner and then take him home to bed. No matter how good he was as a lover, when it was all finished, she was flooded with self-disgust and did not want to see him ever again. Invariably, she would put him out on the street, inhospitably, in the early hours of the morning. By defining her repetitious routine as hypersexual, she did not apperceive its fixation—always a stranger, always the same place, the same seductive power, the same good sexual performance, and the same disgust and peremptory riddance. Hers was not a hyperphilic sex drive but a paraphilic one. Was it merely quirky or pathological? Her own verdict was the latter.

Defining paraphilia as a sexually fixated pathology distinguishable from a quirky sexual recreation or variant is a perilous endeavor that pits biomedical science against the criminal justice system. Before paraphilic sexual offenses were coded in the secular law, they had been coded in the canon law as offenses against God's natural law in accordance with the teachings of St. Augustine. The church decreed that any form of sexual activity which excluded the possibility of procreation was an offense against God and nature. Offenses included oral, anal, and manual sex, autoeroticism, sex with or between juveniles, homosexual eroticism, indecent exposure, sexual peeping, sex with animals, or any other deviation from human penial vaginal insertive sex. Rape did not preclude procreation. It was coded as a crime against property, insofar as the female belonged to her father and, when married, to her husband. Sadism and masochism were unnamed as paraphilias until the nineteenth century. The medieval age of torture and the Inquisition was a heyday for sadistic cruelty. Masochism was regarded as pious penance or as martyred bliss, and it was represented as such in religious art of the era.

The ecclesiastical code of deviant and forbidden sexuality was taken over, holus-bolus, into the secular criminal code. The majesty of the law spoke ex cathedra and defined sexual deviancy, as it still does, with the authority and certainty of ecclesiastical doctrine, not of substantiating empirical evidence (see also chaps. 5, 7).

Pathology/Recreation

AT THE TIME of its founding in the late nineteenth century, sexology made its entry into the criminal justice system by way of forensic psychiatry, notably under the aegis of Richard von Krafft-Ebing 1886/1931. Forensic psychiatry borrowed the nomenclature of the law in classifying sexual offenders as sexual deviants and sexual perverts. Forensic psychiatry also borrowed from the criminal code its official list of the perversions. Eventually, the terms *perversion* and *deviancy* would give way to *paraphilia,* a term brought into American psychiatry by Benjamin Karpman, who borrowed it from his teacher, Wilhelm Stekel, who wrote that he had borrowed it from I. F. Krauss (see Money and Lamacz 1989, 17).

In 1980, paraphilia was adopted in *DSM-III (Diagnostic and Statistical Manual of Mental Disorders, Third Edition)* the official manual of the American Psychiatric Association (APA). Eight paraphilias were listed: fetishism, transvestism, zoophilia, pedophilia, exhibitionism, voyeurism, sexual masochism, and sexual sadism, all of which were liable to legal prosecution. The residual ninth category was for Atypical Paraphilia. This category was "for the many other paraphilias that exist but that have not been sufficiently described to date to warrant inclusion as specific categories."

In *DSM-IV,* the fourth edition of the *Diagnostic and Statistical Manual* (1994), the APA lists a ninth additional paraphilia, frotteurism, i.e., sexually touching or rubbing against a stranger in a crowded, enclosed space, such as a subway car. In the category, "Paraphilia Not Otherwise Mentioned," seven additional paraphilias are mentioned by name only: telephone scatologia, necrophilia, partialism, zoophilia, coprophilia, klismaphilia, and urophilia. Remarkably, rape is not included, the reason being that a delegation of women psychiatrists and psychologists engineered its exclusion. They wanted rape prosecuted and punished exclusively as a nonsexual crime of violence and not subject to diagnosis and treatment as a sexological pathology.

This split in the ranks of forensic sexology on the issue of rape is indicative of a far-reaching philosophical split on the ethics of personal responsibility for illness. Historically, it has been an uphill climb in medicine for a syndrome to be transferred away from the realm of moral responsibility, as in noncompliancy, to that of morally impartial biomedical science. Typically, the transition does not take place until the etiology of a syndrome has been established and an effective treatment set in place. Then it becomes feasible to treat the symptoms, with or without the patient's moral obligation to comply with anything other than treatment. Treatment of syphilis with penicillin is now of this type, whereas it formerly was possible to blame the patient for not complying with a variety of instructions about diet, sleep, exercise, fresh air, smoking, alcohol, work, prayer—the list goes on and on. Putting moral responsibility on the patient always gives the doctor an alibi, at the expense of the patient, for treatment that is ineffectual. A current example pertains to the new impotence drug, Viagra, which, it is warned, does not work in the absence of sexual desire or arousal, for both of which the patient, not the doctor, is held responsible.

In the case of the paraphilias, the etiology still is not understood, and there is no single, sure-fire treatment procedure. Therefore, all patients with these syndromes are easily targeted with moral responsibility for not suppressing their paraphilic behavior. There are some whose paraphilia is minor and may be at least temporarily responsive to moral intervention, whereas those with a major paraphilia are not so fortunate.

Nosological declassification does not solve, as it did in the case of homosexuality, the vexing problem of where to draw the ideological line between normal and abnormal or tolerance and intolerance of paraphilic (kinky) sexuality. Some paraphilic rituals are deadly and some merely quirky. Some are immutably fixated, persistently recurrent, imperiously demanding, and all but impervious to available intervention. By contrast, other paraphilic rituals are erotic recreations, not enslavements. They do not have an exclusive monopoly over erotic arousal. They are engaged in sporadically and are somewhat mutable. Sadomasochism is a made-to-order example.

In most major metropolitan areas around the planet, local inhabitants, visitors, and tourists have access to a network of information regarding meeting places for people with specific paraphilic proclivities (Moser 1998). Some are homosexual only, some are heterosexual, and some are bisexual. They represent a wide variety of paraphilias including infantilism, cross dressing, bondage and discipline, coprophilia and urophilia, foot (but not hand) fetishism, master/slave, threesomes and group orgies, and sadomasochism. The clientele are of adult age range. The paraphilias most prominently represented in metropolitan area clubs are probably some variant of sadomasochism.

In defense of sadomasochism, its apologists point out that it is a mutual agreement between two consenting adults and is nobody's business except their own, whether performed together in private or in a membership club with observers. Although the sadist—the top—appears to dominate the masochist—the bottom—power, it is claimed, is in fact equally distributed: the power of the top lies in gauging exactly how intense the sadistic stimulus should be for the maximum delight of the bottom, and the power of the bottom lies in conveying when the sadistic stimulus is intense enough (Mistress Jacqueline 1991). A signaling system is agreed upon in advance. In addition, the top and bottom roles may be interchangeable, either on different occasions or with different partners. When the top and the bottom are reciprocally well in tune with one another, then the degree of ecstasy may build up to a whole body climax that is reported to surpass the orgasm of ordinary intercourse. Moreover, the genitalia are not necessarily directly stimulated or exposed, so that the procedure cannot be condemned as pornographic. The top expects total submission and obedience, and the bottom expects to be an obedient slave, maybe chained, handcuffed, gagged, blindfolded, tied down, and completely trusting the discretion of the top. The sadistic implements include paddles, straps, whips, piercing needles, urinary catheters, enema syringes, alligator nipple and skin clips, burning cigarette ends, and branding irons. Sadistic stimulation is applied progressively in a crescendo that begins with pain and transforms into painless transcendental bliss.

"People just don't realize that it's such a natural high," wrote a female masochist. "No drugs, no alcohol. And believe me, it's a higher high than any kind of drug could give you. It's extremely spiritual. It involves skill, sensitivity, a kind of psychic awareness and, basically, it's grounded in sexuality, which is always fun!" (Moser and Madeson 1996).

Although the sadistic procedures may stop short of long term bodily mutilation, by mutual consent, it may not. It has been known that mutual consent ends up in the unscheduled death of the bottom induced by, for example, poorly regulated bondage and discipline. In one case from the Midwest, a young sadomasochistic man was on trial for manslaughter. His sadomasochistic girlfriend had come by for an S/M session. It was her turn to be bound and gagged. His scenario called for him to mix himself another martini, while his partner was put on hold. He fell asleep. When he woke up, she was dead. Gagged and wearing a leather face helmet, she had been unable to make any sound or movement to inform him that her harness had slipped and was choking her. Consensual agreement had not been enough to prevent an S/M catastrophe.

In another potentially lethal case, there was a sadist who procured young women prostitutes without informing them of his sadistic propensity. He had what appeared to be a quirky habit of hoarding hundreds of dollars worth of bathroom cleaning supplies. These hoarded supplies were far more dangerous than quirky, however, for they intimated the possibility of sadistic torture, bloodiness, and even death.

By contrast, the top level political or financial power broker by day argues for his right to retain a paid dominatrix (or dominator) by night so that, in bondage and discipline as her slave, he can have the most stupendous orgasms of his life. With his wife, he is impotent. He does not quit his career to become a permanent slave, twenty four hours a day, owned by his dominatrix. However, full time masochistic slavery, with complete humiliation and obedience to the dominatrix, has also been recorded. One such slave, an accomplished musician, forfeited his career, and signed his considerable savings and investment wealth over to his new dominatrix wife and her daughter. Penniless, he managed to contact out of state medical friends and beg to be rescued. They set a time when his wife would be away from home on business. They found him locked away in a cage-like isolation room. They released him and took him to safe haven in New York. Surreptitiously, he made phone calls to his wife. After a couple of weeks, he disappeared to return to his masochistic beatings and enslavement.

As S/M demonstrates, it is indeed difficult to find the dividing line between paraphilia as life-threatening pathology and paraphilia as life enhancing entertainment. There is no absolute criterion applicable to all cases. There are those who would say that paraphilic fantasy is acceptable, provided it is retained in fantasy only. This is not so for the fixated paraphile knows that his fantasy is a rehearsal of a drama that may break loose and become produced as a real live show.

The fear and thrill of such uncertainty is expressed in the writing of a retired archaeology professor, quoted with permission. In the magazine *Drummer*, he advertised his "interest in any form of forcible deprivation of air, including choking, strangling, suffocation, arm across the throat, and even drowning." He received several answers. In this way he met Carlo, of whom he wrote as follows.

> In the past month, Carlo has visited me again. . . . He is now 43 years old. Twice during his 24-hour visit, I lay on top of him, he wearing a spandex shirt and shorts, me with only a jock strap, and choked him with my right hand across his throat while kissing him. He made no attempts to free himself from my grip. He experienced an orgasm during that time. The second time I put a large clear plastic bag over his head with a rubber band around his neck and choked him while we kissed through the plastic bag. Again he got an orgasm. I am no longer able to get an erection, though I do emit a lot of pre-cum. He understands, and I masturbate after he has gone to bed in the guest room downstairs.
> Carlo is the only man with whom I've ever had such an experience. Although my fantasies are often terminal in nature, I never even think of continuing my choking of Carlo to the point that he is helpless. I guess, though, if I have him cuffed or tied to the bed, he is helpless, but even then I don't think of going "too far." I suppose there is always a chance that he (or I) might suffer a heart attack during such a scene. It is more likely to happen to me than to him, I being 75, and he in the very best physical condition. When I meet a man, the idea of strangulation usually comes to mind. I look at his throat as well as his face and then his physical condition.
>
> One man, also 43, who lives in Germany, comes to the States from time to time. He answered my ad, saying that he is strictly a

top. We have corresponded several times and he has been in the States a couple of times, but we did not get together. Now he has just written that he is planning another trip over here and would like to get together with me. In his letters he goes into great detail about what he would like to do to and with me. It is very exciting to me, but I fear that he might go too far. Consequently I am about to write to him declining his offer to pay me a visit.

Male/Female Ratio

ALTHOUGH PARAPHILIAS OCCUR in men and women, it has long been accepted wisdom that their prevalence is greater in men than women. In the absence of a systematic epidemiological study, the male/female prevalence ratio must remain an unanswered question. The popular as well as the scientific stereotype of women's sexual passivity may have allowed the evidence of paraphilia in a female to go unreported. Thus a female exhibitionist (*Baubophile*) in a hotel lobby seated so as to expose her nude genital area might go unreported, whereas a male exhibiting his genitals would be arrested. A female pedophile who sleeps in the same bed as her juvenile son or daughter, is less likely to be condemned than would be her husband if he slept in the same bed as his juvenile daughter or son. If a woman's paraphilia involves a male partner, then the paraphilia is more likely to be attributed to him rather than to her.

Another consideration to be given to the male/female paraphilic prevalence ratio is that some paraphilias are more prevalent in females than males and others less prevalent. Thus, it is a worthy hypothesis that the imagery of women's paraphilias is predominantly contrectative or tactual than visual. In one case, for example (Money 1986, chap. 15), a woman was fixated on rubbing small dogs between her legs. They were a substitute for baby boys. She had a history, dating from early adolescence, when she first began baby sitting, of positioning small infants, boys only, between her legs, genitals to genitals, and doing masturbatory rubbing. After marriage, sexual intercourse was an agonizing burden, but the couple had three children, two of them boys. She was mortally terrified that she would use the boys for genital rubbing but used dogs as putative substitutes.

This same woman had dreams and fantasies that helped relieve the rubbing paraphilic fixation. They were fantasies of "big lovely penises," of men who were black, not white like herself, and of running off with a heavy-built black assailant. Fantasies of fatal attraction, of being swept away and of surrendering to the passionate embrace of a sexually surgent abductor, are widespread among women. Their prevalence in either fantasy or actuality as a paraphilia has not been ascertained. From a feminist perspective, it would be politically incorrect to collect such data.

3

Gender Transpositions

Transposition and Paraphilia

When, in the final quarter of the nineteenth century, forensic psychiatry staked a claim to forensic sexology, it classified homosexuality as one of the perversions. Thus, homosexuality was diagnosable as a disease in need of a cure. It remained so until more than a century later when the term *perversion* was changed to *paraphilia* in *DSM-III* (1980). Homosexuality, having been officially declassified as a disease since 1974, was not listed as a paraphilia in *DSM-III,* nor in subsequent editions.

Declassified, homosexuality is conceptually in a class by itself. Loosely, in popular usage, it is referred to as a preference, orientation, or normal variant. Like heterosexuality, homosexuality is not indexed in *DSM-IV* (1994). In effect, homosexuality as well as heterosexuality have become conceptually orphaned and without a home. Nonetheless, homosexuality belongs somewhere, and that somewhere needs a conceptual name. Hence, the coinage of the conceptual term, *gender transposition* (Money 1984), of which there are diverse manifestations.

Gender transposition means that, in the differentiation and development of natal males or natal females, one or more dimensions of stereotypical masculine or feminine characteristics become, respectively, crosscoded. In its least complex form, homosexual crosscoding is unidimensional and is characterized as erotic attraction toward and response to a member of the same natal sex as the self. In this unidimensional version of homosexual transposition, there is no evidence of other dimensions of transposition, such as cross dressing.

There is no name for the specific, unidimensional type of transposition other than the generic term *homosexual*. It is defined by the natal sex of the partner. It may be manifested either regularly or sporadically. It may signify either exclusive homosexuality or situationally specific homosexuality. Situational homosexuality does not exclude heterosexual attraction and activity. Therefore, it signifies some degree of bisexuality, no matter how consistently or sporadically manifested in the sexological history.

The term *homosexual* is both an adjective and a noun. As an adjective, it applies to a sexual act between two members of the same natal sex. By extension, especially in legal matters, it applies also to a person known to have participated in any way in a homosexual act. Adjectivally, the term *homosexual* does not differentiate between situational and exclusive homosexuality. By contrast, the noun *homosexual* is virtually always used to signify, and usually to stigmatize, a type of person, namely one for whom same-sex preempts other-sex erotic attraction and arousal.

Situational homosexuality may be contingent on male-female segregation in relation to both age and occupation. It is more prevalent in adolescent life than later. In adulthood, it is more prevalent in, for example, sex segregated correctional and military institutions than in sex integrated civilian institutions. Among even long term inhabitants of sex segregated institutions, however, there are many individuals who have no bisexual potential and are incapable of sex-uoerotically responding to a same sexed partner (see Keyes and Money 1993). One youthful prisoner gave a report of being sexually turned on and getting an erection in the communal shower room only if the body morphology of another young inmate metamor-phosed, in his imagery, to that of a nubile female (Money and Bohmer 1980). Once released from prison, this informant resumed an exclusively heterosexual life style.

Multidimensional gender transposition leaves its mark not only on homosexual attraction and practices but also on the other dimen-sions of gender stereotypes: education, vocation, recreation, law, dress, and the societally regulated gender semiotics of etiquette, fash-ion, vocal intonation, and body language. In natal males, one out-come of multidimensional gender transposition is the so-called sissy boy or gay queen feminoid type of natal male. Correspondingly, the virilistic girl or butch dyke is the masculinoid type of natal female. Between these two extremes of unidimensional and multidimension-al gender transposition, there are diverse degrees and combinations of gender crosscoding.

The two extremes of gender transposition have been recognized since antiquity. In Latin, a youthful male with multidimensional gen-der transposition was named a *catamite* (from the Latin *Catamitus*, derived from the Greek, *Ganymede*, lover of Zeus). The ancients had no corresponding name for a natal female. Among males, a catamite was the receptor, never the inserter in anal copulation. There was no specific name for the inserter that would differentiate him from males in general.

Following in the footsteps of the ancients, the Mediterranean area of Europe continues the distinction between male-on-male in-serter and receptor. The distinction diffused from the Mediterranean to the Latin American culture area, where it has been studied no-tably among Puerto Ricans (Carballo-Dieguez 1995), Mexicans of Guadalajara (Carrier 1989; 1995), and Brazilians (Parker 1989). The male who does the penetrating is the *activo*, and the male who is penetrated is the *pasivo*. There is no special name for those who do both. Pasivos are stigmatized. Activos may escape stigmatization altogether, provided they are discreet. Activos, even though bisexual by behavioral history, define themselves as *hombre* (heterosexual).

They claim extenuating circumstances, like being drunk, short of cash, or woman deprived, as the rationale for resorting to having sex with a pasivo. The macho image is damaged not by having penetrative sex with another male but by cuddling and kissing him. The intimacy of cuddling and kissing is macho only if engaged in with a woman partner.

In the sexological literature, natal males who, like activos, have a unidimensional degree of homosexual crosscoding are often characterized as having a masculine gender identity and a homosexual orientation. It is more correct and precise to say that their gender-identity/role [G-I/R] is masculine in all of its dimensions (educational, vocational, recreational, sartorial, semiotical, legal) except for the erotosexual dimension of episodic attraction to, and/or performance with partners who are natal males like the self (Money 1994b, chap. 11). Correspondingly, in the case of lesbianism, the same applies.

Both the unidimensional and the multidimensional expressions of gender transposition may exist with or without evidence of a coexistent paraphilia. That is why it satisfies both common sense and the logic of science to separate gender transposition from paraphilia. Paraphilias are not specifically and exclusively either heterosexual or homosexual. They may be either, or they may be bisexual.

When a paraphilia does coexist with a gender transposition, their coexistence is fortuitous rather than systematically correlated. If they do coexist, it is conceivable that whatever has gone awry developmentally so as to pave the way for paraphilic ideation and imagery also paves the way also for G-I/R differentiation to go awry concurrently. In some instances of homosexuality, paraphilic imagery may escape attention. To avoid this possibility, the sexological history taking should begin with open-ended inquiry that does not put constraints on the replies. Open-ended inquiry is followed by an interrogatory inquiry so as to obtain details, using the sportscaster's technique of a play-by-play account of the sequence of events (Money 1994b, chap. 7).

An example of a heterosexual paraphilia within which a minor gender transposition could not easily be discerned is to be found in the autobiography of an asphyxiophile published in *The Breathless Orgasm* (Money et al. 1991). The author of this autobiography, Nelson Cooper, sought treatment to prevent autoerotic death from self-strangulation. From early childhood onward, he had been over-whelmed with attraction to females who were scared off by his overin-tensity. After puberty, except for self-strangulation, his erotic imagery in dreams and fantasies was of females drowning or being strangled. This imagery was in part borrowed from his home video recordings of TV prime-time movies. Only in the fantasies and practice of self-strangulation did he have the apperception of himself as a girl. He would be standing in front of a mirror in close fitting bikini under-wear, with women's dance tights around his neck, imagining himself to be strangled by a male stealing up on him from behind, as a serial ho-mosexual killer like the infamous John Wayne Gacy might have done.

In the mirror, Nelson Cooper saw his reflection as that of a well proportioned gay boy, not a girl. He did not cross dress and did not have a cross dressed girl's name. It is known from forensic reports on accidental death from autoerotic self-strangulation in males, howev-er, that the deceased was wearing female garments while engaging in the autoerotic ritual of asphyxiophilia (Hazelwood et al. 1983; Bogioli et al. 1991). In some instances, the garments have belonged to the mother. After even years of practice, it requires only a split sec-ond error of timing for the opening of the self-asphyxiating noose to fail, so that blackout and death ensue. The death is that of the stig-matized, albeit eroticized, cross-gendered alter ego.

Another example of gender transposition associated with para-philia is found in the case of a man with an adult history of paraphilic cross dressing which, years later, appeared to have metamorphosed into paraphilic infantilism (Money 1970). Appearances were mis-leading. He gave a demonstration of dressing up in adult diapers and going bye-byes, sucking on a milk-filled baby bottle, and wetting his diapers. The baby's sex was indeterminant at first, but the name eventually became that of a boy and remained so for years. The bridge between dressing as a baby and cross dressing as a woman originated in boyhood when his mother punished him by parading him on the town's main street wearing a girl's dress and diapers. She humiliated him by telling his school friends that he was being pun-ished for bed wetting. His paraphilic baby ritual was repellent to his wife, but it was more tolerable than to have him perform coitus dressed in women's clothes to maintain sexual arousal. After com-pleting his bedtime baby ritual, he would go to sleep. In the morning, he would awaken his wife by sucking on her nipples. Then they would embrace and have sex together.

Kinsey Scaling and Typology

HOMOSEXUAL GENDER TRANSPOSITION can be graded on a quasi-quantitative bipolar scale that ranges from exclusively homosexual through bisexual to exclusively heterosexual. This is the so-called Kinsey scale (Kinsey et al. 1948). It is a seven point scale, graded from six to zero, with six being exclusively homosexual and zero exclusively heterosexual.

A Kinsey rating is uniaxial. Its single axis is prevalence—the prevalence of homosexual and heterosexual acts reported to have occurred at a given age or over a given period of time. The rating may be split in two: one for occurrences in actuality and one for occurrences in ideation and imagery.

A uniaxial Kinsey rating does not differentiate between different homosexual/heterosexual types. Thus, a ranking military officer who conforms to the male stereotype except for being exclusively homosexual in the bedroom would be rated a Kinsey six. The same rating, six, would be given to a natal male transvestite who lives full time as a woman, impersonates a female prostitute, and sexually services men only. That rating would reverse from six to zero if the transvestite lived and dressed full time as a woman at work and at home and had sex, even though rarely, only with his wife and never with another male.

To further complicate the uniaxial system, the same husband's rating would reverse from zero to six if, after undergoing male-to-female hormonal and surgical sex reassignment, he-now-she became her wife's lesbian girlfriend. If, however, having been reassigned as a woman, she took up with a new boyfriend and never again had sex with a woman, the rating would once more flip-flop to a heterosexual zero!

Instead of a uniaxial rating scale, what is needed is a multiaxial one. Such a scale can be depicted metaphorically as a spindle (Money 1998a) pierced by multiple bipolar, male-to-female measuring rods or spokes. There would be separate rods on which to rate adherence to stereotypic masculinity/femininity with respect to sexual partnering, vocation, education, recreation, household arrangements, dress code, cosmetics, adornment, etiquette, mannerisms, vocal cadence, body language, body image, and body morphology.

In multiaxial scaling, each axis has its own Kinsey type of bipolar scale with a continuous distribution ranging from gender transposed to gender nontransposed. The criterion standard is that of the natal sex. For example, on the homosexual/heterosexual dimension, gender transposed is homosexual, and gender nontransposed is heterosexual. On the body image dimension, being gender transposed is manifested as full-time transvestism or transexualism. By contrast, being gender nontransposed on the body image dimension means having a body image concordant with the natal morphological sex.

It is counterintuitive to discover that gender transposition on the body image axis is not necessarily accompanied by transposition on the homosexual/heterosexual axis. But that discordance is exactly what one does discover: in transvestism and transexualism, the individual's partnership is heterosexual in some cases, homosexual in other cases, bisexual in still others, and, rarely, asexual. Multiaxial scaling takes into account the fact that the homo/hetero dimension and the body image dimension are not on the same continuum. Even though they may on occasion overlap, the two dimensions represent a bimodal typology.

Body Image and Body Morphology

AS ORIGINALLY USED, the term *body image* was the counterpart of *body schema* (Money 1994a). *Body schema* is a neurobiological term signifying the representation of the body in the brain. *Body image* is a psychological term signifying the representation of the body mentally and, far from excluding its cerebral representation also, sometimes actually locating it as a "phantom in the brain," to quote the title of the book by the neuroscientist V. S. Ramachandran and coauthor Sandra Blakeslee (1998). Ramachandran discovered that after a limb has been amputated, the nerve cells in the brain that formerly were connected with the missing limb do not wither up and die. Instead, they sprout new dendritic fibers that attach themselves to their nearest neighbor which in the case of the foot and lower leg are the sex organs. With the foot and lower leg gone, the nerve cells left behind in the cerebral cortex join themselves to their next door sex nerves. The outcome for one self-amputee patient was the unexpected discovery of erotic feeling from fondling the stump and an intensification of orgasm if he masturbated at the same time. He had a sexological diagnosis of paraphilic amputeeism (*apotemnophilia*) and had contrived an accident so as to have a body morphology that agreed with his body image as an amputee.

The body image and the body morphology may be either concordant or discordant with one another. Discordance fills the medical and surgical market place with candidates for cosmetological intervention designed to alter the body morphology so that it is concordant with the idealized body image. Some candidates seek the restoration of youthfulness of the natal body and/or the enhancement of its sex appeal—for instance, a face lift or breast augmentation for women, and penis lengthening and enlargement for men, especially gay men. Cosmetological intervention extends to tattooing of the body, an ancient rite of manhood in many parts of the world, and notably in Polynesia. Tattooing is currently in vogue for women as well as men. So also is piercing of various body parts—the ears, nostrils, lips, tongue, nipples, navel, and genitalia—for the wearing of gold rings, bars, and other jewelry. Although piercing of the ears and nose has an ancient heritage as cosmetic enhancement for women, the vogue of these and other piercings for men is recent. Genital, navel, and nipple piercings are a badge of membership in some sadomasochistic circles. These piercings are also fashionable in the gay male community.

Transexualism

THE TERM *transvestism* (the Latin term means cross dressing), was coined early in the twentieth century by Magnus Hirschfeld (1910/ 1991). It filled a void in both the clinical and the forensic vocabulary. It used the criterion of cross dressing generically as the defining characteristic of what would subsequently be partitioned into different entities. One such entity would become known as transexualism (Cauldwell 1949; Benjamin 1966).

In transexualism, the sex of the body image is at variance with the natal sex of the body morphology. The same term is used to name both the phenomenon and its method of treatment and rehabilitation by means of hormonal and surgical sex reassignment (Green and Money 1969). In this way, the body morphology is gender transposed to approximate, as closely as possible, the already transposed body image, unclothed as well as clothed.

Gender dysphoria is an alternative name for transexualism. Its criterion is intrapsychic distress and lack of well being. In *DSM-IV* (1994), transexualism was replaced by another alternative: gender identity disorder of adulthood. In the last half dozen years, transexuals themselves, as an organized medical consumers' group, have favored *transgender identity* (Denny 1998).

Mimetic Transvestism

Transgender, like *transvestism* as coined by Hirschfeld a century ago, is a more inclusive term than is *transexual*. It applies to the phenomenon of transexualism and also of transvestism, the former with genital surgical transformation and the latter without it. In generic usage, *transvestism* means simply being cross dressed. In specific sexological usage, *transvestism* is a typology. One specific type is mimetic (from Greek, *mimos*, mimic) transvestism, namely *gynemimesis* in natal males and *andromimesis* in natal females. In mimetic transvestism, as in transexualism, the body image is gender transposed and is at odds with the body morphology, except that the genitalia are exempted from surgery.

The gynemimetic transvestite is a lady with a penis who lives full time as a woman, dresses only in women's garments, earns a living as a woman, and engages sexually only with a male partner, either casually or in a long term relationship. Correspondingly, the andromimetic transvestite is a man with a vulva who lives, works, and dresses full time as a man and has only a female as a sexual partner.

Mimetic transvestites may obtain treatment with sex hormones to induce a second pubertal hormonalization of the body so that it becomes, as much as possible, concordant with the transposed body image. Hormonal transformation after the first puberty is not, however, as complete as it is if undertaken prepubertally. The sex hormones have been marketed only since they were first synthesized in the 1930s.

Hijras

MIMETIC TRANSVESTISM OCCURS transculturally. It has been differently institutionalized historically and regionally. In India, gynemimetic males are known as hijras (Nanda 1980). Some of them have no testicles, scrotum, or penis, for which the British erroneously named them either as *hermaphrodites* with birth defective sex organs or as *eunuchs,* castrated by one of their own surgical gurus. Traditional hijra treatment includes no technique for the construction of a vaginal cavity and no extraneous source of estrogen to promote breast growth or to suppress the effect of hormonal masculinization. Radical castration, although still a hijra ideal, is optional.

Hijras live in household communities under the supervision of a guru. Several households in a district are loosely confederated, and regional confederations are, in turn, loosely organized nationally. Once in a decade, members gather by the thousands in a national congress.

One traditional way for a hijra household to make a living is by tending a public bathhouse. Another is by being a nuisance, singing and dancing more or less lewdly in the street at an important wedding or announcement of a wealthy family's firstborn son, until they are paid enough to go away. Some individual hijras are supported by a sexual partner, often a married man with a family. Others are available for paid casual liaisons in which they perform as if a female.

Within Indian society, hijras constitute partly a caste and partly a religious cult with its own deity, the goddess Bahuchara Mata. Hijras do not recruit new members but are sought out by those who recognize themselves as candidates. There is no membership for female hijras in male hijra social organization or elsewhere.

Transculturally, there are many variants of the hijra folk tradition but only in India does the tradition include surgical removal of the genitalia (Coleman et al. 1992; Poasa 1992; Wikan 1977; Williams 1986). In modern Western medicine, the recent introduction of surgical and hormonal sex reassignment is an exception.

Theatrical Transvestism

CROSS DRESSING MAY be engaged in recreationally and/or as a theatrical form of entertainment, for example at a Mardi Gras parade or at a drag queens' masquerade ball. Usually named only as *transvestism,* the specific name for this type of cross dressing is *theatrical trans-vestism*. It may be sporadic and situational, as it is for most drag queens. It may be for disguise, as in espionage. Professional entertainers regularly appear cross dressed on stage or on camera as a way of earning a living.

In both the sporadic and the regular variety of theatrical transvestism, gender transposition of the body image is specific chiefly to the external decoration of the body, without alteration of the body itself either hormonally or surgically. The gender transposition of body language, however, is a different story. The perfection of gender crossed body language is a sine qua non of excellence in theatrical transvestism.

Putatively, any great actor or actress could achieve excellence in a theatrical transvestite's role, whether in Shakespearian drama or contemporary cinema or video. Alternatively, achievement of excellence in theatrical transvestism might be contingent on excellence of type casting for the role: only those who have a head start by reason of having an untapped disposition toward mimetic transvestism get the role. If so, then this disposition may involve some degree of gender transposition, although only of body language and body image and not necessarily of sexuoerotic ideation and imagery also.

Actors in the Japanese Kabuki theater provide a case in point. By centuries of tradition, there are no Kabuki actresses. All female roles are impersonated by male actors. They undergo a rigorous training, preferably from boyhood onward, in feminine vocalization and body language. After they graduate, they are not excluded from Kabuki if they are gay. Nor are they excluded if they are the nongay sons of Kabuki female impersonators who, even if to some degree bisexual, were sufficiently heterosexual to have produced a son to follow in the father's footsteps. Being the son who follows in his father's footsteps provides no information about when the following began. It could be the outcome of a genetically transmitted predisposition or of subsequent educational opportunity or a combination of the two.

Paraphilic Transvestism

IN THE NOMENCLATURE of the American Psychiatric Association, the term *transvestic fetishism* first appeared in *DSM-III-R* in 1987. In the revised *DSM-IV* (1994), there was a terminological change to *fetishistic transvestism.* According to the documentary evidence, the fetishistic type of cross dressing occurs predominantly, if not exclusively, in males. Its defining characteristic is that the wearing of women's lingerie or other garments stimulates, and may be imperative for, genitoerotic arousal and performance, including the attainment of orgasm. Deprived of the actual garments, the individual may be able to rely on the stimulation of a replay of a mental video of a former cross dressed performance.

Deprived of a partner, the fetishistic transvestite may masturbate with female clothing as an erotic aid, which is more likely during the period of puberty and adolescence than later. Using or wearing female garments may, as is typical of a fetish, be a substitute for a live partner. However, a partner, if not present in person, may be represented in erotic ideation and imagery—in a masturbation fantasy, for example. The partnership, whether in person or in fantasy, is less likely to be homosexual than heterosexual, though both possibilities exist.

Fetishistic dependency on female garments for genitosexual arousal and performance is the bridge that spans the metaphorical gap between gender transposition of the body image, on the one hand, and paraphilic fixation on the other. As initially manifest in the years of youth and young adulthood, paraphilic cross dressing may be the only overt manifestation of gender transposition in the lovemap. It may remain that way for a lifetime, ensuring adequate copulatory performance in concordance with the natal sex. It commonly happens, however, that copulatory sex becomes subject to progressive apathy and inertia. At the same time, the boundaries of gender transposition may expand beyond cross dressing to fulfill a no longer dormant body image fantasy of complete transexual transformation.

The change from cross dressing to transexualism may be precipitated by catastrophic stress, such as the sudden death of a spouse or the diagnosis of lethal cancer in oneself (unpublished data). It is as though release of the nubile girl long hidden in the body image will ensure a reincarnation and a chance to live one's life again, free from catastrophe. Alternatively, the change toward transexualism may be the long delayed unfolding of a fantasy of gender transposition that becomes insistently demanding. In a unique way, that is what happened to a man with long lived ideation and imagery of becoming more girlish by getting rid of his testicles. From a farming supply store, he purchased an animal castration kit and, in a rented motel room, castrated himself. He expected that his grown children and wife would not need to know what he had done, but a scrotal infection blew his cover.

He was euphoric about being rid of his testicles. He regretted being unable to satisfy his wife with penetrative penile intercourse, whereas he rated sexual relations for himself as never having been better. His explanation was that he was no longer disturbed by having an erection to remind him of not being girlish. Instead, he could be completely oblivious of himself as male while performing prolonged cunnilingus on his wife, all the while experiencing himself in fantasy as a lesbian girl. That he found to be very gratifying.

His wife did not object to oral sex but missed penial vaginal penetration. Nonetheless, she passed up a serious offer by her husband's widowed brother, who had always carried a torch for her, to divorce her husband so that he could marry her. They would all three live together, which would enable her to continue to be protective of her former husband. Her religious scruples were against that. So she and her husband continued their lifelong fidelity, albeit with a progressively diminishing sex life.

Skoptic Syndrome

IN FARM MANAGEMENT, the gelding of male animals is a matter of expediency and not of ethics, whereas in human beings it constitutes mutilation or mayhem. One exception is that, since early times, captured slaves were castrated to make them more docile and more easily subjugated. Boys and youths in training as harem attendants had their testicles removed to prevent fertility. The penis was removed also to prevent copulation, though it did not guarantee the prevention of fondling and oral sex, even though both were forbidden in the harem. In imperial China, boys were castrated so as to be eligible for positions of administrative power as eunuchs. In Europe until the nineteenth century, choir boys with outstanding voices were castrated prepubertally in preparation for a career as soprani castrati in male only cathedral choirs and in operatic female roles in male only opera productions.

In the nineteenth century, compulsory castration of the eugenically unfit was widely debated. The doctrine of eugenic purity, taken up by Hitler, culminated in the Holocaust. Thereafter, the idea of eugenic castration fell into disgrace. In medicine, however, castration became acceptable if the testicles were cancerous or otherwise defective and if their removal as the chief source of testosterone would slow the growth of cancer in other organs. Removal of gonads that had no evident signs of disease came to the ethical forefront again when, in the second half of the twentieth century, sex reassignment of transexuals entailed surgical castration. The ethics of sex reassignment is still open to debate. So also is the ethics of voluntarily requested castration as a surgical intervention for sex offenders.

Opinion in favor of sex offenders who plead for castration to diminish or prevent a recurrence of offending is in the minority. The majority opinion is that sex offenders, especially those who have been apprehended and imprisoned, are unable to give truly informed consent to a procedure that is still advocated as a form of punishment. The outcome is that castration as a form of therapy is disallowed. To a lesser degree, so also is so-called chemical castration (which is reversible) by therapy with an antiandrogenic hormone. As a punishment, however, the hormonal treatment may be enforced, as it is in some United States jurisdictions. Rejected as medical prevention, antiandrogen is accepted as a judicial punishment!

The negative aura that surrounds castration makes it impossible for most people to give credence to those individuals whose entire lives are governed by a fixation on becoming a eunuch. Their condition, the Skoptic syndrome (Money 1988; 1993, chap. 25), is named after the Skoptsi, a breakaway Russian Christian sect founded in the eighteenth century. (See *Encyclopaedia Britannica*, 1958 ed.)

In Russian, a *skoptsi* is a castrated ram. The Skoptsi would read Matthew 19:12, literally, "For there are some eunuchs, which were so born from their mother's womb; and there are some eunuchs, which were made eunuchs of men; and there be eunuchs, which have made themselves eunuchs for the kingdom of heaven's sake. He that is able to receive it, let him receive it." They adopted castration as an act of salvation. In 1771, two of their leaders, Ivanov and Selivanov, were held responsible for the self-castration of thirteen of their followers. The two were convicted and deported to Siberia. Selivanov escaped and led the sect until he died in 1832 at the age of one hundred, self-proclaimed as God of Gods and King of Kings. By 1874, the membership of the sect was estimated at five thousand, including one thousand women. Whereas the badge of membership for men was removal of the testicles and, ideally, of the penis as well, for women it was destruction of the nipples. Outlawed in Russia, some members of the sect found refuge in Rumania. The last survivors died off in the 1920s. They left a few medical photographs that authenticate their surgical practices.

From the knowledge of hindsight, it is quite possible that Selivanov, leader of the Skoptsi, himself had a fixation on being a eunuch for which he found an explanation in the only source of wisdom available to him, the Bible. As a religious ritual, castration elevated him to a position of charismatic grandiosity from which he recruited converts who "made themselves eunuchs for the kingdom of heaven's sake."

Case of Self-Surgery

EVEN WITHOUT CHARISMATIC recruitment, there are in each generation some individuals who independently develop a fixation on becoming a eunuch under the assumption that castration will eradicate what they apperceive as the burden of sexuality. In a few such cases of the skoptic syndrome, an individual, leaving no stone unturned in the search for a surgeon who will castrate him, has presented as a candidate for sex reassignment without removal of the penis. Others have been fixated on a program of self-castration. The autobiographical statement of one such person is reproduced with permission in Money (1988, 1993). As a college student, he succeeded over a period of three years in bilateral self-castration, using only a pocket knife and scalpels made from razor blades. His operating room was a toilet stall in the student bathroom. He used ice or Alka-Seltzer as analgesics and no anesthetic.

> With the removal of the testicles I expected and hoped for a substantial loss of the sex drive and a return to much more favorable emotional conditions, he wrote. In fact there was some reduction in libido and potency but these changes were relatively minor. Underneath the seething madness of desire seemed as strong as ever. This I largely attributed to the remaining genital member and accordingly began to attack it with a scalpel in an effort to sever its nerves. Over several months I cut many of these (very probably), including the dorsal nerve. This had a far more

profound effect than castration, but unfortunately the change was devastating. Apparently my nervous system could not stand the shock of being deprived of the excitation of the penis, a stimulus on which it had come to depend heavily, even though I despised it. . . . So at this point I experienced an almost total loss of ability to feel pleasure in any form, a terrifying feeling of cold and suffocation replacing all the more usual sensations of living. At this time I was in graduate school in Illinois, but being nearly incapacitated, I had to leave school and meanwhile I finally sought psychiatric help. This, however, proved a disappointing and humiliating failure.

Self-denervation surgery was finally discontinued at age twenty-nine, and he was well enough to reenter graduate school where he eventually obtained a doctoral degree in computer science. He wrote:

Life while far from perfect, seems well worth living. In fact, it has so much potential that I have made arrangements to be frozen in the event of death, in case it becomes possible to revive frozen remains at some future date. No longer do I feel consumed by unwanted passion, shackled by self-repression, or even prostrated by loss of feeling. With the cooling of unwanted drives, I no longer feel revolted by nudity or other expressions of sexuality. . . . I feel that sexual abstinence is the best course for at least some of us, and in fact I prefer to be without the sex drive that caused so much difficulty and was such a burden to me. But it hardly seems reasonable to have to go through the sort of drama that has formed such a large part of my life. Surely there must be a better way.

It is not unheard of that the consummation of any type of fixation ushers in an era of contentment. In the present instance, contentment went hand in hand with replacement of the eunuch fixation by a fixation on resurrection and rebirth through cryogenics. By age thirty-eight, the erstwhile computer scientist had a full time career in marketing cryogenic preservation instead of burial or cremation. No testicles necessary for generating a new birth! Such is the wondrous economy of the psyche in self-rehabilitation.

No satisfactory etiology of this man's fixation has yet been discovered. His own autobiographical attempt to find its origin in childhood development is a chronological history but not a scientifically causal explanation. The brain still holds the secrets of its own fixations.

Attractant Morphology

LOOK AROUND THE planet, and it is perfectly obvious that there are no universal criteria of what, in female or male eyes and minds, constitutes the idealized image of sexuoerotic attractiveness. The criteria of attractivity vary transculturally and have a history of changing with the aesthetics of fashion. Hence, it is academically tempting to subscribe to the current social constructionist doctrine that sexuoerotic attractiveness is a socially constructed entity, and that it is transmitted by social indoctrination of the younger by the older generation. Social constructionism has no place for a human sexuoerotic attractant that, like the pheromonal attractant of subprimate species, is innately constructed and transmitted to all new members of the species.

Nonetheless, there is a common denominator shared by all the cultural variations and fashions of sexuoerotic attractivity, namely, the body morphology of the partner. For the majority of males everywhere, the female morphology is a potent attractant, and for females, the male morphology. It should come as no evolutionary surprise that the human species, like all other species, has a phylogenetically built-in method, a phylism, (Money 1983, 1990b) for sexuoerotic attraction and response; the function of which is to ensure that males and females mate and guarantee the survival of the species.

In evolutionary sexology, it is a new theory (Money 1997a, 1998b) that the human brain innately possesses a phyletic mechanism that codes for the recognition of and response to body morphology as a sexuoerotic attractant. It makes sense that if pheromonal smell is not a major human sexual attractant, something must takes its place. Few would dispute the human evidence of the visualization of lust. The majority of males are attracted to the shape and contour of the morphology of the female silhouette as a sexuoerotic attractant. Similarly, the majority of women are attracted to the shape and contour of the morphology of the male silhouette, more, perhaps, if it is partially covered instead of being completely naked. Women are inclined to focus less than men do on particular regions of the body, especially the exposed genitalia. Socially inculcated modesty may override the sexual attraction of the naked genitalia but not the body morphology as a whole, for with or without clothing, the body is a sexual attractant.

As compared with heterosexual attraction, the defining characteristic of homosexual attraction is that the primary sexuoerotic attractant for homosexuals is the body morphology that is isosexual, that is of the same natal sex as their own. This is especially evident in gay male erotica, more so than in lesbian erotica. Like that of all women, lesbian erotica relies more than does men's erotica on tactile or contrectative imagery as a sexuoerotic attractant.

Heterosexual and homosexual people are alike in responding to body morphology as a sexual attractant. They differ in that heterosexuals have a cross-sexed attraction, whereas homosexuals have a same-sexed or isosexual attraction. Bisexuals have some of both; and asexuals, who are few and far between, have neither. No criterion other than the body morphology of sexuoerotic attraction is needed to distinguish heterosexuality from homosexuality. Within the metaphorical garden of heterosexuality, many varieties and species grow, and it is likewise within the garden of homosexuality. Among male homosexuals, the Indian hijra, the flamboyant New York drag queen, and the in-the-closet British army sergeant may share nothing else in common except that the male body morphology is a sexuoerotic attractant. By that criterion alone, they are all three homosexual.

Other than by phylogenetic heritage, there is no satisfactory explanation of the origin of cross sexed body morphology as a sexuoerotic attractant. The origin of the transposition from cross sexed to isosexed body morphology as a homosexual sexuoerotic attraction continues to be a question in search of an empirically satisfying answer.

Neither heterosexual nor homosexual attraction predispose toward attraction that is also paraphilic, regardless of type, nor do they protect against it. Paraphilias overlap with hetero, homo, or bisexual attraction. Precise percentages elude survey methodology, owing to the possibility of self-incrimination in a society in which many paraphiles are criminally prosecuted.

4

Lovemap Development

Educational Sexology
Genetics Research
Prenatal and Neonatal Hormones
Sexological Socialization
Sexual Rehearsal Play
Idiopathic Precocious Puberty
Age Eight
Collusional Pairbondship
Deferred Symptoms
Geriatric Erosion

Educational Sexology

Suppose that an intelligent observer from another planet, someone of the caliber of Alexis de Tocqueville in the nineteenth century, would visit America today, his mission being to write a report on educational sexology in policy and practice in America. He would be surprised at how parsimonious sex education is with respect to information that, at puberty and adolescence, is in the forefront of personal significance and symbolism, namely the ideation and imagery of love and lust coded in the lovemap.

Like foodmaps, languagemaps, and many other informational maps, lovemaps exist synchronously in the brain and the mind. Therefore, they are mindbrain maps.

Attraction, proception, acception, conception, homosexual, heterosexual, bisexual, transgender, hypophilia, hyperphilia, paraphilia—all varieties of imagery and ideation of sexuoerotic arousal and performance are coded in the lovemap. All of it is personalized. In some instances, the lovemap is not only personalized, but it is also highly idiosyncratic. In others it is more stereotypic.

Lovemaps manifest themselves in daydreams, in masturbation fantasies, and in sleeping dreams. Wet dreams in boys culminate in ejaculatory orgasm. Proportionately fewer girls than boys have orgasm dreams in adolescence, according to the evidence available.

A modern day de Tocqueville would find a paucity of lovemap education even in academic institutions of higher education, including medical schools and law schools, not to mention high schools and grade schools, that offer a formal sex educational curriculum. Instructors tacitly obey the taboo on information that is popularly condemned as being so explicit as to be pornographic and dangerous to student morals. Visually explicit materials are more strongly tabooed than printed texts. The tabooed contents include the imagery and ideation of limerence, heterosexual intercourse, contraception, masturbation, homosexuality, and paraphilic lovemaps. De Tocqueville would find that students are obliged to fill in the blanks of these tabooed contents as best they can from media gossip, circumlocutions, paralipses (mentioning things by saying that they are too unmentionable to speak of freely), and the folk knowledge of their own age group.

The taboo on the transmission of sexual knowledge is justified by aphoristic folk wisdom. Aphoristic wisdom carries with it the certitude of its own proof. Unlike scientific wisdom, it needs no substantiating data. Hence, it never stands in need of revision.

The first aphorism of sexual knowledge is that children are innately pure and innocent sexually. The second aphorism is that sexual teaching is redundant as maturity automatically produces breeding behavior, with no teaching required. The third aphorism is that sexual knowledge, like Eve's apple, automatically is loaded with a temptation to put it into practice. Monkey see, monkey do!

De Tocqueville would, of necessity, admit that not all sex education (the term now in vogue is *sexuality education*) follows these three aphorisms literally. But he would be correct in saying that American sex education begins for the very young with scary warnings about good touch and bad touch that leave them afraid of their own bodies. For older children, sexual teaching is mostly of the eggs, sperms, and menstrual periods genre to which are added warnings about sexually transmitted diseases (STDs), including HIV/AIDS, about the so-called epidemic of teenaged pregnancy, and about abstinence until marriage, no matter how delayed the marriage age may be in favor of advanced professional education.

Children who reach puberty with a paraphilic lovemap typically receive no knowledge of how to predict their paraphilic future. Nor do they have knowledge about where to apply for help, about their legal risks and rights, about the possibility of treatment should a crisis arise, and about possible causality. They must go it alone, stigmatized and ostracized. In their textbooks, they are mentioned, if at all, only as sexual deviants or criminals, the likes of whom are written about as if they were alien invaders, not readers of the book, and not oneself or a fellow student.

Paraphilias, whether recreational or pathological, are coded as ideational and imagistic rehearsals belonging to the lovemap's proceptive phase from which the acceptive and the conceptive phase may ensue. The biomedically scientific respectability of the three phases has been historically in reverse order. In the eighteenth century, obstetrics and gynecology embarked on the emancipation of the conceptive phase of pregnancy and delivery from superstitions of folk medicine (Aveling 1882/1977). More than two centuries later, the acceptive phase came under the explicit purview of biomedical science with a big boost from the Masters and Johnson (1970) publication, *Human Sexual Inadequacy*. The proceptive phase has barely begun the transition from criminology to biomedical science. It is not surprising, therefore, that much remains to be discovered regarding the origins of and predisposition to the development of paraphilic lovemaps.

Genetics Research

PARAPHILIA, UNLIKE HOMOSEXUALITY, has no history of studies of its incidence in family pedigrees or in uniovular (monozygotic) versus dizygotic twins; no history of a search for markers of a paraphilic gene; and no history of anecdotal reports of two or more close kin with the same paraphilia. This absence of data may, in part, be attributable to the difficulty in obtaining information that is often self-incriminating. To circumvent this difficulty, an alternative is to change the methodology and to look not for paraphilia in the kin of a known paraphile but to look for paraphilia in men with a known chromosomal anomaly.

This latter method has had some payoff in the case of the supernumerary Y (47, XYY) syndrome. The study of men with this condition does, indeed, suggest an elevated incidence of paraphilia (Money and Bennett 1981; Money et al. 1975; Money et al. 1976; Wiedeking et al. 1979). However, the association is tenuous for the XYY sample was not randomly sampled from the population at large but from a cytogenetic survey of men detained in either prisons or mental institutions. Their paraphilic histories were part of a larger history of impulsive behavior as if the off-switch key was either defective or lost. Their impulsiveness ranged from irrational rage attacks to robbery to suicide. A different sample of 47, XYY men identified by chromosomal typing of blood donors was behaviorally less extreme (Noel and Revil 1974). As compared with the 47, XYY men, 47, XXY (Klinefelter syndrome) men surveyed in the same institutions did not manifest an elevated incidence of paraphilia.

In the absence of additional evidence, it is not presently feasible to postulate a singulative cause-and-effect relationship between 47, XYY or 47, XXY chromosomal genetics and paraphilia. The coexistence of a supernumerary chromosome and a paraphilia is sporadic rather than systematic. The same applies to the coexistence of the supernumerary X chromosome (47, XXY) and gender transposition, notably in transvestism and transexualism.

The data from other chromosomal syndromes point in the same direction. For example, in the 45, X (Turner) syndrome, the evidence of either gender transposition or paraphilia is noteworthy for its absence (Money unpublished). In the 46, XX hermaphroditic syndrome of congenital adrenal hyperplasia (CAH), the prevalence of gender transposition is elevated (Dittman et al. 1992; Meyer-Bahlburg et al. 1996; Money et al. 1984; Mulaikal et al. 1987; Zucker et al. 1996) with no corresponding elevation of the prevalence of paraphilia. In fact, paraphilia in CAH may be virtually nonexistent.

The counterpart of beginning with a chromosomal syndrome and searching for a paraphilia is to begin with a paraphilia and search for evidence of a genetic marker on one or more of the chromosomes. This kind of research, linking molecular genetics with behavioral sexology, got its start with homosexology (Hamer et al. 1993; Hu et al. 1995). The linkage between homosexuality and a specific gene locus is tenuous. Two attemps at replication have not been confirmatory (Rice et al. 1999; Wickelgren 1999). The methodology has not been applied to paraphilic sexology.

With animals, but not with human beings, it is possible to alter the genome by inserting or knocking out genes, and then observing the subsequent sexological development. This methodology was applied to mice that had been genetically altered so that the gene responsible for the synthesis of nitric oxide (NO), a neurotransmitter, had been knocked out (Nelson et al. 1995; Snyder 1992; see also Burnett et al. 1992; Ignarro 1992). Males, but not females, thus deprived of NO were deprived also of knowing when to stop fighting or copulating. Knockout mice attacked other mice brutally and fatally, and they persisted in repeatedly copulating with dissenting females despite screeching resistance. Eventually, the knockout methodology could lead to a more exact explanation of the neuroscience of lovemaps involving paraphilic assault, rape, sadism, and lust murder.

Prenatal and Neonatal Hormones

IN AN EARLIER era, developmental disorders or predispositions were classified as either inborn or acquired. The idea that anything innate might have been acquired in the womb before birth simply did not enter into causal explanations. By contrast, in today's sexology, it is known that something may be both inborn and acquired, by having been acquired in the intrauterine environment before birth. The intrauterine environment is able to carry viral and bacterial infections from the mother to the fetus and likewise toxins from either prescribed or illicit medications or drugs or from nutritional pollutants in the food chain, the water supply, or the atmosphere.

For example, it is well known that androgenic hormonal substances ingested by the pregnant mother or produced endogenously by an androgen secreting tumor in the mother are able to cross the placenta and masculinize the anatomy of a developing female fetus, thus producing an inborn form of intersex or hermaphroditism (Money 1994c; Migeon et al. 1994).

The counterpart of masculinization of the female fetus is not feminization but demasculinization of the male fetus. Estrogenic substances are known to have an antiandrogenic effect. They may be absorbed inadvertently by the pregnant mother and passed on, through the placenta, to the fetus. They are more likely, however, to lead to fetal wastage than to anatomically demasculinized intersexuality.

The demasculinization of mating behavior is a different story, as demonstrated by Ingeborg Ward (1992a; see also O. B. Ward 1992b). She was able to show that experimentally contrived maternal stress in rodents released adrenocortical stress hormones that crossed the placenta and, by competing with the fetus's own hormones, demasculinized the subsequent postpubertal mating behavior of the male pups. It also lowered their fertility rate. Had the experiment been ethically permitted on human beings, then the outcome would have been interpreted as increased prevalence of being homosexually mounted by males with no history of prenatal demasculinization. It remains to be ascertained if human demasculinization is a sequel to intrauterine stress hormones and, if so, how it manifests itself sexologically after puberty in males.

The newest investigations of the intrauterine sexological environment are focused on hormone disrupters, also known as hormone-mimicking environmental chemicals, in particular polychlorinated biphenyls (PCBs). Norwegian Arctic investigators suspect PCBs are the responsible agent for the intersexual abnormality of the clitoris in several polar bear mothers tagged near the island of Spitzbergen.

American and Taiwanese scientists (Guo et al. 1995) have spearheaded research on the overall developmental effects of PCBs on children whose mothers were exposed while pregnant to PCB contaminated rice oil. Boys were born with small penises. PCBs may also affect the fertility of human fathers, whose sperm count has been reducing in some regions by as much as 30 percent to 50 percent or more over the last four decades (Bauman 1996; Carlsen et al. 1992; Ginsburg 1996). PCBs are stored in fatty tissues of carnivores that eat the flesh of other species that are themselves contaminated with PCBs.

In human beings, the possibility of long-term paraphilic effects of pollutant chemicals, whether of prenatal, neonatal, or later exposure, is hypothetical. There is no causal evidence, as yet, of a linkage between the prenatalization of anything and the subsequent paraphilic pathologization of the developing lovemap. More data may, of course, open an entirely new window of understanding.

Clinical human data and experimental animal data both converge to prove beyond any possible shadow of doubt that intrauterine steroidal sex hormones shape the sexual anatomy of the fetus, regardless of whether they originate within the fetus itself or are transmitted to the fetus from the mother by way of the blood supply circulated through the placenta and the umbilical cord. The basic rule is that masculinization is coded by testosterone or one of its derivatives. Feminization is coded not by female hormone (estrogen or progesterone) but by the absence of masculinizing hormone.

Prenatal experimental animal data leave no doubt that sex steroidal hormones are responsible for male/female differences in the sexological brain and its peripheral connections. The prenatal timing of these brain differences is species variable. In some species, it takes place before birth; and in others, in the early days after birth. Since the ethics of human research forbids the definitive types of experiment that can be performed on laboratory animals, the timing of male/female sexological brain differentiation is uncertain. However, fetal autopsy research (Abramovich et al. 1987) has shown that it does not happen during the first six months of gestation when the pelvic genitalia are being formed. Thus, the critical period for male/female brain hormonalization is either during the third trimester or during the early neonatal period.

One piece of evidence in favor of the neonatal period is that in boy babies between two and twelve weeks of age, there is a surge of testicular androgen that reaches a peak in the blood stream that will not be seen again until puberty (Migeon and Forest 1983). Although there is no direct experimental human evidence, the data from newborn rats indicates that the level of serotonin is higher in females than in males during the first two weeks. Correspondingly, during the same time period, testosterone is higher in male than in female rats (Wilson et al. 1992).

In human beings as well as laboratory animals, the sex steroidal hormones from the gonads (testes and ovaries) do not work in hormonal isolation. They are governed by gonadotropins that are synthesized in the pituitary gland which releases them into the blood-stream. Gonadotropins themselves are governed by gonadotropin releasing hormones (GnRH) that are synthesized by brain cells in the nearby hypothalamus. Independently of these hormones, mullerian inhibiting hormone (MIH) is active early in fetal life in males to suppress the formation of a uterus and fallopian tubes (Rey and Josso 1996).

It is a far cry from prenatal and neonatal male/female brain hormonalization to the formation of paraphilic lovemaps and their ideation and imagery in postjuvenile life. More is known about the neuroanatomy of male/female differences in the sexological brain of animals than about the mating functions for which they are the infrastructure. In human sexology, the infrastructure itself is largely unmapped, let alone applicable to the ideation, imagery, and practices of lovemaps whether paraphilic or not. Nonetheless, the very knowledge of the existence of a sexological brain is important as a guide to the expansion of brain neurochemical research from infancy through adolescence.

Sexological Socialization

THE TRANSITION FROM prenatal to postnatal life is also a transition in which sexological hormonalization yields some of its primacy to sexological socialization. A mammal as lowly as a sheep provides an example of how difficult it is to separate the two (Perkins and Fitzgerald 1992; Perkins et al. 1995; see also Money 1997b, 42). At an experimental station in Idaho, ninety-four ram lambs were reared as a sex segregated flock. At between one and two years of age, they remained sexually inexperienced with ewes. Two of the rams were mounted repeatedly by other male pen mates. Eight others were never observed mounting ewes. Two of the eight mounted each other exclusively—which raises the unanswered question of whether they were born or became that way, and if the latter, how and why. Hormonal comparisons of the so-called homosexual rams with heterosexual rams and ewes revealed that the prevalence of estrogen receptors in the amygdalae, bilaterally, of the homosexual rams' brains was lower than that in heterosexual rams' amygdalae and similar to that of ewes. That heterosexual rams had higher prevalence of estrogen receptors is compatible with the counterintuitive finding in many animal brain studies that testosterone must be aromatized into estradiol within the cell

before it can exert a masculinizing effect. The Perkins study was unable to reveal neither whether the prevalence of estrogen receptors in
the amygdalae was reduced prenatally or in the first year of life, nor
why so few rams were affected. As an animal model, the sheep study
is relevant to homosexual lovemap formation but not to paraphilic
lovemaps. There is no animal model for paraphilia, since there is no
way of decoding an animal's prototypic ideation and imagery.

There is also no direct way of decoding the precursor of a newborn
human infant's lovemap. Nonetheless, by inference, it can be attributed
to stimulation of the contrectative (tactual or haptic) sensorium by way
of mother-infant bonding expressed as cuddling, caressing, hugging,
fondling, patting, rocking, and rubbing. All of these activities are forms
of grooming, and they coalesce in breast feeding.

Deprivation of grooming leads to failure to thrive. Premature babies who were grooming-deprived required at least a week longer in
an incubator than did their counterparts who were not grooming-
deprived (Field et al. 1986; Shanberg and Field 1987; Field 1995).
The animal model for grooming deprivation is newborn rat pups.
Their mothers were harnessed so as to prevent the pups from being
licked (tongue groomed) but not from being breast-fed. Grooming
deprivation depleted the level of growth hormone in the bloodstream
of the deprived pups (Schanberg and Kuhn 1985). It also depleted the
level of the enzyme, ornithine decarboxylase (ODC), a powerful reg-
ulator of cell growth in brain, liver, heart, and kidney tissue.

Mother/infant neonatal grooming is one of the phylogenetically
determined ingredients of behavior, also known as phylisms, that in
nature's sexological economy serves a present and a future function.
Its present function is to promote growth and survival of the newborn. Its future function promotes species survival. In the human
species, the grooming phylism is destined to reappear in proceptive
love making and in copulatory foreplay. Pathology of grooming in
infancy paves the way for pathology of grooming in the sexology of
maturity. There is substantiating evidence for their connectedness in
the long term follow-up of sixteen children with a history of early
growth failure (psychosocial dwarfism) associated with abusive neglect and trauma (Money et al. 1990; Money 1992). Five were rated
as paraphilic, five as hypophilic, one as hyperphilic, and only five as
normophilic. While correlation is no proof of causality, it does justify

a more intensive pursuit of hypotheses to explain lovemap formation and deformation in the early postnatal months and years of life.

The hypothesis that bridges the gap between grooming deprivation and paraphilia is the hypothesis of unrequited trust. The young infant must have pairbondant trust in someone, usually the mother, whose nutritive grooming is prerequisite to the maintenance of life. Trust totally or ambivalently unrequited by an abusively depriving mother creates a dilemma (a notorious example of a Catch-22) of being defeated by either maintaining or abandoning the bond of trust. This dilemma has long term, carry-over effects. It has the capacity for disrupting all future relationships that entail mutual trustworthiness, not the least of which are relationships deployed developmentally in the formation of the lovemap.

Sexual Rehearsal Play

THE YEARS OF infancy and childhood are years of preparatory development and rehearsal of the multifarious functions of maturity, sexological functions included. The erectile function of the penis begins prenatally, and it has been recorded pictorially by ultrasound imaging (Sherer et al. 1990; Shirozu et al. 1995). The technology for demonstrating a corresponding phenomenon in girls, either prenatally or postnatally, has not yet been perfected. In boys, spontaneous erections occur from neonatal life onward, awake and asleep. In girls as well as boys, from infancy onward, autogenital squeezing, rubbing, or fingering may be observed. The American culturally stereotypic response is to expunge autoeroticism from the sexological geography of the lovemap.

The same condemnation is culturally stereotypic when, in the years of later infancy and early childhood, children engage playmates in genital look and show displays, in doctor and nurse genital examinations, and in imitation of coital thrusting. Even at so young an age, their lovemaps are being shaped in the cultural mold of prudery and shamefulness.

This mold is not transculturally universal. In Polynesian (Danielsson 1956; Marshall and Suggs 1971; Suggs 1966) and Aboriginal Australian (Money et al. 1970/1977) cultures, for example, the prescribed response is to be pleased that sexological development is proceeding normally. Among the Gond-speaking Muria people of eastern south central India, the culture traditionally provided a special sleeping compound, the ghotul, for juveniles and young adolescents. There, as they approached puberty, juveniles would learn the art of love making and copulation from adolescents (see Money 1997b, 96–98). Muria lovemaps were culturally encouraged to be heterosexual and paraphilia free.

The molding of lovemaps among children in our own culture is exposed to the hazard of mutually dissonant strategies regarding the transmission of sexual knowledge. One is the strategy of licit knowledge. The other is the strategy of illicit knowledge. To illustrate: in the mid-1990s, juveniles who had access to media news about President Bill Clinton and Ms. Monica Lewinsky knew something about sex for which their parents as juveniles probably had no name. Today's juveniles and their parents both know that its name is oral sex. They both know also that oral sex is a topic not to be covered in explicit detail in the sex educational curriculum. If from their peer group juveniles learn that *blowjob, cock sucking, giving head,* and *eating pussy* are slang synonyms for oral sex, then they learn also not to use those terms indiscriminately in the presence of older kinfolk, teachers, preachers, or television talk show hosts.

The oral sex example illustrates the general principle that the lovemap must be double coded, once for what is licit and once for what is illicit. The two codings vary according to time and place; and they also vary according to whether there is an avoidancy taboo on explicit sexual talk between males and females in mixed company and an avoidancy on explicit sexual talk between the younger and the older generation.

Double coding of the lovemap is particularly hazardous for children exposed to an extreme degree of dissonance between what is societally licit and illicit. The personal hazard is increased if personal involvement in illicit sex is of necessity secretive, through lack of a similarly involved peer group with whom to talk and find support. Parent child incest is a classic example. It creates the Catch-22 dilemma of being damned if you do and damned if you don't disclose the existence of the relationship. There is no benign avenue of escape, not even by talking with a professional consultant from whom the law demands mandatory reporting.

The distortion of the lovemap brought on by such an insoluble Catch-22 dilemma varies idiosyncratically. In one case, the daughter postponed escaping from paternal incest until she was old enough to survive alone as a teenager. The day then came when she purchased a one way bus ticket to New York City. In a dazed state of amnesic confusion, she was admitted to the psychiatric service at New York's Bellevue Hospital. Eventually, the amnesic state resolved. The man she eventually married looked old enough to be the grandfather of their young son. He was oblivious to the boy's fixation on becoming a girl and to his wife's phobia of sexual intercourse. Whenever they tried to have intercourse, she would hear a voice whispering over her shoulder: you're fucking your father, you're fucking your father. Once again, she ran away. This time, she became lost to follow-up.

In childhood sexological development and also in many other aspects of development, two principles of responding to a no-win, Catch-22 dilemma are inhibition and adhibition. Inhibition signifies that the individual succumbs to the dilemma and is in some degree incapacitated. For example, some children who undergo unrelenting abuse and neglect become addicted to being abused and neglected (Money 1992, chap. 12), so much so that their rescue is a virtual impossibility. They plead to return to the household of abuse or, if placed in a new household, they provoke new abuse and neglect. Sexologically, inhibition signifies arrested development of the lovemap and the possibility in later life of a hypophilic copulatory dysfunction.

Adhibition signifies that the individual survives the Catch-22 dilemma by becoming a copycat who stage manages its repetition with other players. For example, a juvenile who has been sexologically traumatized by someone older and stronger becomes a playground bully who coerces younger and weaker children into sexual participation. In the psychiatric literature, such coercive replay is usually called acting out. At an older age, it is called psychopathic or sociopathic personality disorder. Children with a history of sexological trauma who are prone to acting out their own trauma with other children commonly become inmates in the criminal justice system which, at the end of the twentieth century, is not yet biomedically equipped to cope with them.

Juveniles and young adolescents in the juvenile justice system as sex offenders occasionally are referred for a sexological evaluation for which the L. C. Miccio-Fonseca Personal Sentence Completion Inventory (1997) is a valuable adjunct. Although tabulated statistics are not yet on record, the childhood sexological histories of young offenders are, it would appear, marked by an extreme discrepancy between their everyday licit sexual knowledge and their personal acquaintance with and participation in illicit sexological pathology. Mostly, they have been reared in a sexually pathological household that has a history of intergenerational, coercive, sadistic, or promiscuous sex among some of its members. In some cases, the juvenile or adolescent has been hired out for commercial sex. Household pathology may include nonsexual abuse, neglect, violence, or other trauma, such as the murder or drug death of a friend, parent, or sibling. The lovemap is fragile and easily distorted in its development. The formula for distortion always involves the Catch-22 dilemma of having no escape from the pathologizing life situation and of being damned whatever you do or don't do to try to prevent it.

Teenagers who run away from home in an attempt to escape are likely to find that street life offers no improvement. Simple survival may entail prostitution or hustling, drug dealing, thieving, and possible murdering. Then follows another installment of institutional detention. That however may prove to be more pathologizing than life on the outside had been. The problem and cost for society is magnified, not diminished.

Idiopathic Precocious Puberty

THE ROLE OF sexological socialization in the ideation and imagery of the lovemap has been well exemplified in the case of children who undergo the spontaneous onset of puberty at a very young age (Hampson and Money 1955; Money and Hampson 1955; Money and Alexander 1969), as young as age three or even sooner.

Far ahead of their contemporaries and without any evidence of associated pathology, children with idiopathic pubertal precocity have a biological chronometer of somatic puberty that is timed prematurely. The physique age races far ahead of the birthday age, with its rate of acceleration being far in advance of that of the social age and academic age. The lovemap age is more mature than would be predicted by the birthday age but is not at the same level of maturity as the physique age.

These discrepancies were well illustrated in a case in which the diagnosis of precocious onset of puberty was made at the age of eight months, the first signs being the appearance of pubic hair and enlargement of the penis (Money and Hampson 1955). Two months after the boy's sixth birthday, the height age was that of a twelve year old. The bone age, having matured precociously to that of a fifteen year old, meant that he would always be conspicuously short as an adult man. The genitalia were of adult size, and the secondary sexual characteristics were fully adolescent.

As early as age four, the boy liked to sing into the microphone used for recording interviews. He sang in tune with a deep bass voice. Two of his favorite songs were about romance:

> *Because of you there's a song in my heart,*
> *Because of you my romance had its start,*
> *Because of you the sun will shine,*
> *Moon and stars say you're mine,*
> *Forever and never to part.*
> *I only live for your love and your kiss*
> *It's paradise to be near you like this.*
> *Because of you my life is now worthwhile,*
> *And I can smile because of you.*

> *They tried to tell us we're too young,*
> *Too young to really be in love.*
> *They say that love's a word*
> *A word we've only heard,*
> *But can't begin to know the meaning of.*
> *And yet we're not too young to know*
> *That love will live though years may go,*
> *And if some day they may recall,*
> *We were not too young at all.*

Six months after his fifth birthday, despite a brief attention span, his talk about dreams included the following lovemap material.

I don't want to tell any more dreams. I dream about ladies. Every day I find a lady and she doesn't have any husband. I tell her to take off all her clothes. Her dress, her slip, her brassiere, and take off this and then I kiss some place on that. On the bust. On the behind. And this is the worst place in the world, on the feet. And then I tell them to get dressed again and I tell them to go back home.

Asked if he liked these dreams, he said: "I hate them. I have ugly dreams; I hate them. I don't want to talk about any of my dreams." Urged a little, he continued telling of the ladies: "Kiss them right here (between the legs); and their legs, and I kiss their belly button, and I kiss their cheeks, their nose, their eyes—I kiss every place on them. I think I'm dreaming about one dream right now. I, oy, it's too hot." (This was during a midsummer heatwave.)

At the age of six and a half, he connected erotic fantasies with masturbatory ejaculations and erotic dreams with nocturnal emissions.

> Huh! You've heard it before, he said with a reluctant laugh. Women! I was thinking about the one I was going to marry. I was thinking that she had a lot of money, and was pretty, and I wouldn't have to buy anything for her. Why do I have to remember it? It's not so pleasant. I can't stop dreaming about it every single night. Asked to tell some more of his dreams, he said: Just women! Women! Women!

Then he went on in silly playfulness about where he kissed them. All of his reported lovemap imagery was about kissing naked females. There was no male-male erotic imagery, no autoerotic imagery, no anal erotic imagery, and not until later than age six, any imagery of the penis penetrating any orifice. Penial vaginal penetration imagery did not appear until after the facts of sexual intercourse became part of his cognitive repertory. Penial vaginal imagery did not automatically accompany the precocious adolescent libidinal energization of the lovemap. In this case, knowledge of copulation supplemented the ideation and imagery of kissing in the lovemap soon enough to prevent a kissing fixation. There was no history of untoward sexual contact with others of any age. Marriage and parenthood took place at the conventional age, following a professional education.

Age Eight

IN THE FOREGOING case, it would appear that the period of sexological development that usually occupies the years from birth to age sixteen or later was condensed into the years from birth to age eight. The fact that the boy was sexologically and reproductively in adulthood by age eight did not jeopardize his future development and career as an adult. Thus, the very existence of idiopathic sexual precocity raises the intriguing question of why the human species has evolved so as to take sixteen years to accomplish what can be done in half the time. It raises also the equally intriguing sexological speculation as to whether our own species evolved from a hominid predecessor which did reach reproductive maturity in half the time that it takes now. What has been the evolutionary gain of the long juvenile hiatus between infancy and puberty?

My own science fictional explanation of this hiatus is that it has something to do with the evolution of the syntactical and mathematical logic of the human languagemap. Language required a brain of greater flexibility and versatility and less biorobotism than is found in the vocal communication (the soundmap) of other species. The sexological connection is that the map for mating and reproduction in subhuman species is biorobotic and stereotyped in its sameness, whereas the ideation and imagery of the human lovemap is widely variable and idiosyncratic. In hominid evolution, derobotization of the lovemap can be viewed as a necessary trade off for the derobotization of the prelinguistic communication map. Derobotization of both the languagemap and the lovemap required, in turn, a hiatus between infancy and pubertal maturity, namely the period of juvenility. The juvenile period, free from breeding and parenting duties, allows time for the development and individualization of the logically complicated languagemap and also of the lovemap. Individualization in both instances may be according to social stereotype, or it may be either creatively eccentric or pathologically idiosyncratic. The duration of the juvenile period extends from plus or minus age eight to the onset of puberty, which is variable, and is earlier for girls than boys. For girls, the age of first menses is around twelve or thirteen. For boys, the age of first ejaculation (semenarche) is around thirteen or fourteen.

In taking a sexological history from someone with a paraphilia, time and again age eight, or thereabouts, turns out to be a pivotal age in lovemap development (Langfeldt 1981, 67–68; Money, unpublished data). For example, in a fragment of psychobiographical prose and verse C. Baby, a cross dresser and infantilist, published a magazine piece under the subtitle, "The Diaper Punishment," as follows.

> I should hate diapers, but I don't. When I was seven years old, my mother used diapers to punish me when I wet the bed one night. At first I refused to cooperate but after she beat me with a

wire coat hanger and an ironing cord, I gave in. The diaper felt good against the welts on my bottom, but the diapers and beatings were just the starters. I was paraded up and down our street wearing a skirt and a diaper. Mother made sure everyone knew what I was wearing under the skirt. She even stopped for coffee at a neighbor's house and I had to sit outside in my diapered state. The diapers and the skirt did not hurt me; the humiliation from the taunting by my peers did. I learned to love diapers and skirts. I learned to hate mother.

Nontraumatizing experiences at around age eight may also have a paraphilic formative influence on the lovemap as revealed in the "Earliest Memories" segment of an interview with a man in his mid-forties (Money and Simcoe 1984–86; see chaps. 5, 6). He sought relief from the ideation and imagery of a paraphilic fixation on female amputees (see chap. 7) which, although never put into practice, had deprived him and each of his two wives of full sexual satisfaction.

I don't like the control that this amputee thing has over me, he gave as his reason for seeking MPA [see chap. 8] treatment. I don't like losing the self-control. I don't like it controlling me, instead of me controlling it. If I see a normal person walking down the street, an attractive girl, I'll stop, and I'll look, and then I forget about it. In the same instance, if it's an amputee, I don't forget about it. The fantasies keep coming back.

I guess, I was about six, seven, or eight, he said, somewhere in that range, and we had gone on a boat ride across the Bay with my parents. I remember my father saying that there was something the matter with this other couple's daughter, I guess she was sixteen, eighteen years old. I remember her sitting across from us on the boat and she was trying to fix lunch and she had only the partial part of an arm. I was fascinated by it at that time. The other time in my childhood that I think about was when I was in school. I was nine or ten years old. We had a substitute teacher. I can remember vividly sitting at a desk and she had only part of an arm. As she walked down the aisle, she got in back of me and someway or another leaned over and put her stump on my shoulder, and I remember getting enjoyment out of that.

Age eight is a developmental milestone, give or take a few months. For example, it is the age when the teeth of adulthood begin to erupt (Behrman et al. 1996). Growth and maturation of the teeth are quite out of synchrony with growth and maturation of the bones.

The bone age advances concurrently with, and is dependent on, the hormonal advance of puberty. In children with idiopathic onset of precocious puberty, the bone age advances with the hormonal age, but the dental age does not. It advances concurrently with the chronological age. This difference between bone age and dental age lends conjectural support to the hypothesis that one aspect of human evolutionary history was postponement of the age of sexological maturity from age eight in eons past to the contemporary age of sixteen.

The eighth year marks also a transition from infantile dependency, in many respects, to juvenile competency and the beginning of autonomy in ideation and imagery. In the use of language, eight is the age of word play and comprehending double meanings in jokes, riddles, puns, rhymes, and conundrums. The constancy principle of one word/one meaning gives way to the inconstancy of two or more meanings even though the sounds remain the same: Knock, knock. Who's there? Percy. Percy who? Persiflage.

Breaking the constancy principle means that things need not be what they have seemed to be, just as *b* revolved sideways changes to *d*. Fixed rules are not necessarily always obeyed: there are ruses for getting around them. In the case of the lovemap, there are ruses for deviously circumventing the official rules while ostensibly obeying them—for example, by masturbating without using the hands.

Dreaming is another age-eight milestone of possible significance to lovemap formation. According to the research of Foulkes (1983, 357), it was between the ages of seven and nine "that fairly substantial and credible self-participation characterized children's dream accounts . . . a larger sense of purposefulness guides the integration of disparate image sequences into a coherent narrative." The coherent narrative may be projected into a dream that is romantic and/or erotic or into a masturbation fantasy. It may or may not be pathological.

Another age-eight phenomenon is that of the phantom limb. If juveniles become amputees prior to age five or six, they do not experience phantom limbs, whereas those who become amputees at age seven or eight do so (Tomkins 1992, 243). The phantom phenomenon is a representation that belongs to both the body image and the neural network of the body schema in the brain. Body image representations that are kinesthetic and tactual occur in orgasm dreams (wet dreams) and in masturbation and coital fantasies. The rudiments of their ideation and imagery in the lovemap are of an earlier vintage than puberty.

Insofar as the lovesong is a sexual attractant, another age-eight milestone to be taken note of is absolute pitch in music. Gottfried Schlaug, using magnetic resonance imaging (MRI) to study hemisphere dominance in musicians with and without absolute pitch, found that musicians with absolute pitch were more left brain dominant than the others. Also, those with absolute pitch had a history of beginning their musical education early, prior to age seven. Among these early beginners, those destined to have absolute pitch possessed it before age ten or else not at all (Kendall 1996; Schlaug et al. 1995).

Transcultural data provide further confirmation of age eight as a milestone in lovemap formation. Among the Gond-speaking Muria people of India, already mentioned (chap. 4), it is around age eight that children leave at night to sleep in the ghotul, the young-people's compound where their lovemap formation is exposed to heterosexual ideation and imagery.

The transcultural confirmation of age eight in lovemap formation is evident also in the tradition, already mentioned in chapter 2, of the Sambia people of New Guinea (Herdt 1981, 1984, 1987). In this tradition, to ensure that a boy will grow up to be not only a husband but also a fierce, man-killing warrior, he is removed at around age eight from the softening influence of females and infants to be reared by men only in the large, central men's house. Their initiation into warriorhood involves stages of what amounts to abusive hazing. The ideation and imagery of their lovemaps becomes heterosexual after a peripubertal and adolescent stage of culturally enforced fellatio. To enter puberty and to ensure subsequent fertility, small boys must suck a lifetime's supply of men's milk from penises of postpubertal boys not yet old enough to be provided with a wife. Until then, all boys must totally avoid contamination by contact with females or their odor. After becoming a married warrior, a young man uses up his semen exclusively in copulatory intercourse with his wife. The paradox of the Sambia tradition is that it institutionalizes sequential bisexuality before marriage so as to ensure a male heterosexual lovemap in adulthood.

Among children of Western culture, in the early school years, beginning at around age four or five, lovemap development includes playway romantic attachments. Mostly, they are boyfriend and girlfriend romances, though not invariably so. Even at an early age, the first intimations of romantic bonding may be isosexual. In boys (the sample of girls was too small), it has been shown in a long term follow up that the first intimations are premonitory of a subsequent lifetime of isosexual (homosexual) attraction (Green 1987; Green and Money 1960; Money and Russo 1979, 1981). Correspondingly, early boy/girl romantic rehearsal play is premonitory of a subsequent lifetime of heterosexual (allosexual) attraction. Rarely are childhood romances long continuing, although some are unbroken beyond the juvenile and adolescent years of courtship rehearsal until they are officially recognized in cohabitation and/or marriage. Age eight, here again, appears to be a year of lovemap significance. It is the age when lovemap rehearsal may become transformed from rehearsal into the authentic experience of limerent bonding, even before the hormonal onset of puberty (Money 1980, 148–50; 1997b, chap. 2). Such early limerent bonding is more likely than not to be associated with genital stimulation and to be heterosexual without pathology, unless the lovemap has been subject to disruptively negative influences.

Collusional Pairbondship

IN THE PEDIATRIC chronicle of a baby's early development, it is conventional to keep track of the age at which various milestones are reached. These milestones include ability to sit up, stand up, take a first step alone, say a word, put two or more words together, get toilet trained, and so on. Sexological milestones, like first infantile flirtatiousness, are not on the list, nor is first playmate romance.

At puberty, first menstruation (menarche) is recorded for girls by the family doctor or gynecologist, even if breast budding is omitted. For boys, sexological milestones at puberty, especially first ejaculation (semenarche) and first wet dream, are almost invariably omitted. For both boys and girls, the milestone of first romance is also overlooked, even though it is popularly recognized and often subjected to teasing and ridicule by younger siblings and acquaintances. Older people also recognize the milestone of romantic attachment by characterizing it as being at the hair combing stage or at the boy (or girl) crazy stage. Condescending relatives refer to it as puppy love or condemn it as infatuation.

The reticence of developmental sexology regarding the milestone of first romance leaves a serious gap in data on the origin of lovemap matching and mismatching. It has long been debated—for example, in nineteenth-century marriage manuals—whether like attracts like or whether opposites attract one another in the matter of mate selection. A more likely scenario is that the first romantic pairbondship is a developmental milestone during the course of which the still unfinished lovemap of each partner is engaged in reciprocally accommodating to that of the other. The process of reciprocation is not limited to the first pairbondship, but the outcome of the first will cast its shadow on any that follow. The ratio of accommodation may be 50:50, but more likely it is lopsided, with one lovemap accommodating itself more than the other, dependent on how closely they were already reciprocated at the outset of the relationship. If the degree of accommodation is too one-sided and the residual reciprocity is insufficient, then the pairbondship is likely to become adversarial and to end in failure.

The idea of reciprocal accommodation of lovemaps is consistent with the phenomenon of pairbonded collusionism that is explicit in some paraphilic cases. It is not uncommon, for example, for the wives or girlfriends of fetishistic transvestites to become collusional in the cross dressing and cosmetic make up of the partner and to appear in public together. Some of the wives or girlfriends put on a brave show of being tolerant and loyal, even though the evidence is perfunctory. Others, by contrast, have a genuinely reciprocal lovemap, so that there is a high degree of sexuoerotic payoff for them in their collusional role as there was for Monica Jay (1995) in her short-lived though intense affair with a transvestite.

Another collusional example is that of the wife of a steelworker who was unable to reach his orgasm in sexual intercourse until he inflicted sadistic injuries on her. The history of their relationship began abruptly when she was sixteen and he was twenty-two. She met him when he was on a visit to her home state. They were married three weeks later. Neither she nor he had previously had sexual intercourse, and neither cheated on the other in more than twenty five years of marriage.

When they married, there had been no signals of the husband's sadism. On the contrary, according to the husband's testimony, during the first week of marriage, they had an argument in the course of which he slapped her and had an immediate orgasm. That was the first time he fully realized that administering punishment was integral to his having an orgasm instead of being anorgasmic.

Nothing was retrieved from the wife's sexological history to indicate that, prior to marriage, she had the makings of a paraphilically masochistic lovemap. Her husband, by contrast, had grown up with sadism. In boyhood, he had shared a bedroom with his father, which is how he knew that his father would sometimes go into the bedroom where his wife slept, empty it of the younger children, and then begin slapping and whipping her.

The father punished his children violently. He would send one of them outdoors to break switches from trees.

> He would take us in, and the one he was going to punish he would strip completely naked, and put him in the middle and tell us what he was going to do. And he would beat us till we bled. He would take a salt shaker or salt box and sprinkle salt into our bleeding hide and make us sit there for an hour or two after he got through with us.

Beating, bleeding, and salting eventually became incorporated into the lovemap imagery and ideation of the oldest son, Denton, the one who grew up to become a sadistic husband. After twenty five years of marriage, this imagery and ideation of beating, bleeding, and salting threatened to break through into an actual performance. As reported by the husband, his scenario was to remove a panel from the bathroom door and reconstruct it as a kind of pillory in which to clamp his wife's head on one side of the door, and her body on the other side. He had already purchased a length of chain with which to lash her back, denuding it of skin, and applying salt, with pauses for rear entry coition, and then more lashes. He did not want his wife to die, but through fear that she would, needed some sort of intervention. His wife was unable to cooperate in finding intervention as it would be tantamount to a public admission of what she considered her private shame.

Her private shame included twenty five years of masochistic toleration of what her husband called punishment: sadistic spitting, slapping, and pinching; hair pulled out by the roots; pins and safety pins counted out and stuck into or threaded through the skin of her back; clothespins clamped on her genitals. Under coercion, she was obliged to cuss out her husband as "you lowdown, rotten bastard, you hairpulling, spitting bastard." The more noise she made, the better for him. There was no oral or anal sex.

She had come to endure these sadistic acts, and even to solicit them, so as to get the sexual act over and done with since her husband could not otherwise get an orgasm and quit. She had never found sex pleasurable and had never had much of an interest in it. "Bedtime behavior" was something that she had to tolerate. When her husband told her about his pillory and lashing fantasy, her reaction was to put it in the same category as all of his bedtime behavior.

What swung the pendulum was her husband's subsidiary sadistic scenario in which sadistic lashing was replaced by a hair cutting equivalent. He would cut her hair short, lock by lock, until she was almost bald. His wife took pride in her long hair. Losing it would be another way of publically advertising her shame. Here she drew the line.

According to the husband, on October 18, they began what became a twenty-eight hour marathon in which he cut off her hair in four installments and plucked out all of her eyebrows. The more she objected, the greater his erotic excitement until he came ten times in penial vaginal intercourse.

The upshot was that the wife called for psychiatric assistance. Twelve days later he was admitted and evaluated for antiandrogenic hormonal treatment (see chap. 8) with the antiandrogenic hormone, medroxyprogesterone acetate (MPA), trade named Depo-Provera (Money 1970). The treatment reduced the frequency and the power of sadistic imagery and ideation, and it stopped the sadistic practices. Relieved of the demands of bedtime compliancy, the wife became increasingly at a loss. Her erstwhile collusional relationship with her husband gave way to a power struggle with neither of them yielding.

Collusional masochism without masochistic lust, as in this case, is not bona fide masochism. It is more precisely defined as compliant masochism, which is akin to martyrdom.

Unquestionably, there are cases in which the recognition of reciprocally matched lovemaps is not incipient but explicit. Thus, the patrons of S/M bars wear colors, jewelry, or keys coded for "top" or "bottom" in an S/M relationship. Instead of going to a bar, they may place highly specific advertisements in the personals column of quasi-underground newspapers or magazines or on the Internet. To be up to date, they will use the Internet to find a well matched partner, ready made, and requiring no period of mutual accommodation.

Although they have absolutely no prior intimation of each other's lovemap, it is possible for two total strangers to be precipitously thrown together as captor and captive and to become locked into an intensely powerful collusional pairbond. This type of bonding has become known as the Stockholm syndrome, after a case of its occurrence following a bank robbery in Sweden's capital. One of the female tellers, who was held hostage for some time, and one of the robbers became so bonded that she broke her engagement to her erstwhile boyfriend, and she remained faithful to her captor while he served time in prison.

The power that one person may have in shaping the lovemap of another resembles so-called brainwashing. Among political prisoners, brain washing is effected by the aid of torture, abuse, neglect, isolation, and privation of the senses. Identification with the aggressor may offer the only promise of salvation.

Without knowledge of the Stockholm phenomenon and brainwashing, it is not possible to comprehend the bizarre and widely published case of Arthur Goode and Jimmy Mannus. Slight of build and twenty-one years old, Goode had a long history dating back to age three of prepsychotic and psychotic paraphilic behavior, chiefly fellatio, either given or received, with male juveniles. In his late teenage years, his diagnosis was given simply as pedophilia, whereas it should have been pedophilic sadism with ideation and imagery of lust murder—a rare multiplex paraphilia.

In 1976, through lack of sufficient evidence regarding multiple child molestations and the murder of a ten-year-old boy, Goode had been returned from Florida to Maryland on probation, provided he report back to the state hospital from which he had previously eloped. He did report but, intolerant of delay, took off and rode a bus into Baltimore City. On the outskirts, he left the bus after seeing Jimmy on a corner folding newspapers for his delivery route. He persuaded Jimmy to leave the papers and go with him. That was on Monday afternoon, March 15. They lived vagrantly, doing yard work when they needed money. The following Saturday, they were standing at a bus stop in suburban Virginia, as was Kerry Dorman.

According to Jimmy's court testimony, Goode talked to Kerry about bicycle paths. The three then took a five mile bus ride to another shopping center where they purchased carry out lunches. They ate lunch in a steeply wooded area. Then they went deeper into the woods. Arthur cleared an area of underbrush and, looking really mean, told Kerry he was going to play a little trick on him and to take off his clothes. Kerry cried, but Goode forced him, put his pants over his head, lying face down, and strangled him with his belt tightened around his neck. Jimmy heard Kerry squealing and then go silent. Goode listened, heard no breathing, and then took Kerry's wallet and clothes to hide elsewhere. Goode told Jimmy he wished he'd had an axe to chop Kerry's head off or razor blade to really cut him up. He said he wanted to kill more kids, in addition to Kerry and a ten-year-old boy in Florida, before the police picked him up. He threatened to kill Jimmy and his sisters, too, if Jimmy should try to run away or tell about any of their doings.

Goode held his captive so completely in thrall that the boy was unable to take advantage of whatever opportunity he might have had to ask for help, as for example when he and Goode were window cleaning for a suburban housewife. It was this woman who, at 11 P.M. that same day, Tuesday, March 23, recognized Goode's mugshot on the late TV news. By happenstance, she had told Goode to phone early the next morning for additional yard work. When Goode and Jimmy arrived at 7:30 A.M., the police were waiting. Only with outside support could Jimmy escape from the thralldom in which he was held by Goode, with his bizarre pedophilic lovemap. In prison, Goode claimed over and again that he loved the boys whom he had killed, and his final wish would be to hold a ten-year-old boy and have sex with him one last time before he went to the electric chair.

Deferred Symptoms

A NEW COLLUSION may be introduced into a relationship that is already collusional. This is what happened in the case of the autobiographer who recorded his story in *The Armed Robbery Orgasm* (Keyes and Money 1993). He was a masochist who met a partner in a girlie bar who perfectly matched in appearance and conduct his lovemap's ideal of a dominatrix. Above all, she would lay him across her lap and paddle his bare behind until he reached a state of ecstatic abandon. She would taunt him by denying access to her body and by withholding another beating until he fulfilled her conditional demands. She had a history of armed robbery which he did not have. He surrendered without protest when she demanded that he collude with her in committing armed robberies of small businesses, while she waited in the getaway car. The ultimate act of her dominance over him was to report him to the police. She received a brief prison sentence, and he received a sentence of fifteen years—not for masochism but for armed robbery.

In the foregoing armed robbery case, the armed robber had a fixation on being spanked with a paddle, on being spanked by a dominatrix younger than himself who had the body build and appearance of his mother and his older sister, on being coerced by his dominatrix into performing armed robberies with her, and on having a dominatrix who made a living as a highly paid prostitute. There is a paraphilic name for each of these four fixations, namely, *masochism* (being dominated, humiliated, and spanked or beaten), *ephebophilia* (being attracted to adolescents or young adults), *symphorophilia* (being aroused by danger and catastrophe), and *chrematistophilia* (being coerced to spend lavishly or be robbed for sexual services). Any one of these four fixations, if occurring alone, would be diagnosable as a paraphilia. Together, however, they do not constitute four different paraphilias: that would imply the existence of four different lovemaps, which would be like saying that a person with four different mouth infections has four mouths, one for each infection. Each individual has only one mouth and, likewise, only one lovemap. That single lovemap may be either simplex or multiplex for paraphilic fixation. In multiplex paraphilic lovemaps, each paraphilic fixation is interconnected around a primary fixation. In the armed robbery case, the primary fixation was masochism. The man himself traced the masochistic fixation to the punishments administered by his mother when he was a little boy and, in her absence, by her deputy, his older sister. When he got a punishment erection, his sister would beat his penis, which put heterosexual ephebophilia into his developing lovemap. Paying large sums of money to a whore separated the impurity of lust from incest. This chrematistophilia became recognized in the lovemap only after the age of earning a living. Soon thereafter, the potential catastrophe of being killed in an armed robbery (symphorophilia) became recognized in the lovemap. Paid sex and armed robbery had not been revealed in the lovemap imagery and ideation of youth but, later, as an extension of masochistic domination and obedience in collusion with a dominatrix whose power was derived from her rarity. She was not a fake lady sadist for hire but a woman with a genuinely sadistic lovemap that matched her client's multiplex lovemap. Diagnostically, this multiple lovemap qualified as being fundamentally that of a masochist.

The logistics of guaranteeing the staffing and financing of a prospective outcome study from birth to age twenty-five are stagger-ing, even if there is a way of identifying the probands in infancy. In *Vandalized Lovemaps* (Money and Lamacz 1989), seven children were being followed in psychoendocrinology for disorders not known to be premonitory of paraphilia. In young adulthood, they disclosed the presence of paraphilic ideation and imagery in their lovemaps. A sample of seven was too few to uncover any consistent-ly occurring juvenile precursors of subsequent full-blown paraphilia, but it did show the early origin of each paraphilia and the coherency of its history.

In the annals of cross dressing, retrospective reports are plentiful of boys who cross dressed as juveniles as a way of relieving stress and also of getting an erection and a dry-run climactic feeling. Postpubertally, cross dressing would accompany masturbating to ejaculation. In a smaller sample of boys, there is retrospective evi-dence in juvenile play of prodromal signs of what will become para-philic ideation and imagery. For example, Nelson Cooper (see chap. 2), who's autobiography is preserved in *The Breathless Orgasm* (Money et al. 1991), had a juvenile fixation on playing strangling games with girl kinfolk, long before self-asphyxiation became a prominent college-age feature of his lovemap. In college, the appear-ance of self-asphyxiation was precipitated, he has since surmised, by an obsession with media coverage of John Wayne Gacy, the Chicago serial killer who strangled adolescent youths.

Another juvenile precursor signal of paraphilic trouble ahead is that of torturing and dismembering animals. Jeffrey Dahmer's well publicized case is an example (Schwartz 1992). As a boy, he collected road kills and displayed them. As a young adult, he was a sadistic se-rial killer who murdered, dismembered, and partly cannibalized young gay males whom he met in gay bars and took home with him for casual sex. He had an elaborate architectural fantasy of building a temple as a shrine in which to display and worship the remains of his victims.

In most cases, if there are juvenile prodromal signs of a paraphilic lovemap, they are overlooked and unheeded until, with adolescence, prodromal becomes syndromal. Imagine the plight of the adolescent boy next door who, on the one had, is on the school's honor roll, is a church leader in Bible study, and is a local sports hero. On the other hand, he secretly peeps through the bedroom windows of the house next door to get glimpses of two teenaged sisters undressing or naked. When he masturbates, the two girls are in his imagery, seducing him. To prevent that immoral catastrophe, they must die. For months, his masturbation fantasies and sleeping dreams incorporate the imagery of their being assaulted, raped, and stabbed to death. He has no way of putting a stop to his imagery. He is too ashamed to confess it and ask for help. Then, one night, the parents return home from a symphony concert to find that the double murder has actually taken place. No one can believe that he is the prime suspect, but he is. The sex murderer is not a space alien, but the eighteen year old from next door.

In such a case as the preceding, the imagery of the lovemap is not revealed in a single tableau, like a crowded mural covering a large wall. Rather, it is revealed progressively, like the unrolling of a Chinese scroll painting, which advances the narrative with each turn of the scroll. All the scenes are there, from beginning to end, but each scene must wait its turn to be revealed. The amount of time needed to unroll the scroll completely may vary from weeks or months to years.

In some cases, the end of the scroll remains forever unrolled. That is to say, the paraphilia does not reach the stage of being transformed from fantasy into actual performance. In this respect, paraphilic ideation and imagery have an as yet unexplained autonomy of their own, beyond personal voluntary control and moral will power. For example, women's paraphilic fantasies of being swept away and possessed sexually are multifarious, but they are very seldom carried through to an actual exposure to the risk of assault, abduction, and rape.

Logically, it is possible that some people pass through adolescence with the ideation and imagery of the lovemap subliminally intact, although virtually dormant, as if in a period of incubation until young adulthood when it bursts into flower. In the Victorian era, ostensible dormancy was idealized for girls. This ideal is currently regaining credence in the political and ecclesiastical doctrine of abstinence until marriage. Traditionally, the responsibility for abstinence has been directed at girls more than boys.

There are, however, some young men with a history of a period of dormant lovemap ideation and imagery between the onset of physiologically normal puberty in teenage and the occurrence of the first experience of being limerently smitten ten or more years later. At the conclusion of the interim period, they recall no history of masturbation or wet dreams, no history of gay or straight romantic attractions, and no erotosexual preoccupations. Without explanation, dormancy yields to affirmative action with the onset of the first experience of falling in love. The love relationship is then at risk of being a too possessive and eccentric one.

Through lack of a sufficient population sample, it has not yet been ascertained how prevalently paraphilic ideation and imagery may be masked in the lovemap during any period of its relative dormancy. Such masking is known to occur, however. In one case, that of a married man, the unmasked phase of his paraphilia was that of three-way sex (troilism) in which the husband would set up his wife to have an affair with a black man—black to complement their whiteness. That would maximize his arousal and prevent the failure of erectile potency. In an illicit and devious way, he tracked down one of his wife's work colleagues and arranged for this man to have an affair with his wife. Then he intervened to accuse his wife of adultery, to accuse the black man of adulterous rape, and to report him to his professional ethics board. Meantime, he himself answered advertisements in the personals section of a local magazine in the hope of finding another woman who would fulfill his paraphilic fantasy of troilism.

Geriatric Erosion

THERE ARE NO consistent changes in the content of the ideation and imagery of the lovemap contingent on aging, per se. There is decline, however, in the frequency with which the lovemap displays itself and in the urgency of its performance. This decline may be of significant advantage to those with a history of imprisonment for a sex offending paraphilia, as it cuts down on the likelihood of repeat offending. Among the nonparaphilic population, the age of the onset of lovemap decline is unpredictably individualistic as is the age of decline in genital erotic function. In women, lovemap decline may be much later than the age of menopause (Frock and Money 1992).

If, with advancing age, there are paraphilic changes in the imagistic and ideational content of the lovemap, one should invariably suspect a corresponding change in the functioning of the sexual brain. The most common change is an erosion of conformity to the sexological standards that formerly one adhered to, such as masturbating or exposing one's nudity in public, making unwanted passes at strangers or associates in inappropriate social situations, fondling grandchildren or other juveniles in an erotically suggestive way, using indecent sexual vocabulary in genteel surroundings, though not explosively as in Tourette's syndrome, and so on. Such signs of erosion of the lovemap may be among the preclinical symptoms of deteriorative brain disease, e.g., in Alzheimer and Huntington disease (Fedoroff et al. 1994), possibly in multiple sclerosis, and also in some cases of invasive brain tumor.

5

Paraphilia: Person and Species

Mythologies
Early Theories
Intrapsychic Determinism
Lovemap Chronicles
Grand Stratagems: Paleodigms
From Biorobotics to Paraphilia
Opponent-Process Theory
Temporal Lobe Sexology

Mythologies

For individuals with a history of paraphilia, the medieval explanation of this condition was demon possession. Only the human species was known to manifest paraphilias, and that uniqueness was attributed to the spiritual uniqueness of the human species with respect to sin and salvation. The *demon possession myth* is nearly moribund although not quite so, witness the sporadic appearance of exorcism as a form of news and entertainment.

In folk sexology and its carryover into professional sexology, various wrong-headed mythologies of paraphilic lovemap formation, even though they lack substantiation, have proved to be tenacious. One such mythology is that paraphilic people, having become jaded with ordinary sexual intercourse, turn to increasingly exotic and bizarre practices. This is the equivalent of saying that drinking milk or sodas leads to alcoholism.

The *jaded myth* is bulwarked by the *social contagion myth*, namely, that people are recruited to the practice of a particular paraphilia by encountering those who already practice it or by seeing or reading about it electronically or on paper. Pornography is the big bugaboo of this myth (Christensen 1990). Its refutation is readily obvious in, for example, paraphilic self-amputation (see also chap. 4). Exposure to even hundreds of hours of videos of this paraphilia (*apotemnophilia*) does not convert a randomly selected viewer into having the lovemap imagery and ideation of becoming a self-arranged amputee. A viewer with a prodromic lovemap of amputeeism will, however, be fascinated by the videos.

As compared with the jaded myth and the social contagion myth, the *hormonal myth* of the origin of paraphilia has more scientific respectability insofar as the pituitary and the gonadal hormones of male/female anatomical and physiological differentiation play a prominent role from embryonic life onward. Their role in the male/female differentiation and governance of the ideation and imagery of the lovemap is far from definitive, however, and is based on reasoning by analogy, namely that male hormone causes all things male, and female hormone causes all thing female (for reviews, see Albert et al. 1993; Siegel and Demetrikopoulos 1993). As applied to paraphilia, this kind of analogical reasoning has been used to associate sexual sadism, assault, rape, and murder with an excess of androgen (Benton 1992; Hucker and Bain 1990). It has been reinforced, no doubt by the success of antiandrogenic hormonal therapy for the control of paraphilias (see chap. 8). However, it does not follow that if antiandrogen helps to subdue paraphilic imagery and ideation in the lovemap, then androgen caused the lovemap to be paraphilic in the first place. Androgen may activate the lovemap, without having constructed it.

Empirically, no endocrine marker has been found that consistently separates those who have paraphilic lovemaps from those who do not. That does not rule out the future possibility that a more systematic endocrine survey of the paraphilias than has yet been attempted will reveal such a marker. There may be hormones or hormone-like substances that will be discovered when new technology emerges. Likewise, there may be hormone disrupters that, in the form of industrial and agricultural pollutants, enter the food chain and selectively disrupt the lovemap. Among the presently known hormone disrupters are PCBs (polychlorinated biphenyls), which are widely dispersed worldwide (Guo et al. 1995; Ginsburg 1996; see also chap. 4). Until more data are available, the idea that hormones or hormone-like substances play a causal role in the formation of paraphilic ideation and imagery must be regarded as a hormonal myth.

The *immunological myth* is of the same order as the endocrine myth except that the possibility of a connection between the immune system and the ideation and imagery of the paraphilic lovemap is totally terra incognita. On the basis of clinical anecdote, paraphilic disorders are not known to have a special affinity for people with immunologic syndromes and, in particular, autoimmune syndromes. Should such an affinity ever be discovered, the responsible immunologic factor could be found to be transmitted in the genome. Alternatively, it could be transmitted from the mother to the fetus through the placenta and have a long incubation period. Blanchard and Klassen (1997; see also Blanchard et al. 1998) proposed the hypothesis that after a series of male pregnancies, a mother may carry a cumulative level of antibodies to her sons' fetal H-Y antigen. They applied this hypothesis to their finding that gay males have more older brothers and fewer older sisters in their sibships than do nongay males (Jones and Blanchard 1998). Whether the maternal antibodies are dormant or active is not known.

Viral determinants of immunodeficiency disorders may begin their influence either before or after birth. The HIV (human immunodeficiency virus) that produces AIDS is not known to have any special association with paraphilia.

Public figures who are embarrassed by the publicity of an arrest for indecent exposure or any other paraphilic offense may call upon the *toxic myth* as an extenuating circumstance. Alcohol, being legal and socially acceptable, is the drug most commonly called upon to construct a toxic defense. Other drugs, licit or illicit, may be implicated, provided they blunt one's judgment and shrink one's attention span from the future to the present. Such drugs may act to release a particular paraphilic episode, but they cannot account for the origin of paraphilic ideation and imagery in the lovemap—hence the appellation, the toxic myth.

Widespread in the mythology of the paraphilias is the *fix it yourself myth*. Adolescent cross dressers, for whom it would be too stigmatizing to "come out of the closet," cling to the myth that by getting married they will cure themselves or, when that fails, getting rid of their entire wardrobe will do the same. The fix it yourself myth applies to all paraphilias. It may owe its persistence to the fact that some paraphilias go through periods of apparent remission, only to flare up again under the pressure of workaday stress or acute trauma. Under conditions of incarceration and coerced treatment, a paraphile's claim of self-cure conforms to the institution's doctrine and policy of treatment, even to the point of using the same shibboleths and platitudes. For example, in the years when Freudianism was in the ascendant, a multiple rapist serving a life sentence was seriously convinced that he would no longer be a menace to society on the outside because he had "found his Oedipals."

Paraphilic rape (*raptophilia* if derived from Latin, and *biastophilia* if derived from Greek) brings up another paraphilic myth, namely, the *violence myth*. In the 1960s era of "make love, not war," the proponents of the sexual liberation and of the women's liberation movements separated lovemap ideology and imagery into consensual and affectionate versus coercive and aggressive. This division gave birth to the violence myth; according to which, paraphilic sexual violence, assault, murder, sadism, molestation, and abuse were sexually deconstructed and reconstructed as crimes of violence and assertions of power, totally devoid of sexuality. The violence myth is alive and well in today's classrooms, text books, and marriage manuals. It has the status of being politically correct but scientifically incorrect. The scientifically correct statement about the paraphilias attributed to violence alone is that they combine sexuality and aggression.

In 1897, Freud replaced his prepsychoanalytic seduction theory of 1895 with his psychoanalytic theory of the Oedipus complex. When seduction theory underwent a revival almost a century later, it gave rise to the *seduction myth* of infantile abuse and molestation (Bass and Davis 1988).

According to this myth, a history of sexual molestation may have begun in infancy, as early as eighteen months of age, or at any time later in childhood. The father is most often accused as the offender. As an adult, the putative victim is not able to retrieve any memory of a molestation history. Nonetheless, repressed memory is held responsible for a wide variety of somatic and psychic symptoms. The putative cure of these symptoms necessitates recall of the molestation history in detail, facilitated if need be by hypnotic suggestion. False recall has led to false accusations and to the concept of the false memory syndrome. Many families have been torn asunder by false memories. Parents, pastors, teachers, and others have been imprisoned on the basis of false accusations which went so far as to include vivid descriptions of Satanic worship with babies sacrificed on Satan's altar. One of the corollaries of the seduction myth is another myth, namely that children never tell lies about sexual events alleged to have occurred in their innocent lives.

Early Theories

PEOPLE STRICKEN WITH any chronic or terminal illness ask: "Why me?" Others with a history of exposure to the same risk factors, even the same pathogen, survive apparently unharmed. Thus, the question, on closer look, calls for two explanations: One is ontogenetic and the other phylogenetic. The ontogenetic explanation addresses the issue of the history and development of a particular person's pathology. The phylogenetic explanation addresses the issue of the history and evolution of susceptibility to that particular pathology in the species as a whole. Why, for example, do paraphilias exist apparently in the human species alone and not in other primate or subprimate species? The question applies not only to paraphilia. Why, for example, does HIV/AIDS affect only members of the human species, so that there is no exact animal model of the disease? There is also no exact animal model of paraphilia.

In paraphilia, there is no single ontogenetic determinant with which to predict the development of paraphilic ideation and imagery in the lovemap. During the first century of sexology's history as a forensic specialty, however, several theories of determinism were tried and found wanting. These theories of determinism were widely applied in all of psychiatry. They included the ancient *theory of degeneracy* caused by loss of the vital fluid, e.g., by masturbation (see chap. 2). Even more popular was the *theory of a tainted heredity* brought into the family pedigree according to the Lamarckian principle of the inheritance of acquired characteristics. Generations of kinsmen, themselves tainted by alcohol, drugs, mineral poisons, epilepsy, malaria, tuberculosis, pellagra, venereal infection, and more, intensified the degree of hereditary taint in the pedigree.

A variant of hereditary taintedness was stated in 1857 by the French psychiatrist, Benedict Morel (see Hoenig 1977). He postulated an *evolutionary arrest* or *regression* ever since the fall of Adam from the state of being God's perfect creation. The idea of evolutionary regression was taken up by the Italian criminologist, Cesar Lombroso (1876/1972), who renamed it *atavism* and associated it with morphological birth defects.

The watershed year in forensic sexology was 1886, the year when Richard von Krafft-Ebing published his once much vilified and now famous *Psychopathia Sexualis*. In the 1931 American edition, the subtitle was *With Especial Reference to the Antipathic Sexual Instinct: A Medico-Forensic Study*.

Psychopathia Sexualis had been the title in 1844 of a book, in German and published in Germany, by Heinrich Kaan, personal physician to the Czar. Kaan made special mention of love of boys, mutual homosexual masturbation, violation of corpses, coitus with animals, and contact with statues (*agalmatophilia* or Pygmalionism, of which the converse is *saliromania,* the defilement of nude female statues and paintings). His causal explanation was circular: an inherited disposition toward morbid fantasy (*phantasmia morbosa*) induces sensual excess, including self-abuse, which intensifies morbid fantasy, which is further intensified by degeneracy induced by eating rich and spicy food; sleeping in a sensual feather bed instead of on a hard mattress; wearing tightly corseted garments; failing to keep fit with exercise and fresh air; and having too much leisure. All of these sources of degeneracy, especially masturbation, were taken seriously in nineteenth-century medicine.

In keeping with the intellectual vogue of the times, Krafft-Ebing's causal explanation of psychosexual pathology began with hereditary taintedness which, together with other sources of degeneracy, was held responsible for a degenerate brain and nervous system. This schema could not be reconciled with the specificity of psychosexual pathologies. However, it allowed Krafft-Ebing to postulate that only a degenerate brain would be unable to resist subsidiary pathological influences, for example those obtained by way of the stimulus-response *principle of associative learning.*

Alfred Binet, the French psychologist famed for his invention of intelligence tests, was the first to use the principle of associative learning to explain the origin of paraphilia. He wrote specifically of fetishism and paved the way for today's behavior modification theory. Krafft-Ebing met Binet's theoretical challenge by responding that only in a degenerative brain could a fetish be established. In the same vein, Krafft-Ebing was able to graft evolutionary retrogression or atavism into his schema specifically to explain sadism and masochism as throwbacks to a primitive evolutionary stage of development. He applied the same explanation to so-called "psychic hermaphroditism," today's transgenderism and homosexuality.

Krafft-Ebing's principle of a brain tainted with hereditary degeneracy was superfluous to the explanation of psychosexual pathology secondary to a *brain lesion* from a head wound, stroke, or epilepsy. In the later editions of *Psychopathia Sexualis*, Krafft-Ebing dealt briefly with three cases of idiocy, two of brain injury, five of late stage syphilis, and twelve of epilepsy. The three cases of idiocy were characterized as having an innate mental weakness, and the other nineteen were characterized as having an acquired mental weakness. Of these nineteen, he wrote: "Perversions of the sexual instinct seem to be infrequent, and here the immoral acts seem to depend on abnormally increased or uninhibited sexual feeling which in itself is not abnormal." With this statement, Krafft-Ebing introduced a new causal explanation, namely perversion of the sexual instinct, with the implication that the sexual instinct exists sui generis. In this way, he lifted the lid off the Pandora's box of *intrapsychic determinism* and introduced the still unresolved issue of organic versus psychogenic causes of psychosexual pathology.

Intrapsychic Determinism

Krafft-Ebing died in 1902, old enough to have left the legacy of *Psychopathia Sexualis* to Freud but too young to leave on record his reaction to Freud's 1905 publication of *Drei Abhandlungen zur Sexualtheorie* (Three essays on the theory of sexuality). One may assume, however, that Krafft-Ebing would have recognized that his own explanation of sexual psychopathology could not absorb Freud's principle of intrapsychic determinism as it had done Binet's principle of associative determinism.

The psychopathologies of sex were, in the vocabulary of Freud, the "perversions," the name they still go by in most of contemporary psychoanalysis (see Stoller 1975). Freud's explanation of the perversions is postulated upon the principles of evolutionary recapitulation and evolutionary reversion.

Ernst Haeckel's principle that ontogeny recapitulates phylogeny was popularized in Freud's time by Wilhelm Boelsche, a novelist who was also a popular science writer. Haeckel had written on gastriculation, the process which he studied in marine sponges, whereby the cell mass invaginates to create a primitive stomach with a mouth and, later, an anal orifice—with, later still in higher organisms, genitalia. Boelsche popularized gastrea theory as portraying the phylogenetic evolution of sexual sensitivity from the external skin to the gastreal mouth, and thence to the primitive cloaca, the anus, and, finally, the genitalia (Sulloway 1979, 262). Boelsche's popularization went further, and it portrayed the parallel between the morphology and the method of reproduction in phylogenetic evolution, beginning with oral fusion and progressing through cloacal exchange to genital union. Recapitulated in individual development and reconstrued as instinctual, these evolutionary stages constitute, in Freudian theory, the developmental stages of infantile "polymorphous-perverse" sexuality—oral, anal, phallic, and genital.

In Freud's intrapsychic explanation of perversion, the principle of evolutionary reversion was dualistic: fixation, if development had been arrested, and regression, if development had progressed and then gone backward. Provided the outcome of either fixation or regression was the persistence of a prior stage of infantile polymorphous-perversity, then it would be named perversion (Freud did not differentiate all of what he classified as the perversions, syndrome by syndrome). By contrast, if the perversion were modified and disguised by the superimposition of repression, then the outcome would be named neurosis.

To be complete, the intrapsychic explanation of perversion must include an explanation of the selectivity of fixation and regression in perverting only a minority of individuals and not the majority. There are various options: degeneracy, hereditary taint, or neuropathology, for example. However, these options are not intrapsychic but extrinsic, and Freud was committed to a wholly intrapsychic theory.

Another option is traumatic interference with development which, in the case of the development of sexuality, might be brought about by premature or illicit sexual stimulation. Traumatic interference is not consistent with an exclusively intrapsychic explanation, insofar as traumatic interference originates extrinsically and is, therefore, a specific instance of associative determinism—as when genital arousal might become prematurely associated with being masturbated by a nursemaid, for example, or with being seduced, possibly incestuously, by an older person. As aforesaid, in 1895, Freud gave credence to both of these possibilities. Whereas he did not ever formally relinquish the possibility of a harmful effect of masturbation, he completely abandoned the formulation of hysterical neurosis as the outcome of premature seduction. Freud's 1897 turning point toward his Oedipal theory of intrapsychic determinism was, in toto, consistently and exclusively intrapsychic. It has long been well known and, at times, acrimoniously controversial (Sulloway 1989; Masson 1984).

Within an exclusively intrapsychic system of explanation, there is a logically finite number of alternative intrapsychic principles with which to explain intrapsychic fixation and regression. One is the intrapsychic principle of idiopathic determinism, according to which it is preordained that fixation and regression will take place in the development of selected individuals only. A second is the intrapsychic principle of chronological sequence, according to which there is a phylogenetically ordained schedule for the various aspects of intrapsychic development, divergence from which induces fixation or regression. A third is the intrapsychic principle of periodicity, according to which intrapsychic development is phylogenetically preordained to take place in a fluctuating, cyclic, periodic, or pulsatile manner, without which fixation and regression will take place.

None of these three principles appears in Freud's system of intrapsychic explanation, although it is known from his letters to Wilhelm Fliess that, after giving due consideration to the principle of periodicity as propounded by Fliess, he did not use it (Sulloway 1979).

A fourth principle by which to explain fixation and regression intrapsychically is the principle of conflict or incompatibility between two or more components of the psyche, one being more powerful or dominant than the other. It is known, also from Freud's letters to Fliess, that the principle of conflict was prominent in two of Fliess's evolutionary formulations: the one of inherent intrapsychic bisexuality and the other of sexual attraction by way of olfaction and the nose versus vision and the eyes. In Freud's formulations, the principle of conflict, transmuted into the principle of intrapsychic conflict, occupied a prominent position in his system of intrapsychic determinism. It applies to instinctual conflict and to hierarchical conflict between the instinctual id, the ego, and the superego. Freud was equivocal about an exclusively intrapsychic origin of the superego. His major intrapsychic contests are in the arenas of bisexuality and the Oedipus complex.

In the arena of bisexuality, the intrapsychic contest is between heterosexuality and homosexuality. Either side may win. Homosexuality, by definition, is a perversion. Therefore, defeat of the perversion entails an alliance with repression. Repressed homosexuality does not disappear but becomes latent homosexuality, and it is able to reappear only in the disguise of neurotic symptomatology, for example, paranoia. What is missing in this paradigm of intrapsychic determinism is that it lacks two principles: one to explain why and in whom heterosexuality will win the contest and another to explain why and in whom homosexuality, a perversion in psychoanalytic terminology, will win without being transformed into a neurosis. The principle of intrapsychic conflict fails to fulfill its promise of providing an explanation of homosexuality as a perversion.

In the arena of the Oedipus complex, the intrapsychic contest is between infantile sexuality and infantile abstinence. The Oedipal triumph of being victorious over the rival, same-sexed parent would be the perversion of incest with the other-sexed parent. The tragedy of not being victorious is ensured by an Oedipal alliance with repression, and the penalty of defeat is castration anxiety. Under the threat of castration anxiety, sexuality can reappear only in the disguise of neurotic symptomatology. Here again, the principle of intrapsychic conflict fails to explain those who survive the Oedipal rivalry without neurosis, to be, instead, if not perverted, then healthy.

One way out of the dilemma of both latent homosexuality and castration anxiety is to make a doctrinal revision whereby latent homosexuality and/or castration anxiety become the intrapsychic forces used to explain all of the paraphilias (perversions in the psychoanalytic vocabulary) as if they were neuroses. The psychoanalyst with a lifetime of experience with paraphilic sex offenders who did precisely this, and used the term *paraphilic neuroses,* was Benjamin Karpman (1954, 579). He wrote:

> Latent homosexuals may resort to paraphilia, or their sexual life may evidence pathology without recourse to paraphilia. Virtually all paraphilias spring from unconscious homosexuality; these perversions give rise to a number of sex crimes. Fellatio, cunnilingus, paederasty [i.e., anal coitus], when enacted in a heterosexual setting express unconscious homosexual trends. (610)

Karpman wrote also that "unconscious incest pervades all neuroses, psychoses, and paraphilias" (603). Karpman was not excessively dogmatic regarding the Oedipus complex and castration anxiety. By contrast, in a brief presentation on psychoanalytic theory and sexual deviation, Kline (1987) espoused Otto Fenichel and his version of castration anxiety, in such statements as:

> The fetish is an attempt to deny the lack of a penis; the male transvestite combines the homosexual's identification with his mother and the fetishist's denial that a woman has no penis; exhibitionism is an attempt at denial of castration; and voyeurs are fixated on experiences that aroused their castration anxiety.

The hazard of intrapsychic determinism is that, as in the foregoing examples, it is too readily converted into dogma. A dogma is validated by the number of its converts and, conversely, of its victims, rather than by the pragmatics of its empirical productivity.

Lovemap Chronicles

WHEN THE FIRST of Havelock Ellis's seven volumes of *Studies in the Psychology of Sex* (see Ellis 1920) appeared in 1897, the entire edition was confiscated as obscene. Its English language publication was then transferred from London to Philadelphia where the final volume appeared in 1928. Purchase was restricted to medical and legal practitioners until after 1930, as the case histories were considered too sexually explicit for the general public. They chronicled the sexual biographies of ordinary citizens, not only of representatives of the clinical and criminal population, and they did so without any particular theoretical bias. Albert Moll in *The Sexual Life of the Child*

(1909/1912) approached the sexology of childhood in a similarly empirical way but on a lesser scale.

There are multiple obstacles to be surmounted in chronicling the development of lovemaps, ranging from informed consent and unbiased sampling to guaranteed financing of outcome follow-up and the trustworthiness of long term recall. Nonetheless, there is plentiful evidence, when the data are forthcoming, of coherency in the way things fit together in the chronicle of a lovemap's multivariate and sequential development. However, they do so with a high degree of personal idiosyncrasy in the timing, strength, duration, and number of variables involved.

Personal idiosyncrasy does not rule out the possibility of some degree of similarity in the chronicle of the development of some lovemaps with the same paraphilic diagnosis. With data pooled from multiple sexological centers, it should be possible to ascertain whether, among assaultive rapists, for instance, there is an elevated prevalence of a boyhood history of incestuous entrapment—not necessarily coital incest, but perhaps sleeping, up to and beyond puberty, in the same bed as the mother or other older female and becoming erotically aroused without consummation.

Similarly, another possibility to be looked into is whether, among seductive pedophiles, there is an increased childhood history of entrapment in a seductive, noncoercive relationship with a pedophilic male or female partner. Alternatively, the outcome might be an increased prevalence of attraction to much older partners (*gerontophilia*). There is no shortage of questions about the possibility of regularities in the chronicles of lovemap formation in all of the paraphilias.

The geography of the lovemap is like the geography of the face in that, whereas all faces are uniquely recognizable, they also have the generic appearance of being a face. Even identical twins cannot count on having lovemaps that are precise copies of one another. If the ethics of human cloning are surmountable, then cloned human replicas will provide a formerly unforeseen reservoir of data from which to distinguish cloned identity from unique idiosyncrasy in the lovemap. The analogy is with language: each of two human clones will have a native language, but which one will depend on the native language of those to whom they listen and with whom they converse.

Study of the developmental sexology of human clones is yet another example of science fictional research. In the meantime, one is restricted to recognizing and formulating whatever principles one can from a systematic examination of such lovemap chronicles as have become available.

From the chronicles of paraphilic lovemaps (Money 1986), the principle of a disjunction between love and lust became evident as a defining characteristic of paraphilia. This is the same disjunction that characterizes the history and ecclesiastical status of sexuality in Western culture. Love is godly. Lust is satanic. Love is pure and is for procreation. Lust is impure and is for sinful pleasure. Love is sentimental and above the navel. Lust is carnal and below the navel.

The paraphilias represent formulas for salvaging lust in a compromise with love. There are forty-odd paraphilias altogether, the exact number depending on how many subdivisions are recognized—how many subdivisions of fetishism, for example. Altogether, the paraphilias cluster in the form of seven grand stratagems by which to salvage sinful lust from its antithesis with saintly love.

Each grand stratagem encodes a paleodigm, that is to say an ancient paradigm of folk wisdom dating back as far, perhaps, as the stone age (Brown 1991). The actual carrying out of a stratagem may, on occasion, be replaced by replaying a mental tape of a prior occasion or by viewing a representative commercial or self-made videotape. The seven grand stratagems are as follows.

Grand Stratagems: Paleodigms

Sacrifice and Expiation. This grand stratagem encodes the paleodigm of sin and its expiation or atonement through sacrifice. In this case, the sin is the experience of lust in genitoerotic arousal and orgasm. The ultimate in paraphilic sacrifice is serial lust murder. Its converse or antipode is the self-arranged risk of one's own accidental death, e.g., by autoerotic self-asphyxiation or by autoerotic self-electrocution should the voltage be improperly regulated. Two cases of autoerotic fatality involving the hydraulic shovels of farm machinery were reported by O'Halloran and Dietz (1993). Their summary was as follows.

> One man developed a romantic attachment to a tractor, even giving it a name and writing poetry in its honor. He died accidentally while intentionally asphyxiating himself through suspension by the neck, leaving clues that he enjoyed perceptual distortions during asphyxiation. The other man engaged in sexual bondage

and transvestic fetishism, but did not purposely asphyxiate himself. He died when accidentally pinned to the ground under a shovel after intentionally suspending himself by the ankles. We compare these cases with other autoerotic fatalities involving perceptual distortion, cross-dressing, machinery, and postural asphyxiation by chest compression.

The risk of one's own accidental erotic death may be stage managed not in isolation but with a coopted partner or partners. One masochistic young man picked up roughnecks on the waterfront and coaxed them into a ritual of squirting him with shaving cream and ketchup (a carry over from puberty) and kicking his head and face with jackboots and cursing him. He audiotaped the episode for subsequent replay to the accompaniement of masturbation. Paraphilic sacrifice may also take the form of punishment inflicted or received in a conjoint sadomasochistic performance. Fasting may also serve to be a form of sacrifice or atonement.

Marauding and Predation. This grand stratagem encodes the paleodigm of capturing and possessing another human being by force, entrapment, or abduction. In military history, when victorious armies raped the women of the enemy they had defeated, rape was defined not as the sexual coercion of the female but as the misappropriation of another man's property, for she belonged to either her father or her husband. In contemporary usage, the heterosexual meaning of the term *rape* has been changed to signify vaginal penetration insisted upon after a female, who may be a wife, paramour, or date, says no to a male (rape of a male by a female is rarely admitted). *Rape* defined in this way bears only a peripheral relationship to the clinical syndrome named *raptophilia* or *biastophilia*. In the paraphilic syndrome of raptophilia, the raptophile's genitoerotic arousal and eventual orgasm are contingent on having or having had a partner who, as a captive, has been forced to yield sexually under conditions of threat, assault, and injury.

Mercantilism and Venality. This grand stratagem encodes the paleodigm of obtaining goods or services by bartering and trade, of which a specific instance is the payment of the bride price or the provision of a dowry in an arranged marriage. A mercantile or venal paraphilia is one in which the paraphile's genitoerotic arousal and orgasm are contingent on negotiating or being robbed of some form of payment. In the orgasm trade, lust is a commodity, bought and sold, independently of love and affection. In some marriages, a mercantile paraphilia takes the form of impersonating a prostitute and client, using play money. In some instances, a second male is the client, and the husband becomes aroused by watching.

Fetishism and Talismanism. This grand stratagem encodes the paleodigm of being in possession of an object or artifact that has extraordinary power of causality that enables its possessor to control events and to make the otherwise impossible come to pass. A paraphilic fetish or talisman is an object or artifact that, as a stimulus of genitoerotic arousal and orgasm, substitutes for the person who is its owner. There are two categories of paraphilic fetishes and talismans. One comprises the touchy-feely or hyphephilic artifacts that are derived from human-body contact, especially with skin and hair. The other comprises the tasty-smelly or olfactophilic artifacts that are derived from human-body tastes and smells, especially sweaty and crotch smells. A fetish may be altered for erotic use. For example, a shoe fetishist drilled a masturbation hole in the heel of ladies' shoes he stole.

Stigmatism and Eligibility. This grand stratagem encodes the paleodigm of love at first sight—the irresistible attraction that draws an observer toward an erstwhile stranger, even at a distance, as if the meeting had been inevitably predestined by an inexplicable fate. Some people explain it as due to the chemistry of love. Since there are, as yet, no laboratory tests for the body's chemistries of love, it is more down to earth to explain the attraction as the observer's sudden recognition that there is something about the stranger that exactly reciprocates the imagery and ideation of his or her brain's own lovemap. An extreme example is the lovemap of *acrotomophilia*, which decrees that the partner must be an amputee (see chaps. 4, 7). The acrotomophilic observer of the amputated stump becomes lust stricken. Other criteria of paraphilic eligibility include race, ethnicity, religion, political allegiance, and wealth. Age is another criterion of eligibility. In paraphilic *pedophilia, ephebophilia,* and *gerontophilia,* the lovemap attractant is, respectively, juvenile, adolescent, and elderly.

Solicitation and Allure. This grand stratagem encodes the paleodigm of what is known in the animal kingdom as assortative, conspecific mating while being in season or in heat. It may take the form of a mating dance or courtship display, the gestures of which are an overt presentation of the sex organs as an invitation to copulate.

Except in live shows and movies for erotic entertainment, in the human species, the mating dance is more likely to be a debutante ball or disco dance than a display of the naked genitalia. Solicitation and allurement become paraphilic when, instead of being a flirtatious invitation to courtship, preliminary to bilateral erotosexual involvement, they are engaged in unilaterally, and themselves constitute the trigger on which orgasm is dependent. Thus, the person being solicited or allured needs only to look, and is spared the defilement of genital contact. Many people fear that the paraphilic exhibitionist, as well as the peeping Tom (voyeur), will be a rapist as well. That combination does exist, but paraphilic rape belongs in the category of marauding and predation and does not routinely overlap with paraphilic solicitation and allure.

Protectorship and Rescue. This grand stratagem encodes the paleodigm of rescue and deliverance. The one who is rescued is the victim of someone else's lust (see also chap. 7). A paraphilic protector is one whose lust becomes released only if he/she rescues a victimized partner from an inept or abusive partner. This paraphilic scenario occurs in some instances of adulterous infidelity and also in some instances of incest. In some instances of incest, one parent connives to be rid of the spouse's unwanted affection. Some prostitutes serve as agents of rescue, payment notwithstanding. Protectorship and rescue may be either heterosexual, homosexual, or bisexual.

Paleodigms illustrate the principle that information coded in the mind and the cerebral cortex may influence behavior, even though the connection between the paleodigm and the behavior is not explicitly recognized by the person concerned. A paleodigm is not, per se, causative. However, in syndromes characterized by selectively ritualized behavior, the performance of which has an effect on someone else, paleodigmatics may be of explanatory significance.

From Biorobotics to Paraphilia

THE SEVEN GRAND stratagems illustrate the diversity of imagery and ideation that can be incorporated into the lovemap, even though much of it bears no apparent relationship to the biorobotic elements (phylisms) of mammalian mating and procreation. *Phylism* is the term used to refer to one of the phylogenetically determined elements of behavior that belongs innately to all members of a species. A phylism is characterized by an innate detection or recognition system, and an innate responding system, both of which work in synchrony at an innately determined phase of development, after which they leave a long lasting, if not indelible imprint. The classic example comes from the literature on ethology (Lorenz 1952): a newly hatched gosling or duckling recognizes a squat shaped waddling stimulus, usually though not inevitably its mother, follows it, and becomes imprinted to it. When Lorenz himself impersonated a mother bird, the young ones became imprinted to him as their surrogate mother.

Phylismic stimulus-response systems do not need to be learned. They are stereotypically the same for all members of the species, and they are closed to individual variation. Observe, for example, the ritualized pattern of canine mating in free roaming urban dogs. It has the quality of being biorobotic. The mating of four-legged subprimate mammals is more biorobotic than that of subhuman primates, and it is least biorobotic of all in human primates. Human lovemaps are so variable as to be not only eccentric but also, in many instances, downright bizarre in the way they deviate from the bare essentials of reproductive biorobotism.

Only the human species has the wherewithal to narrate the ideational and imagistic contents of its lovemaps for the benefit of listeners, whereas body language and a limited repertory of sounds must suffice for other species. In other words, the human being has not only a lovemap but also a speechmap to go with it. As already adumbrated (see chap. 4, "Age Eight"), there may be an evolutionary connection between the two maps.

According to this hypothetical conjecture, evolution of the human speechmap transcended the biorobotics of the soundmaps of the prelinguistic mammalian mindbrain. Evolution of the syntactical language of symbolic logic and numerical reasoning necessitated flexibility and versatility beyond the capacity of any biorobotic map which, in turn, necessitated emancipation from the restrictions of all biorobotic maps, including the biorobotic matingmap. The gap between the robotic soundmap and the emancipated speechmap may have been bridged by the prototypic songmap. Emancipation from the robotic system of squeaks, squawks, hoots, howls, growls, screams, clicks, chatters, and other sounds of alarm, warning, threat, mating, or feeding would not have sufficed to form the speechmap without a merger with the melodic cadences, inflection, rhythmicity, syllabic intonation, cooing, crooning, humming, chanting, phrasing, and mimicry of the songmap. The first intimation of human language might well have been the lullaby or the love song. Song and dance are ingredients of the lovemap, worldwide, especially in the culture of adolescence. The maps for music and speech are differently represented in the hemispheric laterality of the cerebral cortex (Money 1998b).

The foregoing evolutionary sequence may have been contingent on prior hominid emancipation from quadrupedal to bipedal locomotion. Bipedal locomotion may itself have evolved, not according to the familiar neo-Darwinian doctrine of accumulated random mutations in the DNA, but according to the more recent serial endosymbiosis theory (SET). Serial endosymbiosis signifies evolutionary change through long term proximity of different bacterially small organisms. Eventually, two or more of them merge their DNA within the nucleus of a single cell (Margulis and Dolan 1997). An everyday example of symbiogenesis is the merging of a fungus and green alga to form a lichen.

Quadrupeds have the nose and the genital organs on the same plane. They are sexuoerotically aroused by smell rather than vision and in periodic or seasonal synchrony with hormonal or pheromonal cycles. The bipedal human species, by contrast, is emancipated from the nose in favor of the eyes and contrectative (skin) senses and from exclusively dorsoventral (doggie) to ventroventral (missionary) and other coital positioning, without dependence on periodic or seasonal cyclicity.

With an evolutionary history of being emancipated from the confines of biorobotism, each individual human lovemap was free to splice extraneous ideation and imagery, derobotized from other nonsexual brainmaps, into its own formation—as in fetishism, for example, or violence and self-mutilation. Hence, the seven paleodigmatic grand stratagems of paraphilic lovemap modification became a human possibility.

Opponent-Process Theory

SEXOLOGICAL BRAIN RESEARCH, in brain imaging for example, will need to advance far beyond its late twentieth-century limitations before it will be possible to trace the formation and activation of paraphilic lovemaps. Meanwhile, the most promising hypothesis is that paraphilic ideation and imagery begin getting grafted or spliced into a lovemap in childhood and become consolidated after puberty. Centuries of stigmatization, criminalization, and brutal punishment have been relentlessly unsuccessful in achieving their ostensible purpose, namely, ridding the species of its paraphilias, even the most gruesome ones. The rules of reward and punishment training simply do not apply. There was no explanation of this failure until Richard Solomon (1980) formulated and experimentally tested opponent process theory (LoLordo and Seligman 1997).

Opponent process learning theory turns regular stimulus/response, operant conditioning theory upside down. Opponent process converts negative into positive, tragedy into triumph, and aversion into addiction. Two recreational examples of opponent process reversal are bungee jumping and riding a gravity defying roller coaster. The novice whose apprehension amounts to sheer terror at first may, after very few trials, discover that terror transmogrifies into exhilaration and ecstasy as if the brain had released a flood of its own opiate-like endorphins. Thereafter, the thrill returns with each repeat, totally replacing terror.

As applied to paraphilia, the coding of lovemap ideation and imagery that should be negative flip-flops and becomes positive. The ideation and imagery that other people disapprove of and punish if translated into action reasserts itself repetitiously and insistently demands a live performance, consequences notwithstanding. Even one's own life and death may be at stake, as in the process of paraphilic armed robbery (Keyes and Money 1993), or of paraphilic self-asphyxiation (Money et al. 1991).

The opponent process flip flop manifests itself also in *hybristophilia,* the paraphilia of fixation on partners known to have raped, killed, robbed, or otherwise have committed crimes. It is recognized more often in women than men. In its most malignant form, the woman subtly precipitates a rage attack in her partner, and then she has him arrested and imprisoned for domestic violence. Subsequently, she visits him in prison and sexually frustrates him by her unavailability. The prison argot for someone with this paraphilia is a death row groupie.

The following biographical summary (Money et al. 1990) of an opponent process flip-flop is that of a woman originally seen in pediatric endocrinology for growth failure secondary to deficiency of pituitary growth hormone which itself is secondary to pathological child abuse and neglect at home. Growth hormone level and growth rate both normalize following transfer to a benign domicile. Known eponymously as the Kaspar Hauser syndrome (Money 1992), this reversible type of hypopituitarism is known also as psychosocial dwarfism. In the present instance, the early history of pathological neglect and abuse was not suspected or investigated in the course of multiple clinic visits. The girl was nine and a half years old when the medical record tersely noted that the home situation had been complicated by a fire which destroyed the family dwelling and critically burned the father. At the age of twenty, the patient's own account was as follows.

> One night they [her parents] got into a fight again. She had caught him on his oyster boat with another woman. She threw a combination lock at the woman's head and busted it open. . . . When he came home they fought some more. He fell asleep that night. He was drunk. She got some gasoline and poured it over him, and lit the match.

Homeless, the mother and her four children were taken in by family and friends until, after fourteen months, the mother was sentenced to life imprisonment. The patient's behavioral problems—for example, writing sexually explicit notes to ten-year-old twin brothers—got her evicted from foster homes. She was fifteen when her paternal grandmother took her in. When angry, this woman would call her "a mother lookin' bitch, damn fool, and stupid. She said I act like my mother and look like my mother."

The girl visited her mother regularly in prison. She said that she had always felt the guilt of responsibility for her father's death because of something she might have done but could not identify. From late teenage onward, there were mounting problems of sex, delinquency, depression, self-mutilation, and suicide.

By age nineteen, she had a baby daughter. The two of them were abandoned by the baby's teenaged father. The mother was unable to combine the responsibilities of single parenthood with a career in prostitution, her only source of support. A local community service agency arranged for the baby's adoption at the age of sixteen months and for the mother's sexological evaluation and possible rehabilitation. In the course of this evaluation, she revealed the ideation and imagery of masochism in her lovemap.

> I was sixteen when I met this black guy and played hooky from school. We went to his house, and while we were having sex, he slapped me on the face, one time. It didn't hurt. It excited me. It felt good. But it really wasn't until I was age eighteen that I really got into it. I was going steady with Mark who lived in the same group home that I did. And we would fist fight when we were having sex, or before having sex. It was better when he slapped me. I think he got turned on by it, too.

There was an earlier childhood antecedent to this eroticization of fighting. It traced back to the constant fighting of her parents which the patient could recall from as far back as when she was probably five years old.

> My father and mother were fighting constantly, she said. And sometimes it looked sexual to me. One time they were fighting in the dining room. My mother had on this real suggestive, slinky black negligee, and my father was just standing there, calling her bitch. And he slapped her.

When they fought, he would slap her in the face and push her around, as well as yell at her.

> Sometimes [the patient said] when I'm having sex with a guy and I ask him to slap me, if he does, I'll get sexually excited and find myself thinking back to that time when my mother was standing there in that black negligee, and my father was screaming at her and getting ready to hit her.

By the age of twelve, the girl had been exposed to coercive sexual harassment by a sixteen-year-old foster brother whose mother's reaction was to threaten the girl with a hysterectomy "if anything happened." She also suffered sadistic humiliation and injury by a same-aged girl friend who was showing off to boys. At age twenty, she was quite articulate about the lure of street life.

> I guess it's the excitement I like. The pimps trying to get you, the cops after you, the drug dealers trying to chase after you. The cops are looking at you all the time, because they know you're a prostitute, and that's illegal. That alone is excitement to me. So are the fights. Some of the girls get into standing around, watching. A girl who's not a prostitute will ride by and make fun of us.

A prostitute will pull her out of her car and start messing her up, and all the other prostitutes will start beating her up. That's exciting. The threat of getting put in jail is exciting, but not actually getting in jail. . . . And just going in and out of bars, and everything in there is exciting. The city, and the night time, and how people might get wild sometimes, it's thrilling, I guess.

Of the tricks whom she picked up, she said:

They just treated me like a piece of shit, after they got done with me. . . . There was one trick with whom it was more enjoyable for me because he was my type, which is important. He was a young black male, and he looked nice to me.

Her attraction to black male clients was because they were:

more aggressive. I just feel that they know how to express themselves better, doing sex. I just feel an attraction toward them. It's almost an obsession. . . . I haven't come across any who didn't have a big dick. You can feel it more. I just feels better to me.

Her ideal was to have a black man who would treat her rough and slap her around, on the face and arms or legs.

There was this incident with drug dealer whose name was Black Jack. At a bar, one day, he asked me if I wanted to have sex with him. . . . I went up to his room. We got undressed and we started having sex. It seemed to me that the more he got excited, the more violent he became; and right before he was going to reach orgasm, he started hitting me. After we were finished, I said, well, what did you do that for? And he said, well, because it gets me more excited.

For her, it was also exciting. It did not hurt but was sexually arousing. In fact, it was possible for her to reach orgasm just by being slapped, without intromission. She had had no history of difficulty in reaching orgasm and was able to do so two or three times in fifteen or twenty minutes. After finishing having sex, she would be ready to begin again in about ten minutes. She estimated that, if she would try to set a record, she might be able to service twenty-five men between 9 P.M. and 3 A.M. In actuality, the maximum number of tricks had been three or four in one evening.

On the sentence completion test, the patient wrote: "The worst thing I ever did was to be a prostitute." Contradicting herself, she also claimed that she didn't find anything wrong with being a prostitute. Rather, it was getting paid that made her feel bad, she conjectured. She had sometimes felt that she should be paying, especially those men who, honoring her request to slap her up, gave her the most ecstatic orgasms of all, without themselves being turned on by slapping a masochist.

With respect to the future, the patient was candid in saying that prostitution as a lifestyle continued to appeal to her. Though she had no other prospects of financial support, her plans included another pregnancy.

> I'm upset, she said, because I just gave my first child up for adoption. I figure if I get pregnant again, I keep saying to myself, this time I want to get pregnant by a black man, and this time I can keep my child. Social services won't be involved. I feel like having a child is—it's something that I could have that would love me and depend on me.

There is no technology for retrieving data for or against a gene coded infrastructure of masochism. By contrast, there are data in this young woman's history, from early life onward, of an infrastructure of masochism environmentally coded into the developing lovemap where, by opponent process, the tragedy of violence became the eroticized triumph of masochistic ecstasy.

Paraphilic lovemaps are multivariately and sequentially determined. The ascertainable determinants, whatever they are, are not identically replicated in every similar case. However, the common circumstance present in all cases may very well be the Catch-22 dilemma of irreconcilable alternatives. In the present example, the young girl's dilemma was to be damned if she condemned her mother for immolating her father, to whom she was closely attached, and damned if she condoned her mother, to whom she was also attached, as a murderess. The paraphilic compromise in the daughter's own lovemap was the eroticization of the tragedy of her assaultive father's murder by his retaliative wife into the masochistic triumph of achieving superorgasms by being assaulted by the men she picked up as a prostitute.

Temporal Lobe Sexology

A PARAPHILIC LOVEMAP formulates and reveals itself autonomously, like a dream or nightmare. It does not require the intervention of conscious awareness, voluntary intent, or planning. Unlike a lesson, it is not learned, and it cannot be discarded by moral resolve or will power.

After 1950, a still small literature on temporal lobe epilepsy and impaired sexuality began to be published (Gastaut and Collomb 1954; reviews by Money and Pruce 1977; and Lehne 1986). Impotency in males was the most noted symptom. Hypophilia prevailed over hyperphilia and paraphilia. Among the paraphilias, fetishism prevailed. If temporal lobe seizures yielded to temporal lobectomy, the fetishism did also. Huws et al. (1991) published a case report on fetishism and hypersexuality in which magnetic resonance imaging (MRI) showed lesions of the frontal and temporal lobes of the brain. Monga et al. (1986) reported on three cases, two women and one man, with a history of poststroke temporal lobe lesions, demonstrated by CAT (computerized axial tomography) scan, associated with seizures, altered sexuality, and in the two women, with loss of appetite control. Langevin et al. (1988) in a literature review, concluded that forty percent of paraphilic sadists manifested subtle signs of temporal lobe brain abnormalities.

Lehne (1986) published a temporal lobe case of particular significance in that temporal lobe seizures and paraphilia were absent from the sexological history for thirty-one years at which time they were synchronous in onset following an "open skull fracture over the right frontal bone." The patient had been thrown from his bicycle when it hit a rock. For the following month, he was in a coma and required treatment for hydrocephalus, diffuse encephalitis, and hemiparesis. He underwent rehabilitative treatment for impairment of speaking, reading, writing, and calculation, and to prevent masturbating in public. He remained apathetic and withdrawn, and the continued to have an abnormal EEG, intermittent epileptic seizures accompanied by peculiar drooping of the face, a blank stare, and a confused postictal state.

Five years after the accident, the patient was rehospitalized for five months and two years later for another four months. At this time, the "EEG was abnormal with diffuse slowing, right greater than left, and suspicious activity in the right frontal central region, but with no spikes." The chief complaint was that there had been an escalation of unacceptable sexual behavior of a paraphilic nature, namely attempts to see the breasts of his seventeen-year-old stepdaughter and, sporadically, to fondle them. He had tried to observe her undress by looking through her bedroom and bathroom window and through a hole he had drilled in the wall.

The girl herself said:

> He was spacy whenever it happened. The most that ever happened is he would grab my breasts, not physically hurt me. He always turned very pale, and his right eye would get red and glassy. Whenever it happened it was like a seizure. He would look right through you. I could always tell when something would happen.

No genital contact was ever attempted. The patient's own report was that he was not sexually aroused. The presence of other family members did not inhibit an episode of staring, but he would cease if told to do so. They all recognized the signs that he was undergoing a seizure. Only the one stepdaughter and neither of her two sisters nor her mother were stared at in the same way, though other girls might have been. It was once reported that the father had made obscene telephone calls, but further details are lacking.

There are four components to this man's brain-injury induced paraphilia: peeping (*voyeurism*), touching (*toucheurism*), breast specificity (so-called fetishistic partialism), and telephone scatologia (*telephonicophilia*). Thus, the paraphilia is said to be of the multiplex, not the simplex type. Voyeurism (peeping) was its principal component. Since genital arousal and eroticism were not involved in the paraphilia, it qualified as incomplete or partial. In content, it was restricted to the proceptive phase of sexuoeroticism, the phase of wooing and foreplay. The acceptive phase of sexual intercourse was not involved.

Loyalty and affection between the husband and wife were not impaired. Before the injury, their timetable for sexual intercourse was between one and three times weekly. After the injury, the frequency was not recorded.

This case exemplifies the paraphilic principle of disjunction between love and lust. The patient's loyally affectionate relationship with his wife was not abolished by the paraphilic ideation and imagery of lust on the loose, peeping at nubile female breasts.

After seven years of trial and error treatment, the patient was steered to what was then still a new treatment for paraphilic temporal lobe seizures, namely with MPA (Money 1970). On this treatment, paraphilia and epilepsy were both brought under control. Love and lust were reunited. They remained reunited provided the MPA dosage was optimal. On one occasion, when the dosage was decreased by 25 percent, the symptoms of both paraphilia and seizures returned until the missing 25 percent was restored.

If state of the art brain imaging technology (Hendricks et al. 1988) at some future date allows precise monitoring of paraphilic brain pathways involved in such cases as the foregoing, then it will probably be necessary to synchronize the monitoring procedure with an actual paraphilic attack. With sufficiently sophisticated technology, it may also be possible to test the hypothesis that paraphilic disorder may actually be the first detectable precursor of a more pervasive brain disorder.

An actual example (Money 1986, chap. 16) is that of a man with a peculiar form of pedophilia for which he sought treatment successfully with MPA. He would set out on a business trip and arrive inexplicably at the wrong destination after undergoing a paraphilic attack. Once he had such an attack which made him an hour late for a clinic appointment. Usually he was half an hour early so as to avoid being late. Lateness on this occasion gave him a chance to describe what had happened. On the expressway ahead of him, two school buses carrying early teenaged boys had turned off at an exit ramp. Like an automaton, he took the next exit.

> If somebody was with me, he said, they would want to know why, and I would have to explain what I'm doing—and I can't explain it. Also, it's easier just to carry on a conversation and keep going so that it doesn't happen, anyway.

Taking the next exit ramp, he experienced a familiar premonition, namely of seeing the spire of a village church and driving around until he would find a peripubertal boy with whom he would engage in conversation. While talking, he would, while still acting like an automaton, violently assault the boy, kicking and punching him, and then immediately drive away.

The church scenario was derived from his boyhood with his mother who had a diagnosed delusional psychosis in which she persuaded her son that the Almighty was conversing with her. Under MPA treatment, his pedophilic paraphilia was ameliorated. By long-distance telephone he maintained annual follow-up for a quarter of a

century. By age fifty-two, he had become progressively and completely incapacitated by Parkinson's disease.

In the clinical annals of paraphilia, there are too many cases associated with either definitive or so-called soft signs of neurological and
brain disorder to be attributed to fortuitous coincidence. One example is that of the sadistic husband who had plans to convert the bathroom door into a kind of pillory in which to secure his wife's neck
while he lashed her back (see chap. 4). This man's entire body writhed
with athetoid movements noticeable as neck twisting, blinking, facial
grimacing, and dysarthric speech. Suddenly and without warning, his
right arm would occasionally lurch forward into the air. "It happens
every now and then," he said. "Don't pay any attention to it."

Instability of the autonomic nervous system may also be implicated.
For example, the paroxysmal gasping of paraphilic self-asphyxiation
may be associated with a history of paroxysmal asthmatic gasping for
breath. The colon may also become involved, as in a case (unpublished)
of constipation for which the most successful reversal was to engage in
the multiple performance of fellatio in public places where the risk of arrest was high.

Among teenaged boys arrested for serious sex offenses, there are
many in whose sexological history there are data indicating central
and autonomic nervous system premonitory warnings of an oncoming fugue state (Miccio-Fonseca personal communication), known in
the vernacular as zoning out. These warnings include: headache,
dizziness or giddiness, blacking out, a warm feeling all over, hand
tremors, butterflies in the stomach, and diarrhea. In many of this
same population, the history includes mention of accidental head injuries, and also of language and learning disability, and attention
deficit. Miccio-Fonseca's Personal Sentence Completion Inventory
(1997) enables one to pick up these ancillary signs and symptoms.

6

Fugue and Altered States

Paraphilic Fugue
Sleepwalking, Sleepsexing
Alter Ego
Bimodal Mindbrain Coding
Two Syndromes Interlocked

Paraphilic Fugue

Psychomotor epilepsy (Niedermeyer 1974) is synonymous with temporal lobe epilepsy. Seizures are known as psychomotor when they originate in either of the brain's temporal lobes (interior at the upper ear level). Unlike a grand mal seizure with loss of consciousness, a psychomotor seizure is characterized by an altered state of consciousness. Although altered by a covert seizure, motor and psychic functioning may not appear unusual to a nearby observer. The duration of the seizure is usually measured in minutes, not hours, but may be longer. The electroencephalograph (EEG) is not invariably abnormal. It has not been customary to link psychomotor epiptology with paraphilic sexology and altered states of consciousness, nor to research the possibility of such a linkage, either before, during, or after an actual altered state.

For seven years after the bicycle accident and brain injury of Lehne's case (see chap. 5), it was recognized that the patient had epileptic seizures and a sexual disorder, but the two were not connected. In fact, the sexual disorder was misconstrued as incest, for which he was placed in the custody of the county criminal justice system and not permitted to live at home. With the knowledge of hindsight, the data on the case indicate clearly that, sexologically, he was undergoing an altered state of consciousness when he made advances to his stepdaughter. The evidence, especially the glazed look of his eyes, was readily recognized by members of his family as indicative of a seizure. It was confirmed by the bilateral abnormality of his brain function demonstrated on the EEG. Moreover, both the EEG and the behavioral signs of an altered state of consciousness could be reversed by treatment with the hormone MPA (Depo-Provera) (see chap. 8).

This case is not unique, but, even if it were, it would alert one to the possibility of an altered state of consciousness in other instances of paraphilia in which there is no documented history of brain lesion or EEG abnormality.

Paraphilic fugue is the name for the altered state of consciousness associated with paraphilia and identifiable on the basis of observable behavioral data, the patient's own verbal report, and possibly by laboratory measurements of brain function taken while a fugue state is in progress.

The term *fugue* is derived from Latin *fuga*, meaning flight. In music, a fugue is a polyphonic type of composition. In psychiatry, according to the *Oxford English Dictionary,* a fugue is "a flight from or loss of awareness of one's own identity, sometimes involving wandering away from home, and often occurring as a reaction to shock or emotional stress." A paraphilic fugue is associated with licit or illicit sexuoerotic ideation, imagery, and behavior of a pathological type or degree. For the duration of the fugue, the paraphile has flown away from himself or herself to be transformed into someone else.

In legal doctrine, paraphilic fugue states are either ignored or denied. Like the M'Naghten insanity rules, they challenge the legal postulate of personal culpability irrespective of extenuating circumstances for engaging in illicit acts. The general public mostly follows the law in holding paraphiles wholly responsible for their acts for which the fugue state is no more than a putative excuse to avoid punishment. Even practitioners in sexology are disproportionately likely to take the side of legal condemnation rather than the side of biomedical science regarding paraphilic fugue.

The paraphilic fugue state may be experienced as subjectively distressing, as was articulately expressed by an amputee paraphile (Money and Simcoe 1984–86; see also chap. 4, "Age Eight"):

When I see an amputee, he explained, I get a feeling in my stomach. If I was on my way to dinner I would lose my appetite. I get, I guess, it's a warm feeling. I feel flushed. I feel as though this is the only thing there is for me to look at. There could be a multi-alarm fire going on and the only thing that I would look at would be this person. I get nervous. I get edgy. The feeling in my stomach seems like all encompassing. It's the only thing that I can focus on right then. It's worse if I'm caught by surprise. Like if I see this individual without any warning, it seems just for a minute that there's nothing else around me, and that that's the only thing there is. And then after a few seconds the initial shock, I guess that's a good word, wears off and I try to get control of myself. That's basically it. . . . What I'm concerned about is work outside. I'm a foreman. I don't want to get in a position where I would have to make a decision, be in the process of making a decision, and then see an amputee where I would lose, for a second, my train of thought, job related. It's happened a few times but I've recovered fast enough, at least I thought, and it wasn't noticeable. . . . I don't think I get a full erection. Oh yeah, I guess I do. Not all the time. Sometimes a partial erection, sometimes full erection but there is always at least a partial erection I would say. If I'm on the job, of course I can't masturbate, or if I'm out with my wife, but normally that's the only type of relief that I'll get. It's just a built up feeling like I'm almost ready to explode. She has said that I get extremely quiet. Like either intercourse or masturbation is a relief.

Recorded and transcribed interviews with paraphilic sex offenders many times do contain evidence of an altered state of consciousness or fugue state. Their wording is never the same, for there is no idiomatically shared expression for it in the English vernacular. After a head injury in a motor cycle crash, the patient, who was reported in Money (1990a), became first a serial rapist and then a serial murderer. When he prepared to pick up and murder another roadside prostitute after having had sex with her, he said it was like going on automatic pilot and being unable to stop except by external intervention.

In the case of the pedophile who developed Parkinsonism (Money 1986, chap. 16; see also chap. 5 above), the first clue from which an altered state of consciousness could be inferred was his story of setting out to drive from Washington to Ohio and arriving in South Dakota instead. He could not explain why he was there. He had no recall of the journey but knew he must have driven himself, as he had credit card receipts from the gas stations where he had stopped on the way. On the day when he was late for a clinic appointment, when he did finally arrive at my office, he appeared still to be in an altered or fugue state, as judged by trembling, sweating, fast breathing, and a fearful tone of voice. His mouth, he said, was dry, and his pulse had been racing.

In the case of Frank/Joey (see also p. 147), Frank, the patient, at age nineteen had been hospitalized for some weeks when one of the staff observed that, while watching television, he would go into a dazed state of fixed staring. When this happened, the image on the screen was of a young boy. Upon inquiry, Frank explained that the image of the boy on the television screen would become transformed into Joey, Frank's murderous alter ego. Joey's own paraphilic fantasy imagery would then displace the broadcast image and take over the screen until Frank's transfixed fugue state was interrupted or came to an end (Money 1986, 129).

The wording that another patient, a musician, used to characterize his own exhibitionistic fugue state was as follows.

> I know that I become distant. I've seen that in the past I become distant. I be concentrating on wanting to do it, where can I do it at, things like that. And maybe you might ask me questions and I might not hear you; and you being a doctor probably would pick up on it. . . .

> It's a thing where the urge does come so strong that you really want to do it. You just blocks off everything that could make you stop from doing it, because you want to do it so bad. . . . In this case I was driving very slow, and the urge just came out of nowhere to go do it—you can stop here, go in this store and expose yourself. I must have passed up about ten or fifteen places that I would have did it, and trying not to do it. While I was driving, I knew that if I didn't stop, then I couldn't do it. So I just kept driving. But it just kept tingling with me: stop here, stop there. Stop here. Go ahead. You can do it, and the feeling that I had inside was one like, if I didn't do it, I'd be missing out on something very, very great. I just kept on going. I ended up driving all the way to Glen Burnie, trying not to do it, just passing up places. And it just got so strong, I just had to do it. I just had to get out and do it.

> When I went into the store I pulled my zipper down and got myself ready to be exposed. My penis was ready to be exposed; and

as I was walking around the store, it just came out. I didn't single anybody out, like I normally do, and masturbate. I didn't do any of that because I was still fighting, trying not to do it. So I was just like walking around. My mind told me to steal something. Then I would leave. I would get out of there. So I picked up the first thing I saw which happened to be a bracelet. I put it in my pocket, and then I started leaving. That was enough to make me want to leave. I zipped up my pants and was leaving.

On the parking lost, the security police were waiting for him for indecent exposure, reported by a woman customer. That same evening, he recorded by phone a detailed account of what had happened and a week later he recorded an interview in person from which the foregoing was excerpted.

His arrest wrought havoc with his career as a musician who was breaking into the big time with a recording contract. He had just returned from a successful engagement overseas, and he had become overconfident that he could postpone further treatment with MPA until his finances were in better shape. Without the hormone, however, there was invariably a relapse into paraphilic exhibitionism.

In the case of the sadist with the pillory fantasy (see chaps. 4, 5), he first made mention of having "spells" while hospitalized and away from his wife. In two of them, he said, "I tried to fuck my hand," to the accompaniment of sadistic imagery. The third occurred after a visit to his wife. He laid his pants over a chair in his hospital room and "imagined" them to be his wife. He then began beating the empty chair with his belt. He had an erection and almost ejaculated before the spell ended.

Nelson Cooper, the former asphyxiophile who contributed his autobiography to *The Breathless Orgasm* (Money et al. 1991), has the equivalent of paraphilic fugues that, like nightmares, present themselves with eidetically vivid detail. The characters in these episodes are chiefly actresses, the majority of whom are recalled from television shows watched from as far back as the age of four. The actors and their shows, *Dark Shadows*, for example, are recalled in photographic and auditory detail. The recall may include a show in which the plot incorporates a drowning or strangling. More often, the plot is mostly a recurrent one in which a familiar actress drowns or strangles another. Similar imagery often intrudes itself, unsolicited, into a masturbation fantasy, as the orgasm approaches. Masturbation is hyperphilically frequent, medication notwithstanding.

There is no history of putting the imagery into practice; on the contrary, Nelson Cooper has no history of any social dating, and no history of sexual contact of any variety except in dreams and fantasy, where it is always heterosexual. He is shy to the extent of being socially inept in a schizoidal way, much to his dismay. Nonetheless, he is obsessed with women as sexual attractants with whom he would like to engage in sexual intercourse, but he is frozen in his tracks.

Up until a dozen years ago, he went through a period of being beleaguered by a paraphilic fugue of self-asphyxiation. Typically, it would begin as imagery in a dream in which he would become aware of an insistent erection. In the next phase, he would be standing in front of a mirror in bikini underwear, strangling himself with women's dance tights, still with an erection but no orgasm. At the near point of blackout, he would collapse on his bed. Then the imagery would change to that of two females, one strangling or drowning the other, until his masturbation culminated in orgasm. On treatment with MPA, the imagery and practices of self-asphyxiophilia ceased and did not return when the medication was withdrawn after three years. Various other psychoactive medications have been prescribed for his overall mental health problems, but with only limited, ameliorative success.

When Ken, the exhibitionist (Money 1981; see also below), was first arrested as a young man, aged twenty-six, he had told a court examiner: "It seems like I'm two different people."

Exposing his penis and masturbating was a form of solicitation gone awry.

> It's really stupid. To expose yourself is stupid, anyhow. . . . If I knew the answer to that, I wouldn't be sitting here, would I? . . . You think that I know the answer, but I don't. . . . When I exposed myself to women on the street who ran, that excited me more than if they stood there. And if they stood there and said dirty things to me, and told me how common and rotten I was, that excited me too. So maybe that's why I was doing it.

After six years, treatment with MPA was withdrawn on suspicion that it might be responsible for blurry vision secondary to high blood pressure. After one more year, there was a relapse, and the unharnessed exhibitionistic alter ego roamed the streets again.

Sleepsexing/Sleepwalking

THE NELSON COOPER case of asphyxiophilia (see above) shows that paraphilic ideation and imagery crosses the boundary between sleeping and waking. While asleep Nelson Cooper had two kinds of erotic experience: one of which he called a nightmare and the other an ordinary dream. The nightmare resembled a delirium in its eidetic vividness of himself masturbating to paraphilic imagery in which one woman strangulated another until the victim succumbed, whereupon he would hallucinate an orgasm. Then he awoke to discover the whole scenario had been a delirium. He had not been masturbating, did not have an erection, had not ejaculated, and had no inclination to begin masturbating. The ordinary erotic dream overlapped with masturbation fantasy in that he did have an erection and ejaculation. The content of the accompanying paraphilic scenario varied but, as the orgasm approached, it automatically switched itself to a scene of two fighting women in which, the one overcame the other. The combatants were recognizable as friends or in many instances as characters from the television movies and serials familiar to him in meticulous detail since childhood until the present.

Such a case as that of Nelson Cooper raises the question of the relationship between paraphilic fugue and sleepwalking or, more specifically, having sex while sleepwalking (sleepsexing). Although sexology lacks systematic information about sleepsexing, there is occasional anecdotal information about, for example, the partner who falls asleep while having sexual intercourse; or the sleeping husband who wakens his wife and asks her to feel his hard penis and play with it, and who recalls nothing whatsoever about the incident when in the morning she mentions it; or the partner who initiates and consummates sexual intercourse with his/her sleeping partner who does not awaken.

Sleepsex, it would seem, is for most people a joke rather than a serious concern likely to come to either medical, scientific or legal attention. One case that did come to medical attention (Rosenfeld and Elhajjar 1998) is that of a man whose self-referral was precipitated by his live-in girlfriend's realization that, one night while having intercourse, he was snoring loudly. Also, he had a history of regularly, every night, initiating and engaging in an entire sexual episode while asleep. It included varied positioning, oral sex (both ways), ejaculation, orgasm, and lasted upward of half an hour. Subsequently, he had no recall of the episode. By contrast, early morning intercourse, engaged in regularly after they were awake, was always recallable.

In addition, there were also episodes of sleepwalking, sometimes aimlessly, and sometimes in connection with sleepeating when he would go to the kitchen and snack on readily available food. Sometimes, he would bring food back to bed for his girlfriend. Often, though not invariably, an episode of sleepeating preceded sleepsexing.

Morning sex and sleep sex were different in manner and style. Sleepsex, according to the girlfriend, was a little more "kinky, and probably not normal." He was more aggressive, dominant, and more forcefully playful in erotic biting and talking dirty. The girlfriend would have liked more of this in morning sex.

Rosenfeld and Elhajjar (1998) present a second case, that of a forty-five-year-old male, with a lifelong history of sleepwalking and somnambulistic automatisms since childhood. He was arrested one morning at 2 A.M., while still sleepwalking, after having briefly fondled the genitals of his teenaged daughter's girlfriend who was asleep in a sleeping bag downstairs. Typically for a somnambulist, he was disoriented and confused as he began to wake up and had no recall for what had happened. He was charged as a sex offender. Another somnambulistic automatism which may be wrongly charged as a sex offense, namely indecent exposure, occurs when a sleepwalker who goes to bed nude is found somnambulating, still nude, outside his house, in public.

"Sleep and Sexual Offending" is the title of brief but comprehensive monograph, with illustrative case data, by Peter Fenwick (1996). In it he wrote:

> Sexual behavior can be carried out during slow wave sleep, and is associated with sleepwalking. The sexual behavior can be either simple or complex and will typically last for a few minutes. In the simple cases the sleepwalker may caress or stroke the partner's body; these movements may sometimes apparently be more sexually directed, with groping or caressing of the partner's genitals. Sexual intercourse is not reported in sleepwalkers but because it is now accepted that the somnambulistic episode merges into a dissociated state, on theoretical grounds it is perfectly possible for a sleepwalker in the later stages of somnambulism to become

sexually aroused and have intercourse. In the more complex cases a sleepwalker will leave the bed and if there are other sleepers in the house may get into bed with them or may interact in a sexual way with other members of the household.

One of Fenwick's cases illustrates the continuity and complexity of sleepwalking and sleepsexing. It is the case of a young man with a lifetime history of sleepwalking and a present history of duress at home and at work. On the night of his somnambulatory sex offense, he had visited the local pub for a pint of beer and was home by 11 P.M. His top floor apartment neighbor was a young woman whom he knew in passing and, likewise, her boyfriend.

> On arriving home that fateful evening, the patient went to sleep in his boxer shorts, and as it was a hot summer's evening, he had his window wide open. The window opened onto a ledge which ran the length of the house and was about two and a half feet wide. About one hour after retiring, while still asleep, he climbed out of the bedroom window and crawled along the ledge to the window of the next door flat. This window was also open and he entered the flat's kitchen. He walked through the kitchen into the girl's bedroom. There was some evidence that he had handled her digital clock which was on the table in her bedroom before going and lying down beside her bed, his hand under the bedclothes so that it came to rest against her genitals.
>
> He remained asleep until the girl woke up to find a hand against her genitals, which she initially thought was that of her boyfriend who was in bed with her. She then realized the hand was coming from the opposite side of the bed, started up, saw the defendant asleep beside her and shouted to her boyfriend in alarm. The kerfuffle woke the defendant, who in a confusional state stood up, wandered out of the room, opening the door with some difficulty, went through the kitchen and back onto the ledge. He unfortunately fell three stories into a flower-bed and received moderate head injuries, but he survived the fall.

This case has all the major features of a sleepwalking incident. He arose while in slow wave sleep about an hour after sleep onset. He had a long history of sleepwalking, and was tired and stressed at the time of the incident. He had also had a pint of beer. Most important was his bizarre behavior in the girl's room. Had he been awake he would have seen that her boyfriend was in bed with her, and that it was clearly inappropriate to go to sleep beside the bed with his hand on her genitals. His confusional arousal is also characteristic of awakening from slow wave sleep.

The case appeared before the Crown Court and sleepwalking evidence was given by a sleep expert. The jury had difficulty in understanding how an act as complex as this could be carried out during sleep and brought in a verdict of guilty. The defendant was put on probation.

Engaging in some form of sexual activity with a sleeping partner occurs not only in somnambulatory sex but also in *somnophilia* (from Greek, *somnos*, sleep + *-philia*), a paraphilia which is also known as the sleeping princess syndrome. The somnophile is not asleep but in a trance-like paraphilic fugue state. Fedoroff et al. (1997) briefly report such a case, taken from a law enforcement file, as follows:

P, a 43-year-old divorced factory worker, presented with a long history of "sneaking into the bedrooms of female house guests." He was extremely aroused by thoughts and fantasies of a partner whom he could control completely. Although he denied specific arousal from the fact that his victims were sleeping, he admitted that if his victims awoke and began to actively participate (an event which he insisted was not uncommon) he would lose interest. Although he denied being aroused by physically hurting his sexual partners, he enjoyed tying them up and coercing them into his preferred sexual activities. He came to the attention of the police after spending eight years training a female relative to be the perfect sex slave by repeatedly assaulting her while she slept. This "training" began when she was three. On examination he was also found to have alcohol dependence, major depression and antisocial personality disorder.

Coercion, as in this case, is not an essential characteristic of somnophilia. Nonetheless, the sleeping woman, if she wakens, is justifiably stricken with fear of being kidnapped or raped. Her first call is for the police to catch the intruder, which may be quite easy to do, as he saunters away with no plan of escape.

Being asleep is itself an altered state of consciousness. In a quite literal sense, therefore, the episodes of sleepsex were carried out in an altered state of consciousness that, in this instance, corresponds to the altered state of a paraphilic fugue. None of the sexual activities carried out while asleep, however, qualified as paraphilic, though they were less inhibited than the activities of waking sex. Sleeping sex did not interfere with successful everyday living and working.

Alter Ego

THE DISJUNCTION BETWEEN paraphilic lust and nonparaphilic loyalty and affection in the lovemap may, in some cases of paraphilia, enlarge to become a disjunction between two personalities: the one paraphilic and the other not, each of a different age. This phenomenon is well exemplified in the case of the transvestophilic naval officer, subsequently a sex reassignment case, reported under the title of "Two names, two wardrobes, two personalities" (Money 1974). It is also well exemplified in the case (see above) of nonparaphilic Frank whose alter ego was paraphilic Joey. Frank's transformation into Joey could be observed when he was looking at the image of a male juvenile on the hospital television screen.

Frank, in his own words, gave a secularized version of death and reincarnation to explain how it had come to pass that he had phoned his neighbors advising them that he wanted to kidnap and kill their six-year-old son, Calvin.

> My desire was to kill myself and kill Calvin, and somehow be born as Calvin. I don't know how that would have worked out. I wanted not only to be Calvin; but [his parents] Jeff and Kay seemed like such good parents toward Calvin that I would have loved to fall into their hands. I wanted them as my parents. I was suicidal at the time; and, because it seemed so close to actually happen, I thought: "Let's go all the way with it." So [it seemed as if] I accelerated the desires, and the feelings intensified more, and I didn't—I wanted to be Calvin, but deep down inside, I didn't really want to hurt the boy. So I started sending letters, threatening letters, and I started making phone calls. . . . I said I was going to kidnap Calvin, and I was going to kill him.

Earlier in his teenage years, Frank had gone through a prolonged period of intense religious obsession:

> I felt that you not only had to pray seventy times a week, but if you remembered something that God did for you, or something good, you had to drop everything and pray, and thank Him, or say you are sorry, that very second. I had a document that I had

drawn up, about the size of this desk top. I had nothing but rules on it, and prayers that I had to follow . . . like you couldn't use old English handwriting, except for religion. You can't use a green pen, but only for religion . . . I was up to 500 prayers a week . . . I was so overwhelmed by all of this . . . I prayed to God to help me, and slow it down.

The time consumed by Frank's praying decreased by age eighteen, and it was filled instead by Joey's kidnapping and killing fantasies which had become explicitly eroticized and were masturbation fantasies. Previously, Joey's fantasies had not been accompanied by masturbation but sometimes by an erection induced by live or pictorial images of young boys and by thoughts of touching them. "It was sexual," Frank said, "but I didn't know it was sexual. I didn't know what it was."

Frank's prior sexual history had been one of total deprivation of sexual learning at home and among peers who had teased and stigmatized him because his behavior did not conform to their standards. There had been, at age six, a traumatic incident, confused in the recall but confirmed by the parents, of spying on him in the bathroom, and three times beating him on one occasion for not desisting from masturbating while taking a bath.

Frank was an early adolescent when Joey came into existence as his alter ego. Joey was only six years old, and he never grew older. Joey was destined to be kidnapped, murdered, and reincarnated as a better person. At first, his death was scheduled to be effected by suicide but that failed on at least three different occasions. Then it was effected pictorially. The technique was to tear out magazine fashion pictures or take actual photographs of young boys in shorts or T-shirts, and to superimpose over them an acetate sheet on which he painted wounds and blood, strategically placed to represent inflicted injuries and, ultimately, lust murder. The composite pictures served as a stimulus for sadomasochistic and lust-murdering masturbation fantasies. The stimulus figure could represent either Joey or the boy who had posed for the picture or photograph. Disassembled, neither the acetate sheet nor the picture betrayed their conjoined sadomasochistic and murderous secrets. Calvin, the boy next door, was one of those whose photograph had been used under an acetate sheet.

Eventually, the pictures became an insufficient substitute for sex-uoerotic contact. That was when Calvin and his parents began receiving phone calls and letters. The caller was Joey, but his voice was recognized as Frank's, the quiet religious neighbor who attended the same church as Calvin and his parents. The upshot was that the patient was summoned to the police station.

> I thought to myself this is the perfect opportunity to grab a gun
> . . . and just blast your brains out. But I didn't want to do it until
> after I made my confession, because I don't want to be pictured
> as a child killer, or a child murderer. I wanted people to under-
> stand where I was coming from. . . . I just poured out my
> guts. . . . We tape recorded the conversation . . . what I wanted all
> along was to get to jail. I said I wanted to be arrested and to go
> to jail . . . and I wanted to kill myself.

Bimodal Mindbrain Coding

To those who met him, Frank/Joey was one person with one body, one brain, and one mind. He himself knew that his mentation was bi-modally divided into Frank and Joey. His mindbrain schema for Frank was positively coded as the quiet, religious, high achieving, sexually pure, good boy. Joey was negatively coded as the sexually impure bad boy who masturbated to fantasies of sadistic lust and murder of the six-year-old boy next door.

Frank and Joey are illustrative of a general principle of mind-brain schemas or maps, namely that they are bipotential to begin with and then become bimodally coded. For conduct to be assimilat-ed and positively coded as conforming to a standard of correctness, conduct that is nonconforming and incorrect must also be assimilat-ed but negatively coded. Positive and negative are not universally exact mirror images of one another, for usually there is only one stan-dard or stereotype of conformity but more than one alternative way of nonconformity. Positive and negative bimodal coding applies to all brainmind schemas or maps—foodmaps, languagemaps, gender-maps, everything mappable.

There is no guarantee that bimodal coding will be orthodox, and there is no guarantee that it will be stable over a given period of time or for a lifetime. Unorthodox coding is in the very nature of paraphilic lovemaps. What other people condemn as unorthodox and negative, the paraphile experiences as positive. It is not that the paraphile is unable to distinguish between orthodox and unorthodox, but rather that, for reasons inexplicable, the coding is reversed, according to the process of opponent process (see chap. 5).

The opponent process reversal may weaken as it did in the Frank/Joey case, when he phoned and wrote to the parents of his would be victim and gave them a warning in advance. Then, as is not at all atypical in paraphilia, Frank made a confession. "I poured out my guts," he said.

A similar thing happened in the case of Ken, the burglar-exhibitionist (see also p. 154). He was arrested on the basis of incriminating evidence found in his car. In the police station, he recalled years later,

> I ran my mouth and told them everything I ever done. That's how
> I got 28 years. I was always glad it was, because sooner or later I
> would have hurt somebody real bad [had he been interrupted
> during a robbery]. I snitched on myself.

A full paraphilic confession signifies that the usual coding of the paraphilic schema has, for the time being, been reversed from positive to negative. The paraphile agrees with his prosecutors and condemns himself/herself. Apart from a full confession, there are other, more subtle ways to hint at a paraphilia. For example, a paraphilic serial lust murderer (with two names, Dennis and Dude, and with a masturbation fetish for his mother's underclothes) had several emblems of death tattooed on his arms, shoulders, and penis. There were heraldic designs pierced with daggers, two of them emblazoned with girls' names, another with the name, Wild Irish Dude and one with the words, Never Again. Among the other designs were griffin-like monsters, one with the caption DEATH (in very large letters) To All My Twelve. Yet another design was a portrait of the grim reaper wielding an oversized scythe.

Another example is that of a sadist who wore tell-tale gold jewelry of miniature handcuffs and other paraphernalia of sadomasochism and dressed with a studded belt and chokingly tight necktie. Yet another sadist appeared at a reception with his submissive wife who wore a transparent blouse through which one could see pierced nipples fitted with gold rings joined by a gold chain. Obedient to her husband, she unobtrusively asked him for permission to eat each mouthful of food and, at his command, agreed to show, in private, her pierced genital jewelry. In another case, a self-asphyxiating high school aged youth carried a miniature rope noose and used it as a conversation piece.

Bimodal mindbrain coding is exemplified not only in self-incriminating confessions and subtle hints but also counterintuitively in the phenomenon of falsely confessing to someone else's paraphilic crime. This is what happened in the above mentioned case of Dennis/Dude. After the drug intoxicated Dude had been arrested and charged with murder, his mother overheard his roommate on the telephone, talking to the police, and claiming that he himself had committed the murder. Since there were established factual details that he either could not supply or else fabricated, charges were not brought against him. His confession was false.

This phenomenon of borrowing someone else's criminal sex offense belongs in the category of *folie à deux* (French for madness of two). In borrowed madness, one of the pair borrows the delusions and schemings of the other and becomes, so to speak, a psychiatric clone of the other. An extreme case occurred forty years ago in New Zealand when two teenaged girls murdered the mother of one of them by bashing her head with a brick in a sock (Medlicott 1955). Their shared delusion was that the murder would prevent the breakup of their friendship by family emigration and divorce. The case returned to public attention in the 1994 movie, "Heavenly Creatures." The one girl who was not lost to followup had become rehabilitated and led a quiet life as a writer of murder mysteries.

In the case of the false confessor of Dennis/Dude's murder, nothing is known of how much the two may have shared the same or similar fantasies of lust murder, except that they had a shared lifestyle and both were exposed to mind-fracturing drugs, including the psychosis inducing PCP (phencyclidine).

Another example (Money 1991a, chap. 11) is that of a young man with the supernumerary Y (47, XYY) syndrome which is notorious for sudden impulsiveness. He and two gay friends went home with a third gay man they hustled in a gay bar. Robbery was their intent. A knife fight ensued, and "I just went berserk," he said. Then, to exonerate his two friends, "because they can't take jail as well as I can," he claimed responsibility and turned himself in. Four years later, in long-term solitary confinement after attacking two guards, he threatened suicide unless he was transferred away from the noise of a prison riot to the quiet hospital wing. There he would be able to see his prison lover. Refused the transfer, he hung himself, as he had threatened to do.

Bimodal mindbrain coding, as aforesaid in this chapter, is not restricted to the coding of lovemaps and their paraphilias. On the contrary, bimodal coding applies far beyond the boundaries of lovemaps, paraphilic and otherwise, to all mindbrain schemas or maps that require discrimination between alternatives of what elements should belong in the map and what should be excluded. Bilingualism provides an example. Babies who grow up hearing and responding to their parents in English, exclusively, and to their nanny and playmates in Spanish must code a languagemap for English that excludes Spanish and another for Spanish that excludes English. Then they have two native languagemaps.

By contrast, bimodal mindbrain coding of the disparity between masculine and feminine begins in the brain prenatally under the influence of sex hormones, whereas conformity or nonconformity to the cultural criteria of masculinity or femininity is subject to postnatal determinants. Postnatal stereotypes of masculine or feminine are transculturally different, despite similarities. To meet the criteria of either a masculine or feminine gender identity and role (G-I/R) necessitates having a mindbrain map or schema for both, one marked mine, and the other thine (with some people being mixed).

Bimodal coding applies even to such routine practices as eating. The criteria are those of etiquette, and they differ transculturally as well as within one's own culture. Thus, nonoriental American restaurants do not provide chopsticks, nor do they serve rice and condiments to be kneaded, Indian style, with the fingers of the right hand and transferred directly to the mouth. By contrast, eating finger food at an American cocktail party or cookout is acceptable, whereas cutlery is required at a formal dinner. Food itself is bimodally coded as edible or toxic, native or foreign, vegetarian or carnivorous, and organically versus chemically grown.

Without limit, bimodal mindbrain coding applies wherever human values are dichotomized as in orthodox and unorthodox, approved and disapproved, obedient and disobedient, correct and incorrect, right and wrong, good and bad, licit and illicit, moral and immoral, faith and heresy, and so on and on.

Reversal of bimodal coding may be reversed by fiat, which is what happens when military killing is mandated, whereas civilian killing is criminalized as homicide or murder. It does not require a war to bring about the reversal of the bimodal killing code: it may occur in the context of an individual life under the influence of determinants yet to be fully deciphered.

More than one bimodally coded map or schema may undergo reversal concurrently with one or more others. Three concurrent reversals constitute an unnamed syndrome of pathological lying, thieving, and sexing. In this syndrome, lying is not an alibi feigned to exculpate oneself from punishment. Rather it is, like a novel, a fiction narrated to entertain and intrigue the listener. Its formal name is *pseudologia fantastica,* which means fantasy that seems logical enough but is fictional.

Such a fictionally transparent tale was circulated by a teenaged girl with Turner (45, X) syndrome. She had been humiliated at school when a close girlfriend in whom she had confided betrayed her trust and spread the news of her syndrome, namely, that she had no ovaries and was, therefore, doomed never to conceive. The boys at school then talked about her as a potentially "good lay" as there would be no likelihood of pregnancy. After the long summer break, she returned to school with the story that she was no longer her former self but her look-alike cousin who had had fabulous film star experiences during the summer. That only worsened the torment handed out by her peers.

The three part syndrome of lying, thieving, and sexing was exemplified in the story of an upwardly mobile minority youth who, as a seminary student, spun a fantastic story of his experiences before he was asked to leave. His history as a shoplifter became public after a police investigation of his apartment revealed a kleptomaniac's hoard of shoplifted silver, more than he could effectively display or use. The sexing component of his syndrome was that, forfeiting the chance of higher education and superior earning power, he became a street hustler.

Pseudologia fantastica is related to impostoring which, when it is good is so very, very good that it can easily pass undetected unless corroborated by outside observers and written records. This being so, in taking the sexological history of a sex-offending or other paraphilia, it is necessary to supplement the informant's account with confirmatory sources and persons who are certifiably not in cahoots with the patient. One authentic story is that of a very elegant and intellectually superior male-to-female transexual who, at another medical center, posed as the mother of an eighteen-year-old male-to-female applicant and gave a fictional transgender history of the boy without being discovered.

The erosion of memories of events long since past and their telescoping and omission of details produces a coherent history, but one that is not a photocopy of what actually happened. This also bespeaks the value of obtaining historical records.

Pseudologia fantastica is universal in young children as they progressively differentiate the imagery and ideation of fantasy and fiction from that of actual encounters and historical events. Fantasy is readily cast into the mold of fact, and vice versa. That is why the reliability and validity of young children's testimony in court, as in cases of abusive violence and neglect, sexual or otherwise, is equivocal. They are as likely to falsely incriminate themselves and to cover for their parents or other adults as they are to level false accusations against them in the form of pseudologia fantastica.

Two Syndromes Interlocked

THESE TWO INTERLOCKED syndromes are abuse martyrdom and paraphilic exhibitionism in, respectively, a wife and husband, Katie and Ken (Money 1981). The couple appeared to be the proverbial couple made for each other. As never before, each felt the fulfillment of being truly wanted and needed, each as the rescuer and protector of the other. He rescued her from abandonment and abuse, and she rescued him from social rejection and stigmatization as a sex offender. The going was not easy, and they both had episodes of backsliding. Nonetheless, they were sure that they were too dependent on one another ever to separate.

In her infancy, Katie's father had been killed in a fall, and a year later, her older brother was drowned. Unable to cope, her natal mother gave the girl, aged three, and her younger brother to her childless sister for adoption. The boy was favored. The girl became the victim of child abuse. As she subsequently recalled an alleged incident, her stepmother approached her in the bathtub with a threaded needle and, puncturing her vulva, threatened to sew her up as punishment for playing with herself. When the girl was eleven, the stepmother died of cancer. Soon thereafter her stepfather, whose favorite she was, began making sexual approaches. After he married again, Katie and her new stepmother antagonized one another. At age fourteen, the girl ran away from home and lived in a series of institutional and foster placements. In one of these placements, she met a behaviorally disturbed teenager and, at age sixteen, married him. He was a physically assaultive husband and also a cross dresser. They stayed together for three years until he was put in jail, leaving her and their infant daughter destitute until Ken took them in.

Ken's early history, obtained retrospectively by self-report, is sketchy. As a child, he was subject to severe temper tantrums, learning disability, and academic underachievement. He quit school at age sixteen in the seventh grade. He grew up in what would now be called a dysfunctional household. His father was quick tempered and beat his children violently. He was reputed to have once been arrested for indecent exposure when drunk. Several siblings and others in the family pedigree had a history of having been in trouble with the law, one woman for murder. As juveniles, he and his girl cousins would show their genitals to each other while playing. When he was entering puberty, a teenaged cousin introduced him to sexual intercourse, which they continued to engage in until she was nineteen and pregnant. He was suspected of being the father. Once in early adolescence, he recalled, he and some friends exposed their penises to girls riding horseback in the park. The girls' reaction was one of amusement. Otherwise, he had no explanation of what led up to his becoming a sex offending exhibitionist. As a young husband and father, he spent two years in military service with a clean record except for stealing an automobile, for which the charge was dropped. He did not drink, smoke, or take drugs.

He met his first wife when she was fourteen and he sixteen. They married three years later. During the next seven years, they had six children; three more than she wanted. According to Ken, she said "that I raped her into the last three kids, and I probably did." He attributed her withdrawal from sexual intercourse to her being "an underlying lesbian," as she subsequently "came out." This was the period in his life when he first became in jeopardy as a sex offender. The marriage ended in divorce after he was sentenced to twenty eight years in prison.

He was twenty six when he first went to prison. After serving ten of the twenty-eight year sentence, he was released on parole. Aged forty, he married his second wife, aged twenty. They had one child before he was locked up again for indecent exposure. Subsequently, they were divorced.

For the second time, he was released on parole, only to be rearrested, again for indecent exposure. This time he was given a suspended sentence, provided that he attended group therapy sessions in a court ordered program. This eventually led to his being directed to the then new program (Money 1970) for sex offenders in which therapy sessions were augmented by hormonal treatment with the antiandrogenic hormone MPA (see chap. 8).

While waiting for official permission to transfer to the MPA program, he met twenty-year-old Katie, whose stepfather he resembled. They set up housekeeping together and then married three years later. His age was forty three. In the same month that they married, he began taking weekly injections of 400 mg of MPA, and she underwent surgery for removal of the gall bladder (cholecystectomy). Her weight at this time was 268 lb (122 kg); height 5 ft 5 1/2 in (166. 4 cm). It had fluctuated during the preceding five years to as low as 200 lb (91 kg). Postoperatively, during the next eighteen months, it decreased to 201 lb (91. 3 kg), after which it progressively increased to 300 lb (136. 3 kg) over the next five years. Then it began to diminish again until, two years later, when admitted as an inpatient, she weighed 150 lb (68. 2 kg). Her goal was to weigh 130 lb (59 kg).

As her weight changed, up or down, she complained of chronic vomiting after swallowing either solids or fluids, which she attributed to "a nerve that quivers in my stomach." Eventually, it became evident that she was taking a laxative ostensibly to prevent constipation and had induced vomiting by thrusting her fingers down her throat until, eventually, vomiting occurred spontaneously. Sometimes she brought up only a watery fluid.

Concurrently with her loss of weight, her husband began to gain weight. As a side effect of MPA, his appetite increased, especially for sweet foods. From 154 lb (70 kg), height 5 ft 11 in (180. 3 cm) his weight increased to 215 lb (97. 7 kg). Like his wife, he began vomiting. He attributed it to the accumulation of mucus in his throat if he ate something sweet, which led to persistent coughing and throwing up. His vomiting, however, was episodic rather than chronic like that of his wife.

His wife's vomiting became incorporated into the daily routine as something that, like eating or elimination, had to be accommodated. It remained that way until, at the age of thirty, she became an inpatient for a neurological and psychiatric evaluation. In addition to vomiting, she also had leg pain, constipation, facial swelling, occipital headaches, and, of major concern, seizure-like episodes. The seizures were without convulsions, but they did include a period of apparent loss of consciousness for ten to fifteen minutes, followed by dazed confusion and amnesia for what had happened.

The seizure workup yielded no definitive data to support a differential diagnosis of either seizures or pseudoseizures. Irrespective of etiology, they were significantly dangerous in that they had occurred in sleep and in places where the patient could fall and suffer head injury. The effect of antiepileptic medication in suppressing them could not be properly tested as oral medications were subject to being vomited up. Eventually, however, the seizures were brought under control so as to allow the woman to take a sales job to augment her husband's meager pay as a buildings' maintenance man.

By contrast, the husband, temporarily off MPA, became more bellicose in fiercely protecting his wife. He threatened to blow the place up if he was not satisfied with the way his wife was being treated in the hospital, in particular by a psychotic woman patient.

The wife's various symptoms of suffering and ill health served to elicit her husband's protectiveness of her as one whom he had rescued from abuse. They both agreed that there had been, at most, three occasions when, over some trivial matter, he lost control of himself and all but physically injured her. With the benefit of MPA treatment, he said his rages were more controllable.

Alone or together, husband and wife were both able to talk openly about their sex life. About orgasm, the wife told a woman interviewer:

> I get a tingling feeling all through my fingers and my body. My whole body just tingles you know. It's like a sensation that you can't stand, like you want to scream or something, you know. It feels really good. That's how it feels. I just like quiver. My body quivers. And then when it goes away, I'm tired. . . . I don't get an orgasm every time I have sex. Ken thinks I should, but I don't

think it's abnormal. . . . If I'm really in the mood to have sex, I know that I can have an orgasm, if I'm really hot and bothered, you know. But there's been times when I've been really hot and bothered and ain't had an orgasm.

She enjoyed receiving oral sex and less so giving it, but that was in part because her husband hadn't shaved or showered beforehand and had an odor attributed to hemorrhoids, the correction of which was perpetually procrastinated. They did not engage in anal sex. Only rarely was he given to cuddling, fondling, kissing, and caressing, without which she felt deprived and neglected. Nonetheless, she remained sure that she did not want to lose him, and he was committed to not losing her.

Early in their relationship, there had been a prolonged period when she had become sexually indifferent to Ken because of a fabricated story which he told to her and the police as an alibi. He had been picked up for indecent exposure. His alibi was that he had not been exhibiting himself, but following a woman home to have sex with her. His wife believed this cock-and-bull story, and she felt betrayed.

The imagery of betrayal intervened each time they tried to have sex for several months thereafter. She was able to attribute her nonresponsiveness to being too weakened most of the time by vomiting to be interested in sexual intercourse. Her husband echoed this explanation especially after he began treatment with MPA which, as expected, diminished his own sexual performance level. His own explanation of his diminished sexual frequency was that MPA made him too fatigued to be bothered with sex. Erections were less frequent, but not totally suppressed. Ejaculation was much less frequent. Orgasm did not occur in penial vaginal intercourse. In masturbation, orgasm at times coincided with a minor release of watery fluid or with no ejaculation at all. The latter he once called a psychological orgasm. He did not masturbate at home as a substitute for intercourse with his wife, but as a method of tension release when he could not fall asleep. The imagery then was of "just getting a head job from a girl, not anybody in particular, just anybody that would pop into my mind at the time." Or, it might be the imagery of different positions of intercourse. He did not dream about sex, and neither did his wife, and he recalled seldom having had sleep ejaculations in adolescence or subsequently.

Despite the impediments to their sex life together, they were not, in the long run, without some good times, whereas at other times "the sex could have been better." On one of the worst occasions, after he was already experiencing the sexually suppressant effect of MPA, the husband had an outburst of violence and threatened to rape his wife if she didn't respond to his approach. He hit her, threw her against the couch, and left the house. In the distress of being abandoned, she cut her wrist with a razor blade and had to be taken to the nearest hospital emergency room. Her explanation was that she had only been teasing him, and they had planned an afternoon session together. Her teasing was consistent with her subsequent statement: "Sometimes I think I'd love to tell him to rape me."

Ken could not explain why an orgasm by flashing was more exciting than by ordinary intercourse:

> I can't answer that [he said]. It, it, it, it, it's a stupid thing to do and, and, and I've asked myself the question a million times. I asked myself the question why I was doing it, you know? What the hell you doing this for? You've got a wife at home, you've got a baby at home, you've got people home that care about you and all you're going to do is wind up getting in jail, but I just had to do it. If I didn't do it, the world was going to come to an end, you know, or something tragic was going to happen if I didn't expose myself, until I ejaculated. Something terrible was going to happen, you know.

No matter what the risk of getting caught, once he began exposing himself, he had to keep at it, masturbating until he ejaculated: "Even if I couldn't keep a hard on, I still had to come." The greater the noise and commotion he created and the greater the risk of being caught, the higher the level of sexual excitement. Hence the attraction of exhibiting in the vicinity of a police car, or a police station, or of phoning the police in advance to warn them that he would be exposing himself.

His was the thrill of the forbidden turned upside down by opponent process (see chap. 5). "Having sexual relations with a girl in a fantasy doesn't do anything for me. . . . In prison, I wanted to choke them to death, and this fantasy always set me off," he said, in one interview. Out of prison and even when on MPA, the idea of exposing himself was more enticing than ordinary intercourse.

The imagery that predominantly accompanied masturbation while exhibiting was of receiving fellatio, a practice forbidden by his religion. Also forbidden, but not recurrent, was the occasional imagery of exposing to a woman police officer, a nun, or a pregnant mother. During his long imprisonment as a young man, he had a masturbation fantasy in which "I used to get this whole family, the policeman, his wife, and his daughter, and I used to make his daughter go down on him, while I made his wife go down on me, and then I balled all of them." By contrast, during the "first period of six months I was in prison, sex didn't mean nothing to me then."

Although MPA did not abolish all memories or thoughts of indecent exposure, it dampened them, so that they lost their imperiousness and did not have to be translated into action.

> Sometimes when I pass certain places, you know, that appeals to me like when I used to expose myself, I'd say that would be a good place for that to happen. And I say, what the hell is the matter with you? You going crazy again. You want to go back to jail? And I get it out of my mind. But the thing is, before Provera (MPA), I couldn't get it out of my mind. It became a thought, then it became an obsession. And then I had to do it. I didn't give a damn if I stayed out in the streets till the sun come up, you know, it had to be done. But now, if I get the thought, I transfer it to something else. . . . I'm scared to death to come off the medicine, because I know what's going to happen. I know that I couldn't control it before, and it used to tear me up inside. I always said you can control anything you want. If you don't want to eat a whole lot, you just eat so much and you stop. Smoking. I said I'm going to quit smoking. I quit smoking. Drinking. I quit drinking. I said I'm going to stop exposing myself, but I never did stop. Every time I got out of jail, I'd be straight for about four or five months, and then I'd start all over again. It was the fear that kept me the four or five months. I just can't explain myself. I can remember peeping in windows. Maybe a woman would be changing her clothes, and I'd be reaching a climax, and she'd go into another room, and I'd stand there and stamp like a little kid . . . I'd pick up something and throw it through the window. That was before I first went to prison.

He was imprisoned on charges of breaking and entering, burglary, peeping (*voyeurism*), attempted rape, and rape (*raptophilia*). Following release from prison, his arrests had been on charges of indecent exposure (*exhibitionism*) only. He himself conjectured that "stealing and sex came from the same thing, hostility, which is all I've ever known. . . . I didn't break in for nothing. If there was no money, I'd steal something," even if it was an unwashed table knife lying on the table.

On at least three occasions, there had been a woman in the house, reclining or dozing. Rationalizing that she might respond favorably to his solicitation, he would expose himself. Then he might attempt rape, after which he would feel sorry and apologize. He always had prepared an escape route through an open window or unlocked door. After the ten year imprisonment, the peeping, burglary, and rape scenario no longer held sway. In its place, the scenario of indecent exposure in public held sway exclusively. It is possible that the change was interconnected with trying to kill off his sex-offender self by suicide, attempted while in prison by tying his belt to a light fixture and hanging himself.

Exhibitionism was the paraphilia for which he was referred by the court to the MPA program. Its relatedness to the offenses for which he was originally imprisoned demonstrates that his was a multiplex paraphilia and not several different simplex paraphilias in the same individual (see chap. 4).

As well as exemplifying the multiplex nature of paraphilia, the case also exemplifies the paraphilic split between love and lust. The glitzy excitement of lust belonged to the forbidden act of exhibitionism, not to the grooming and affectionate tenderness of making love to his wife. Sexual intercourse with her was more of a take-it-or-leave-it chore than an erotic joy. His wife's illnesses and chronic vomiting relieved him of some of the burden of making love to her. She herself said in an interview, "I think I was more in love with Ken when I first met him than he was with me."

On MPA, something similar to what happened to Ken's exhibitionism happened also to his outbursts of destructive rage and violence, of which he had a vivid history. They became less frequent and were more likely to be vocal than physical. MPA did not, however, change his stance of intransigence. For seven years and more, he and his wife were in a state of episodic bickering and contentiousness. There was much to be contentious about: housekeeping duties, joblessness, unpaid bills, car breakdowns, television programs, household pets (five dogs, two cats, one bird), overcrowding with needy kin, child discipline and chores, his hemorrhoids, fraternizing with neighbors, and his irrational jealousy lest his wife pay attention to other men who would find her loss of weight sexually attractive. The two topics exempted from their arguments were matters of illness, weight, and vomiting for her; and matters of sex and the law for him. There lay the common ground on which their lovemaps met in a pairbonded relationship that kept them together through thick and thin. Their syndromes interlocked.

7

Phylismic Underpinnings

Phylisms

From the viewpoint of sexological epidemiology, paraphilic love-maps are expressions of sexual imagery, ideation, and practice that are distributed worldwide. So far as can be ascertained, they are phylogenetically restricted to the human species. Among individual members of the human species, however, paraphilias are sporadically, not universally distributed. Therefore, a two tiered explanation is required, one phylogenetic and the other ontogenetic, neither of which, like much else in contemporary science, fulfills the intellectually satisfying demands of being wholly complete.

The phylogenetic explanation of how the human species became a paraphilic species belongs in the conjectural realm of evolutionary sexology, as adumbrated in "From Biorobotics to Paraphilia" (see chaps. 4, 5). In brief, derobotization of all the maps or schemas in the mindbrain took place concurrently with the evolution of the human languagemap. Derobotization of the procreative map transformed it into the lovemap. Thus emancipated, the lovemap has been able to exclude or relocate its own phylismic elements or to graft in phylismic elements from other mindbrain maps. A phylism or phylismic element is a building block of behavior that is built in to all members of a species.

Yawning is an example, and a particularly apt one, for in some primate species it is a signal of sexual invitation. In human beings, yawning is usually associated with sleepiness or exhaustion. It is also contagious and thus a signal of reciprocity. Although not usually present in the human lovemap, in some few individuals it may be translocated there pharmacologically by clomipramine (Anafranil), a medication usually used for either unipolar depression or obsessive compulsive disorder (OCD). In four cases reported (McLean et al. 1983), sexual arousal up to and including orgasm and, in one male, ejaculation, occurred concurrently with yawning. One woman "was able to experience orgasm by deliberate yawning." In all four cases, the association between yawning and sexual arousal ceased within days after withdrawal of the medication. Harrison et al. (1984) linked the phenomenon to the "stretching-yawning syndrome" experimentally associated in animals with the release of hypothalamic releasing hormones. They attributed the clomipramine effect to an increase in the brain's level of the neurotransmitter serotonin. Holmgren et al. (1980), in experiments with rats, showed a relationship between neuropeptide hormones, testosterone, and pharmacologically induced yawning and genital arousal.

The diversity of the paraphilias can be accounted for by phylismic rearrangements, exclusions, or inclusions. Rearrangements take place within the lovemap, as when genital display gets central instead of peripheral prominence as a sexual solicitation. Exclusion is exemplified in the eligibility paraphilias. Pedophilia, for instance, excludes partners of all ages except juveniles. Inclusion is exemplified in the olfactophilic (smelly-tasty) fetishistic paraphilias. Smelly underwear is an example, when their inclusion in the lovemap surpasses a live partner as a stimulus to sexual arousal.

The wide diversity of phylismic rearrangements, exclusions, and inclusions that are possible in the lovemap accounts for the wide diversity of the paraphilias. Their diversity is such that, at first glance, the paraphilias may seem to be chaotically unclassifiable and likewise their phylismic underpinnings. However, it is possible to classify paraphilic phylisms under the same everyday headings as the grand stratagems (see chap. 5). First, however, an illustration is in order.

The case would not have been recognized as one of paraphilia until it entered the public domain in the criminal justice system. The person concerned was found guilty of having had a consensual sexual relationship with a young woman who was legally underage. He and the girl's mother had been having a long running adulterous affair. On her own initiative, the girl intervened and claimed attention. By the letter of the law, he was guilty of pedophilia, more accurately ephebophilia since the girl was no longer a juvenile. Actually, the case was more complex than one of simple age disparity and had a history dating back to the boyhood of the accused at the age of eight (see chap. 4).

He was a big boy for an eight-year-old and physically attractive to adolescent girls in the neighborhood who elicited his participation serially, as they tried to have penetrative sexual intercourse with him. Although he was cut by a sharp garden tool in the garage, first time around, he did not give up, but sporadically played at the same activity with the same girls, and with their successors, until he was twelve and began to undergo his own puberty. At this same time, his family moved to a new address. In the new location he did not resume his former sexual activities. By contrast, beginning at around age fourteen and continuing until he married at age eighteen and then throughout thirty years of marriage, he masturbated with incessant regularity, even as frequently as up to ten times a day when younger, and five to six times daily when older. Sometimes his penis became chafed and sore.

An episode of masturbation would be stimulated by somebody or something that reminded him of the sexual activities of his early years. He would then be overtaken by a compulsion to repeat each childhood experience serially, as if on a mental videotape and in vivid detail, until he ejaculated. The culmination of ejaculation was contingent on repetition in eidetically vivid mental replay of all of the childhood episodes of coercive sex with an estimated fifteen different female partners. He worked long hours at heavy construction work so as to help reduce exposure to masturbation stimulation.

In retrospect, he recalled that he had never in his life initiated a sexual relationship, but had always had women put the make on him until he couldn't back out. By coincidence, it turned out that his wife proved to be sexually anhedonic; so that after two pregnancies they discontinued having sexual intercourse. Nonetheless, he continued to have a series of extramarital partners.

He began MPA treatment in pill form, 30 mg twice a day, supplemented with antidepressant medication. Within three weeks, he no longer experienced the obsessional replay of masturbation imagery. He could recall what it had been like, but it no longer exercised its pervasive tyranny. The change coincided with a lifting of suicidal depressive despair, which on at least half a dozen earlier occasions had all but culminated in a suicidal leap.

Six general principles are exemplified in this particular paraphilia. The first is that paraphilias have a developmental history traceable in many instances, as in this one, to around the age of eight. The second is that a paraphilia, like a narrative painted on a Chinese scroll, takes time, variable in duration, to be unfurled from beginning to end.

The third principle is the separation of love and lust, in this case represented by affectionate love and attachment to a sexually anhedonic wife, on the one hand, and, on the other hand, lust expressed autoerotically and only in association with an obsessional mental replay of the imagery of sexual encounters dating back to prepuberty.

The fourth principle is that paraphilic imagery, ideation, and practice cannot be written off as a so-called normal variation, simply because the paraphilia does not involve violence and coercion of a nonconsensual partner.

The fifth principle is that, despite their unique and eccentric individuality, paraphilias are classifiable. In the present instance, the general category is masochism. The man took the submissive "bottom" role in response to the "top" role of dominant females who thrust their demands upon him, even though he did not enjoy their attention.

The sixth principle is that legal and biomedical definitions of paraphilia do not necessarily agree. In this instance, the law defined the paraphilia as pedophilia, whereas in actuality it was an idiosyncratic form of masochism and only coincidentally age discrepant.

The seventh principle is that paraphilia may coexist with a second diagnosis or condition, in this instance suicidal despair at being paraphilic. Also the man had an extraordinary degree of eidetic (photographic) memory. He could recall numbers and prices of catalog merchandise dating back for several years. He was also a workaholic, working two jobs for many years of his life in a vain effort to be sequestered from stimuli that might trigger another round of masturbation and its reiterative fantasies.

Sacrifice and Expiation

THE BEGINNING AND the ending of life are antithetical mysteries. Except for the late twentieth-century technology of cloning, the beginning of life is marked by haphazard uncertainty as to which one among several hundreds of millions of rival sperms will conjoin with a single ovum to create the beginning of a uniquely new life. There is nothing uncertain, by contrast, about the ending of life: death is the one ineluctable mystery that applies universally to all members of the human species. Its uncertainty lies not in its ineluctability, but in when and how we will die.

Apoptosis, programmed cell death, is an essential contingency of programmed cell differentiation and growth from embryonic life onward. It, too, is a late twentieth century discovery. Like blood pressure, kidney filtration, hormonal balance, and other bodily maintenance systems, apoptosis takes care of itself without intruding on conscious awareness until it runs amok, as it does in cancer. Cancer cells that should have died proliferate until they produce deadly symptoms.

Sexological processes that are beyond the reach of conscious awareness do not necessarily guarantee indifference to them. Quite to the contrary, they may generate obsessional and hypochondriacal anxiety lest they harbor hidden pathology. Obsessional worry about the possibility of exposure to a sexually transmitted disease is an example. It becomes the source of phobia and irrational avoidance of sexual contact. More specifically, the phobia may apply not to the proceptive phase of flirting and courtship, but to the acceptive phase of penial vaginal penetration. In the male, penetration phobia may be manifested as impotence, and in the female as vaginismus. Whatever the clinical manifestations of penetration phobia, they belong in the general category of hypophilia, not paraphilia.

Whereas hypophilias are anhedonic, paraphilias are hedonic. Some defy the ineluctibility of death by erotizing it. The death they erotize is not of insidious, cellular origin. It is death that is sudden in origin and that, with greater vigilance, might have been avoided. It is death that originates in five phylisms of aggression and dominance. One is the carnivorous phylism of fighting to kill or be killed for food. The second is the territorial phylism of fighting to expel and maybe kill ecological intruders. The third is the phylism of dominance rivalry and fighting to retain hierarchical status. The fourth is mating rivalry and fighting to eliminate procreative competition. The fifth is protective fighting in defense of the young.

All five of these phylisms are shared by the hominid species, ourselves included, but each species is distinct and different. Males and females in all hominid species share the five phylisms, but respond differently. Thus, females more than males resist the intrusion of a young female who has left her home troop in search of a partner, whereas males are extremely violent toward male intruders in search of breeding females. Within the troop, dominance rivalry and mating rivalry are more violent between males, whereas females are more likely to set up alliances that will enable them to follow the victor, and thus upgrade their social hierarchical power. Females are more fierce in guarding the young, whereas in some primate species an intruding male may kill the baby and take over its mother as a breeding partner (Roes 1998; see also p. 173).

All five of the fighting phylisms are dangerous, there being no guarantee of who will be the winner and who the loser. Human adolescent males deal with this precariousness by being impervious to it, perceiving themselves as omnipotent and eternal. The more they triumph, the more are they in demand by celebrity seeking young women. Today the big rivalries are not raw phylisms but those of celebrity sport, music, film, and television stars. The raw phylisms are not lost and gone, however. They may maintain themselves by becoming harnessed in the service of the sadomasochistic paraphilias. In masochism, being potentially vanquished and subordinate is erotized. In sadism, being potentially victorious and dominant is erotized.

The phylism for the erotization of being the loser is less evident in the human species than in the bonobo species of ape, formerly known as the pygmy chimpanzee. Bonobo genitalia are phylismically endowed to be used not only as organs of procreation, but also as organs of appeasement and reconciliation (de Waal and Lanting 1997; Kano 1992; see also Money 1997b, chap. 2). To illustrate, a female who shares her mate's dominance status approaches him as he lies on his back munching a bundle of leaves. His penis is erect. She backs onto it, inserting it into her vagina. He hands her the bundle of leaves. She eats her fill and then returns the leaves. Again, two young males end a dispute when the loser lies on his back with his penis emerging from its sheath. Then the winner massages the loser's penis, though not to ejaculation, as if to guarantee the loser's safety. Alternatively, the winner may mount the loser from behind, though without penetration or ejaculation. Although both postures are phylisms of conflict resolution, they do discriminate between dominance and submission. The female counterpart is genitogenital rubbing, done in the missionary position. It functions to avoid conflict by bonding two females in a mutual alliance. The phylisms that are erotized to form human paraphilic lovemaps of sadistic dominance and masochistic submission are not only phylisms of conflict and its resolution. Phylisms from other systems may also be erotized so as to contribute to the formation of a sadomasochistic lovemap. One such phylism observed among subhuman as well as human primates is the slapping, shoving, or shaking of infants if they fail to quit pestering their mothers or guardians.

A glimpse into the phylism of self-mutilation that may prove relevant to the brain biochemistry of masochistic mutilation is provided by the Lesch-Nyhan syndrome. This is a rare genetic disorder in purine metabolism secondary to a congenital deficiency of an enzyme (hypoxanthine-guanine phosphoribosyl-transferase). One of its most distressing symptoms is compulsively painful self-mutilation of the fingers and lips by biting (Anderson et al. 1992). The lips may be completely eaten away. Self-mutilation is not specific to any one syndrome, however. Among primates it is widespread as a response to prolonged social separation, isolation, and sensory deprivation. Individual human beings report that it induces tranquility and relief of tension. In a less pathological degree, self-mutilation takes the form of biting the fingernails to the quick.

In infancy, a prototypic form of self-mutilation takes the form of head banging and rocking. Although painful at first, head banging brings on a state of euphoric tension release, perhaps as a sequel to the release of opiate neurotransmitters in the brain. Infantile head banging and rocking may give way, in later years, to explicit self-mutilation by cutting or scratching the arms, legs, or other parts of the body with sharp or pointed utensils. It is done under the pressure of compulsion so great that it may lead to suicidal slicing of the wrists or neck as a method of escape.

Another phylismic response to severe sensory and social deprivation in subhuman and human primates is the smearing of feces and eating them (*coprophagia*). The paraphilia that incorporates this excremental phylism is *coprophilia*. It may be associated with *urophilia*. Either or both may be self-directed, other directed, or alternatingly shared.

In paraphilia, feces and urine have yet another possible phyletic linkage, namely in the maternal licking of the nether parts of their infants to keep them clean. This practice can be observed in the great apes. Human mothers may, in prehistoric times, have transferred the duty of licking feces to small dogs domesticated specifically for that purpose. Margaret Mead (personal communication) observed such dogs in the course of her research in Bali, years ago.

The phylism of coprophagia provides a unique example of the complexity of what still remains to be discovered empirically about the phyletic infrastructure of the paraphilias. One example is the relationship of coprophagia to immunology as revealed in the rat experiments of Moltz (1984) and Moltz and Lee (1983). Newborn rats are immunologically incompetent to resist acute infection of the gut and death from necrotizing enterocolitis. Fourteen days after the onset of lactation, the mother begins to release a fecal pheromone, a prolactin-induced derivative of cholic acid in bile. The pheromone attracts the young to eat their mother's fecal pellets. The pheromone-containing pellets are rich in deoxycholic acid, also a derivative of cholic acid in bile. It protects against bacterial endotoxin, for example, of *E. coli*. The young need protection beginning at day fourteen, which is when they first ingest bacteria-containing solid food. By day twenty-eight, the young produce their own deoxycholic acid and cease eating the mother's fecal pellets which no longer contain the pheromonal attractant.

In human species, necrotizing enterocolitis is more prevalent among premature than full-term babies (Moltz 1984). The premature are less efficient in bile-acid production. There is no known human counterpart of neonatal coprophagia in rats, so the possible relation of this phylism to human adult coprophilia is speculative.

Similarly speculative is a hypothesis put forward by Hopp (1980) regarding coprophagia, incidental to ingestion of feces from the gut of the prey eaten by carnivorous predators. Bacteria ingested in this way eventually are shed in the feces of the predator. The proximity of the anal and genital openings allows for the transfer of microorganisms from the gut into the female genital tract at the time of copulation. In this way, Hopp conjectured, genetic information from another species may splice itself into the DNA of a chromosome belonging to an embryo about to be formed and become a permanent feature of its genetic code. Complex transformation of genetic information is thus achieved at a rate far more rapidly than is possible by random mutation alone, as postulated in neo-Darwinian evolutionary theory (see also SET in chap. 5).

A significant feature of coprophilia and urophilia is that they involve the phylism of eating and drinking, both of which are rarely incorporated into a paraphilic lovemap. Ingestion of semen is a possible exception. So also is drinking milk from a baby bottle as part of the "adult baby ritual" of paraphilic infantilists. Paraphilic cannibalism is known, though its rarity is extreme.

In the males of four legged mammals, an olfactory (pheromonal) component of urine serves as a territorial marker and warning against intruders. However, this phylism is comparatively insignificant in primates, including humans.

The phylism of breathing or, more correctly, of paroxysmally not breathing (apnea) may be paraphilically enchained in the lovemap of *asphyxiophilia*. Induced asphyxiation may be applied to the self, the partner, or both together. The phylism of prolonged apnea is observed in young children undergoing a rage and crying tantrum. It is also observed as a paroxysmal manifestation of an acute asthma attack. Asphyxiophilia has been known also as hypoxia, on the basis of the supposition that a deficient supply of oxygen to the brain is an erotic enhancer, but there is no empirical proof. Moreover, the masochistic peril of autoerotic death from self-asphyxiation is paralleled by autoerotic death from a self-induced electrical jolt applied to the genitalia (Cairns and Rainer 1981), which does not entail hypoxia. Autoerotic death is, by definition, a solo event. However (see chap. 5), a partner or partners may be enlisted, as in a prearranged paraphilic mutilation or sacrifice of oneself (*autoassassinophilia*).

Marauding and Predation

A SACRIFICE REQUIRES an offering, and expiation requires penance. Both the sacrifice and the expiatory penance may be self-performed, or they may be performed on or by someone else. The two roles may also be interchangeable. They may be performed with informed consent or without it.

Informed consent is, at best, actuarial, for it is impossible to foresee in every most minute detail the outcome of any performance. At one extreme, only advice or mild persuasion may be needed to obtain participation. At the other extreme, participation may be coerced or violently imposed without informed consent. The paraphilias of marauding and predation are in this category. For the most part, so also are those of abduction or kidnapping.

Insofar as the paraphilias of marauding and predation involve coercive force and violence, they draw on the same phylisms of aggression as do the paraphilias of sacrifice and expiation. In particular, they draw on the phylism of mating rivalry and fighting to eliminate procreative competition. In the human species, predatory marauding is paraphilic rape (its Latin name, *raptophilia;* its Greek name, *biastophilia*). In the vernacular it is also known as molestation. In extreme form, paraphilic marauding is manifested as lust murder, singly or serially, possibly in association with *necrophilia*.

Among primates, the phylism of mating rivalry may connect with the phylism of dominance rivalry and the phylism of age-dispersal. The age of dispersal is the age when offspring are sufficiently mature to leave the home troop. Those who leave may be sons only, daughters only, or a combination of sons and daughters. In the case of bonobos and other species of troopbonding great apes, a mother can always be sure which are the offspring she bore, whereas a father cannot be sure which are the offspring he sired. Thus, there is an incest preventing logic of sorts in the fact that daughters, who cannot identify their fathers or his sons, are the ones who, like human brides, leave home and migrate to live with the partner in his troop's territory. Hence the phylism of mating rivalry works in conjunction with the phylism against incest (see p. 204).

This conjunction is far from perfect, however, for the bachelor males who do not leave home cannot identify either their own father or the daughters he has sired. However, they have only limited access to nonmigrating females who remain in the troop. They are monopolized by the males of high rank in the social dominance hierarchy. One solution to the mating deprivation of young bachelorhood is for an assertive young bachelor to challenge and dethrone a higher ranking male. Alternatively, a predatory young bachelor may maraud a neighboring troop and capture a nubile female or more than one with a view to setting up a new troop of his own. He may sacrifice his life in trying to grab or defend territory for his new troop. Provided the lives of his females are spared, a young male's life is expendable in battle as many females can be impregnated by a single male survivor. Thus, population growth is not diminished or retarded.

Another phylism that might be enlisted in the service of a marauding and predatory paraphilic lovemap is the phylism of infanticide. In males, the killing of infants is an extension of mating rivalry in that it follows the conquest of the former male leader and the takeover of the group by the victor. According to de Waal and Lanting (1997, 118), infanticide is "now known to occur in a wide range of species from lions to prairie dogs, and from mice to gorillas." The proportion of infantile deaths attributable to conspecific infanticide is "estimated to be 35% in grey langurs [Hanuman monkeys]; 37% in mountain gorillas; 43% in red howler monkeys; and 29% in blue monkeys."

Loss of a nursing infant disrupts the lactating mother's hypothalamic-pituitary-ovarian hormonal balance and allows a return to ovulation. Thus, the infanticidal male has a good chance of being the father of her next offspring, which may itself fall prey to infanticide, however.

A completely different phylism for ensuring paternity and avoiding incest is regulated through the sense of smell by pheromones and has been most intensively studied in prairie voles, a rodent species that live in family groups (Carter et al. 1997). After reaching the age of maturity, females in a family group are incapable of copulating with male relatives; their vaginas remain closed. The trigger that opens the vagina and begins ovulation is a pheromonal genital odor released by a male stranger, whereupon the couple copulate repeatedly over a twenty-four hour period. Their copulation releases neuropeptides by way of neurosecretory cells in the brain's hypothalamus (Gainer and Wray 1992), oxytocin in females and vasopressin in males. Oxytocin is associated with female parental behavior and lactation and vasopressin with male parental behavior and aggression (Morell 1998). Oxytocin has also been proposed as a social bonding hormone.

It is rare to find monogamous fidelity among mammals, even those that stay together and cooperate in rearing the young. One species, the California mouse is an exception (Morell 1998). In rearing the young, parental bonding is more common among birds, but DNA testing proves that not all the hatchlings are from the same father. Among human beings, according to Popovich in Oregon, United States labs screening for inherited diseases typically expect to find that about 10 percent of children are not sired by the putative father (Morell 1998).

At the risk of being pedantic, let it be repeated that the significance of the foregoing phylisms of marauding and predation—like those of sacrifice and expiation—is not that they explain the genesis of paraphilia in a particular individual; their significance is phylogenetic, not ontogenetic. That is, they explain why the human species is sporadically capable of producing marauding, predatory, sacrificial, or expiatory lovemaps in some of its members.

Mercantilism and Venality

THROUGHOUT NATURE, THERE are examples of symbiont species that cannot exist alone, but only in paired cooperation with one another. The sulphur ingesting bacteria of the newly discovered deep-ocean volcanic vents (black smokers) are a spectacular example. In the total absence of sunlight to convert carbon dioxide into nutriment, these bacteria synthesize nutrients from volcanic sulphur instead and supply them to their symbiont giant tube worms in which they are housed.

On land there are many plant and animal species that colonize other species and use them parasitically for nutrition or procreation. Other pairs of species are true symbionts: each gives to the other something in return for what it takes. Among mammals, symbiont species are those that can be domesticated or enslaved. In return for services performed, they are guaranteed, at a minimum, nutrition and shelter. One of the great milestones of domestication in hominid evolution was the extension of direct reward and punishment method of training to the operant conditioning method of token-economy training. By the third millennium B.C., silver smelted from lead ore and cast into coins had become the chief tokens of exchange in the Near East, whence they spread rapidly (Niragu 1998). Coins made eminently suitable tokens received in return for goods received or physical and mental services rendered. Among the services rendered were, and still are, those provided by sex organs. Those lacking wealth paid for services in public harems, whereas the wealthy and ruling class maintained their own private harems.

The symbiont relationship between two people in a relationship of sex worker and his/her clients may be transient and nonparaphilic, as is usually the case. For some few men and women, however, being a sex worker or a client becomes a permanent paraphilic feature of the lovemap, for which the technical term is *chrematistophilia* (see p. 105).

Fetishes and Talismans

IN THE ANIMAL world, odors function not only as sexual attractants. In laboratory rodents, a pheromone regulated by testosterone in the urine of mature males accelerates the onset of puberty in juvenile females. If a female is newly impregnated by a cage mate, a pheromone in the urine of a male intruder induces abortion, thus allowing the female to become pregnant again by the intruder. An oily male pheromone, also synthesized under the influence of testosterone, is stored in territorial marker glands in the neck or rump of the males of some mammalian species. When smeared on home boundary markers, it serves to warn intruder males to keep out.

As compared with rodents and other pheromonal species, primates are sexually more visile and tactile than they are olfactile (see also chap. 1). Neither subhuman nor human primates are characteristically smell blind, however. In the human species, when smell blindness (anosmia) does occur, it is a symptom of some other disorder or possibly a side effect of medication. It is congenital in origin in Kallmann's syndrome (Bobrow et al. 1971). In this syndrome, embryonic cells that normally form two clusters, one of which migrates to the olfactory lobe of the brain and the other to the hypothalamic-pituitary region, fail to do so (Bick et al. 1992). The respective outcomes are anosmia and pubertal failure secondary to failure of the hypothalamic, pituitary, and gonadal hormonal axis. In addition, individuals with Kallmann's syndrome are loners with impairment, presumably in the region of the hypothalamus, of the attractant for becoming love smitten.

Despite the research efforts of the perfume industry, there is no perfume that is a sure fire sexual attractant. As mentioned on p. 29, women who live in close proximity, as in a college dormitory, progressively synchronize their menstrual cycles. The responsible factor is an odor contained in underarm perspiration (McClintock 1971). The significance of this finding remains elusive, however. It happens without conscious awareness.

Some women find the odor of male crotch sweat to be a sexual attractant, and some men are intensely turned on by the smell and taste of the female vulva in oral sex. In both instances, there are no substantiating statistics, and there is no way of predicting who will and who will not find these odors to be sexual attractants.

In many mammalian species, the maternal and infant odors of licking and sucking are essential to the establishment of the mother-infant pairbondship, without which the infant is neglected, unfed, and dies (see also chap. 1, "Grooming"). Under the general rubric of failure to thrive, there are some mothers and infants whose olfactory and tactile bonding fails or is deficient. In extreme cases, the infant dies or is killed (Money 1992), and the mother is diagnosable as having Munchausen's syndrome by proxy (Money and Werlwas 1976).

The phylisms of mother infant pairbondship are olfactory and tactile or contrectative. The phylisms of fetishism or talismanism belong to the same two categories and constitute, respectively, the *olfactophilias* and the *hyphephilias*. The olfactory (smelly-tasty) fetishes may actually carry smells of the human body, as in fetishes for worn or soiled underwear, bras, menstrual pads or tampons, sweaty T-shirts, boots, and shoes. In the older literature, they were called collectively the *mysophilias* (from the Greek for filth). In a particular high-profile case that hit the society pages of the media, the fetishist proved to be a personal manager who took shoes from his employer's closet. He is the one, above mentioned (p. 124), who bored a hole in the heel of the shoe through which to insert his penis and masturbate. The alternative practice for an olfactophilic fetishist is to sniff or chew the smelly fetish object while masturbating. Odorous feet far surpass odorless hands in fetish formation.

The hyphephilic or touchy-feely fetishes derive in the ultimate analysis from the feel of human hair or skin and the fabrics or garments worn to cover them: fur, velvet, silk, and leather, for example, or flannel, linen, cotton, and synthetic fabrics. Fabric fetishes change together with changes in synthetic fabric technology and fashion. Garment fetishes follow the styles of the fetishist's youth rather than those of contemporary fashion.

Especially in adolescence, the hyphephilic fetishist commonly masturbates into his fetishistic garments and then conceals them. He may take them from his sister's or his mother's closet and wear them. This practice manifests a linkage between paraphilia (fetishism) and gender transposition in boys (see also chap. 3, "Paraphilic Transvestism"). If there is a corresponding phenomenon in girls, it has yet to be brought out in the open.

In the popular media, the term *fetish* is frequently applied to all forms of paraphilic, atypical, or censured sexual expression. For example, it may be said that someone has a fetish for feet, big buttocks, large breasts, long flowing hair, bald heads, blue eyes, huge penises, and so on. In *DSM-IV* such a focus on a part of the body is defined as partialism and listed under 302.9 "Paraphilia Not Otherwise Specified." Here, in this book, the term *partialism* is not used. Instead, partial attractants are listed under stigma and eligibility where, although they may be idiosyncratic or even quirky, they may be not so fixated and exclusive as to qualify as paraphilic pathologies.

Stigma and Eligibility

NATURE DID NOT have the opportunity to consult Darwin on the evolutionary merits of introducing sexual (diecious) reproduction to compete with asexual (monecious) reproduction. In each system, species have proved quite capable of holding their own and not becoming extinct.

Among vertebrates, whiptail lizards are a rare but apt example (Crews and Fitzgerald 1980; Crews 1987, 1989; Moritz 1983). Some whiptail species are diecious. They have both males that produce sperms and females that produce ova. Other whiptail species are monecious. They have neither males nor females, but are parthenogenic. That is to say, all members of the species are able to produce ova, whereas none is able to produce sperms. Without being impregnated by a sperm, an ovum is able to initiate the process of embryogenesis that culminates in the hatching of a baby whiptail lizard.

Parthenogenic reproduction, whether in blue-green algae or whiptail lizards, is a form of cloning. It demonstrates that species survival is not invariably contingent on the interchange of genetic material by way of the chromosomes of the ovum and the sperm. On the contrary, it demonstrates that species survival is compatible with the exclusion of genetic material from a mating partner.

The tension represented here between the evolutionary merits of parthenogenic and diecious breeding has its counterpart in the merits of inbreeding versus outbreeding in diecious species, our own species included. In animal husbandry, inbreeding of a pure blood line increases the chances of producing more thoroughbreds. On the debit side, inbreeding of a genetically transmitted defective line increases the chances of producing more defective offspring.

Cross breeding or hybridization may produce a prodigy superior to a thoroughbred, but it may also produce a mongrel. Then inbreeding of a mongrel line produces more mongrels.

Animal breeding in the wild is conspecific. That is, individuals mate with members of their own species, even if they could hybridize with a neighboring subspecies.

The phylism for conspecific breeding is the phylism that underpins transcultural legal, religious, and familial rules and customs regarding miscegenation, inbreeding and outbreeding (endogamy and exogamy). It is the phylism that underpins individual lovemaps of the stigmatic and eligibilic type, which range from the culturally tolerated to the culturally ostracized or condemned.

The two main categories of stigmatic and eligibilic paraphilias are the *morphophilias* and the *chronophilias* (see below). Morphophilias pertain to select features of the appearance or morphology of the body as sexual attractants.

The majority of the morphophilias constitute fixations on bodily organs and features that are distributed among the population in general. Thus, a morphophile may be not simply fascinated by hyperplastic breasts or buttocks, but fixated on them to a degree incompatible with an erotic response to breasts of small or medium size. Sexuoerotic fascinations or fixations on the size of bodily parts have not, for the most part, been subject to social censure. Consequently, they have not been brought to the attention of either the court or the clinic, and they have not been given Greek or Latin derived names in the official nomenclature. In the vernacular of Personals in the print media, however, many of them were given descriptive and sometimes picturesque names, and even more so, as likeminded people set up web sites on the Internet. *Gainers* is one such term. It is used to identify people who are extremely overweight or who seek sexual partners who are extremely overweight. Catering to heterosexual men, pictorial pornography magazines were popularized under such titles as "Big Fat Mamas." In homosexual argot, there are chubby chasers who seek heavily overweight partners; muscle queens whose turn on is to body builders (Lorefice 1991); and size queens who maintain a constant search for very large penises (macrogenitalia). On the Internet, *macrophilia* refers to an interest in people who, although not necessarily overweight, are very tall and brawny, and a tall hawk is someone who stalks tall people. Gregersen (personal communication) recognized the need for two new terms, *gigantophilia* and *nanophilia,* for paraphilic fixation on the very tall and the dwarfed, respectively. He also proposed the terms, based on Sheldon's three body types, *endomorphophilia, mesomorphophilia,* and *ectomorphophilia,* to refer, respectively, to paraphilias for fat, muscular, and skinny body morphology (Sheldon 1970). Today's equivalent to statues in *agalmatophilia* (see chap. 5) might be life-size inflatable or molded plastic dolls.

Morphophilic fixations include also racial features and skin color, which are recognized only in folk taxonomy. A rice queen in homosexual jargon is a caucasian attracted only to orientals; a potato queen, an oriental attracted only to whites; and a dinge queen, a white attracted only to blacks. Each has its unnamed heterosexual counterpart. It is politically incorrect and socially inept to mention racial morphophilias, for miscegenation is too traumatically connected with the history of slavery and colonialism. American slaves had no legal rights and, therefore, could not be legally married. It was acceptable for white plantation males to have colored concubines, as the offspring could be classed as colored slaves. By contrast, if a white plantation girl had a colored boyfriend, his relationship was defined as one of rape, and he was in danger of being lynched.

Social stigmatization notwithstanding, mutually compatible interracial unions are, per se, no more prone to paraphilic morbidity than are uniracial unions. A morphophilia of any type is morbid if its fixation is so restrictive and immutable that it excludes alternatives and, at the same time, is incapable of maintaining its own promise of fulfillment.

An example of this type of morbidity is encountered in the stigmatic and eligibility paraphilia in which the criterion of eligibility the possession of is one or more amputated limbs or digits. This amputation paraphilia has the Greek derived name of *acrotomophilia* (*akron*, extremity + *tomé*, a cutting) when applied to the partner (Money and Simcoe 1984/86) and *apotemnophilia* (*apo*, from + *temnein*, to cut) when applied to the self (Money et al. 1977; Money 1993, chap. 23; see also chap. 3, p. 68).

Unlike cosmetic plastic surgery, amputation upon demand is virtually unknown. Those would-be amputees who are sufficiently desperate are, therefore, reduced to contriving injuries that will necessitate surgical intervention. In one case (Money et al. 1977, and unpublished followup), after thirty years of postponement and psychotherapeutic failure, a patient contrived a putative hunting accident which led to amputation of the left leg above the knee as planned. The primary sexual attractant in this case was the stump of young males with the same above the knee amputation. In other cases, acrotomophilic attraction is heterosexual. Attraction to male amputees or cripples in wheel chairs (*abasiophilia*) occurs in females as well as in males (Money 1990c).

At first glance, it would appear logical that a posttraumatic or postsurgical amputee would be the ideal match for someone with a paraphilia for the stump of an amputation. A lovemap that recognizes a stump as a sexual attractant is not, however, the same as one that recognizes the whole person as a sexual attractant. Either one or both of the two partners eventually comes to this realization, and their relationship becomes devoid of lust although not necessarily of affectionate caring. One man married to an intact woman wrote:

> I know that my present wife is not at all comfortable with my paraphilia. She says that she cannot accept my "sickness," nor allow it to continue. Otherwise, I would have to be as sick as

you, she believes. She likens it to adultery, in that my thoughts drift to anonymous women amputees for erotic arousal. She has gotten on my case so heavy that I can no longer get aroused around her, so she now charges me with impotency. In my efforts to submerge my natural emotions I have inhibited all arousal capabilities. I now feel so guilty about my feelings that I can't allow myself to think sexy thoughts about her. I used to be able to caress her and become aroused with full performance, but now I can't bring myself to try. (Money 1986, chap. 23)

The split between lust and love in the amputation paraphilia is exemplified also in a woman's biographical statement (Money 1990c):

In my fantasies, sometimes the man is handicapped; other times I am; and at other times we both are. They are generally fantasies of a highly romantic nature. In my mid-twenties, I attempted to live out my fantasies. Most of these attempts were very short lived. After the initial contact, I am often "turned off." I did enjoy one relationship, however. In addition to being handicapped, he was bright, funny, attractive, and we shared a number of interests. It was with this man that I enjoyed my first gratifying sexual relationship. By then I was totally hooked and "in love." However, I also experienced a great deal of guilt and anxiety. He did not know about my paraphilia and I was torn between needing to tell him and a tremendous fear of the effect it might have on him and our relationship. His physical problem was a congenital one and I soon learned from him that it was a taboo subject. We later broke up and during a night of mutual confessions, I told him how and why I was initially attracted to him. About two years later we got back together, but it did not work out. Since then, I have not attempted to live out any more fantasies. This is partly due to a hesitance on my part as well as an extremely limited number of opportunities.

From the foregoing quotations, it can be recognized that a morphophilic lovemap may have the appearance of being not only harmless, but also of self-sacrificing devotion to a handicapped person. On the contrary, it may be abusively destructive if one partner is beseeching the other to submit to amputation or to approve of one's own becoming an amputee.

A more acutely morbid example of morphophilic destructiveness is serial lust murder followed by attempted orgasm from oral or vaginal penetration of the corpse (*necrophilia*, from Greek, *nekros*, dead). Serial lust murder and necrophilia are not invariably coupled, however. The true necrophile is fascinated not with killing but with corpses. Thus, he/she might find employment in a morgue or in the embalming rooms of a funeral home.

Since the time of the Pharaohs, corpses of the rulers have been embalmed, painted, bejeweled, and gilded, so that even in death the rich, powerful, and famous are assured of maintaining their allure in the next world. In contemporary American funeral customs, corpses are made up with cosmetics so as to appear as lifelike and alluring as a painted doll. The pathos of death is an exquisitely aesthetic experience for some people, among whom are those for whom the experience overlaps with sexual arousal. This overlap is exemplified in a case of necrophilia from the Internet (Malin 1987; Davison personal communication) first brought to attention by an inspector in a photo processing lab. The offending pictures were of two early adolescent girls, the photographer's daughters, posing like cosmetically made-up corpses in fancy silk-lined coffins. Their father, a successful business man, was sentenced to a long imprisonment on charges of pedophilia, as the girls were not yet eighteen years old.

Investigation of the case eventually revealed that part of the buildup to sexual intercourse between husband and wife was to have her pose as a corpse in a coffin and to remain immobile while having sex. The husband had experience with actual corpses by volunteering to work in the embalming room of the funeral home owned by one of his friends. There was no record of actual sexual contact with the corpses. His necrophilic imagery and ideation was put into practice in play with a collection of Barbie Dolls which he kept locked away in the trunk of his car. Using cut-outs from clothing catalogues, he made composite necrophilic pictures. None of the dolls or pictures had been mutilated. They were used as masturbation aids. Sexual intercourse was too big a burden for both marital partners and so fell by the wayside. The prepotency of necrophilia to his sexual arousal was attributed by the man himself to his exposure, in boyhood, to dead people at scenes of accident or disaster. He would be there in the company of his father who belonged to a rescue squad. He requested MPA treatment, even while in prison, for the control of necrophilic fantasies, but the criminal justice system disallowed his request.

Toward the end of World War II, the morgue building of a sprawling state hospital was a place of secret fascination for a hospital orderly recently discharged from military service. While on active duty overseas, he and his buddy huddled together in terror in the course of an enemy artillery bombardment. A shell exploded and took away his buddy's entire head. He himself was not injured. Thereafter he became obsessed with corpses. On off-duty days at the hospital, he would return on the midnight train and invariably check the morgue as he walked across the campus to his sleeping quarters. He was too diffident to disclose what he did in there and was adamant about being unaccompanied.

Although the phylism that underpins the stigmatic and eligibilic paraphilias works to keep members of a species breeding with others of their own kind, it may be contravened. Sexual relationships may take place between two species that do not hybridize. When an infant of one species is reared by a foster parent of another species, the young one may grow up to bond only with members of the foster species. Housebound pets of two species sometimes grow up to bond with one another. Crossbonding of animal species has been documented by Maple (1977).

Human beings bond with their pets. They pet them (from which comes the human erotic term *petting*). They stroke them, kiss them, and curl up beside them to sleep. That, however, does not constitute *zoophilia*. Nor is it zoophilic to rescue stray pets, to house them in overcrowded, disease-ridden apartments, and to skin their corpses for wall decorations, though it is extremely bizarre to do so (Worth and Beck 1981). It is also not zoophilic when young adolescent farm boys without a partner have sporadic contacts with farm animals as a substitute for masturbation. It is believed to occur less in females than males, but there is no solid evidence.

Although not a danger to other people (Matthews 1994; Shepherd unpublished, 1996), zoophilia may be morbidly noxious to the zoophile. This was so in the case of a young Buddhist man who sought help at age twenty-eight for what he called "my disgusting habit," *formicophilia* (Dewaraja and Money 1986). He traced this to age nine when, as a very shy and introverted boy he began keeping "a little zoo" of ants, later expanded to include cockroaches, snails, and frogs. He liked "the ticklish feeling of having them crawl on my legs and thighs." That feeling comforted him after he was deprived of his only friend, the family's houseboy, at age ten. The houseboy was seen performing interfemoral sex on him. His father gave him a severe thrashing and took the houseboy to the police station where he, too, was thrashed.

By age twelve, he found further consolation with his little zoo after the cancer death of his mother, with whom he was very close. He blamed his father. Depressed, he ceased achieving at school. He consoled himself with his zoo. He would undress and let the insects stimulate his genital area. The snails would slide over his nipples and the tip of his penis, biting "as if they were eating a leaf with their little mouths." When he pressed a frog in the palm of his hand against his penis and testicles, the frog would vibrate them. In a single three or four hour episode with his zoo, he would masturbate to orgasm up to five times, as often as four times a week.

At age eighteen, he witnessed his father having sexual intercourse, "just like an animal" with a woman friend and found it offensive that a woman would do that. He failed to get an erection when he tried to masturbate while looking at porno pictures. He was twenty-five when a woman of thirty "tempted me and made me do dirty things with her." Despite intromission and orgasm, it was not pleasurable. Subsequently, he avoided the woman. He had dreams that his mother was watching him performing sexual intercourse with the woman, "with an expression of horror on her face." Although he was able to work to support himself, he was a diffident loner who had trouble in "relating to other people, particularly women. I cannot look at their eyes when I talk with them," he said. "It makes me nervous. I feel that they can read my mind and know what a disgusting man I am."

In the middle ages and up until the end of the eighteenth century, bestiality was a capital crime for which the death penalty was imposed upon both the animal that had been sodomized and the mostly young men in their teens and early twenties convicted of having sodomized the beast (bestiality). In Europe, uncounted numbers of offenders, men and beasts together, were convicted and hanged or burned alive at the stake (Evans 1987; Liliequist 1992). Bestiality in colonial New England also brought the death sentence for the animal as well as the human offender (Bullough 1976).

Horses, cows, pigs, sheep, and other animals were executed for bestiality on the basis of the Christian theological doctrine that they had been possessed of the demons of the sin and crime of buggery. In other religions, zoophilia may have the status of being sacred, as in the Hindu case of Hanuman, the monkey, and Ganesha, the elephant.

In China, there is a fourth-century work, *Sou shen chi*, which in Japan became a sacred ballad, "oshirasama saimon," still chanted or sung by shamans (blind women, often) in the north. Shorn of detail, it tells of a rich man's daughter, Tamaya-gozen, and her beautiful chestnut horse, Sendan-kurige.

> Every day the girl used to feed the horse with her own hands, until one day, struck by his beauty, she said: If only you were a man I should like you for my husband. From this moment the horse conceived a burning passion for Tamaya-gozen, so consuming he could neither eat nor drink.
>
> The rich man called in diviners to discover what ailed the horse. When they told him that the horse was sick for love of his daughter the rich man in a rage had the horse killed and skinned. Tamaya-gozen went to say a requiem mass over the skin, when it suddenly wrapped itself round her and carried her up to the sky. Presently there fell down a shower of black and white insects, which alighted on the mulberry trees and began to eat the leaves. As they ate, they gave out a fine thread. They were the first silkworms, and in consequence the rich man became the greatest silk merchant in the land. (Blacker 1975, courtesy of the musicologist, Dr. Gerald Groemer)

The phylism for conspecific breeding may be rehearsed in the juvenile years prior to the onset of fertility. It is not irrevocably linked to actual breeding, for it may be exercised by those who, for whatever reason, are chronically infertile. It may also be exercised in the postfertile years, the onset of which is marked in women by the menopause, with no corresponding marker in males. Its exercise is compatible with the use of contraception to limit breeding.

Chronophilias pertain to the development age limits within which sexual attraction takes place and beyond which its does not. Around the world, mating and breeding within one's own generation is the prevalent chronological custom, regardless of whether the relationship is transient, romantically inspired, or family arranged. Age mismatching, if it occurs between members of the same generation, typically favors an older, economically established male and a younger female ready for motherhood.

Intergenerational age disparity typically favors an older male of paternal or grandpaternal age and a young nubile female with many premenopausal years of fertility ahead. Intergenerational disparity favors males of wealth and political power sufficient, perhaps, to sequester a harem of wives or concubines. The social institutions of mating and breeding and the means of producing and distributing wealth are mutually contingent in all cultures.

The age of one's self-representation in one's own lovemap does not necessarily keep pace with one's birthdays (Berezin 1975). For many people, it maintains itself at the age of young adulthood for forty years or more. If one's image in the mirror does not agree with that of the lovemap, then the outcome may be a visit to the plastic surgeon to reinstate one's more youthful appearance. Eventually, the age of one's self-representation in the lovemap begins to age and to catch up with one's birthday age.

Rather than stabilizing in young adulthood, the self-represented age may be incongruously too young, as it is in infantilism, juvenilism, and adolescentism. Infantilism is also known as *autonepiophilia* (from Greek, *auto*, self + *nepon*, infant). Infantilists call themselves adult babies (see also chap. 4). Being dressed and displayed as a baby in public by his wife or girlfriend is a sexual stimulant for a male infantilist. In one case, the man had his bedroom designed and furnished as a adult baby's nursery. His paraphilic ritual was to be diapered and put to bed with a baby bottle, while his wife played cards with a group of women friends downstairs. When she discovered that the baby had wet his diapers, she took him downstairs to scold and humiliate him in front of her guests. That set the stage for him to be able to have an erection and to perform sexually with his wife when she came to bed.

Another infantilist remembered an incident that occurred at around age six when he was chastised in public for having wet himself. Subsequently, he had recurrent nightmares of relentless ridicule by the ghost man who went away as soon as he put on a diaper. His first successful masturbation had been with a diaper, and his adolescent wet dreams always featured diapering. He suffered for years for being unable to quit wearing diapers even as an adult. It was exciting for him to price and order a supply of adult diapers and to secretly wear them.

The converse of infantilism is *infantophilia* (also known as *nepiophilia*). The one does not necessarily predicate the other. Infantophilia alone was the diagnosis of a young lesbian who dressed mannishly. For several years, she sought help in vain for sadistic infantophilia. Her sadistic ritual began with volunteering her services as a baby sitter in a household with an infant daughter too young to talk fluently. Her sadistic arousal was contingent on the infant's screams of induced pain. With a cigarette lighter, she would set fire to the end of a pencil and extinguish it by inserting it into the infant's vagina. She had no explanation of why she did it, nor of why the state hospital released her back into the community to do it again.

In the current era of resurgent antisexualism, it has become commonplace to equate parental fondling, cuddling, bathing, and drying of young children with molestation and abuse—the legal terms for infantophilia. A toddler who has been taught good touch and bad touch may in complete naiveté tell that a beloved grandfather or other relative touched her/him in a bad place while wiping her/him down after a bath. If that sets the wheels of child advocacy in motion, they may turn until the grandfather is falsely accused of sexual molestation and abuse and, quite possibly, indicted and imprisoned. Teachers and daycare providers are subject to the same erroneous accusations.

The converse of juvenilism is *pedophilia* (from Greek, *paidos*, child). Although the one does not necessarily predicate the other, the existence of juvenilism as a sexological syndrome of adulthood, independent of pedophilia, has not yet been diagnostically certified. Whenever juvenilism has been recognized, it has been in association with pedophilia. A pedophilic juvenilist may be so engrossed in the life of boyhood that he is a Peter Pan (Birkin 1979), socially inept in the presence of adults, with no topics of conversation to share with them. The pedophilic juvenilist engrossed in the life of girlhood is an Alice in Wonderland (Cohen 1978) who relates to the mothers of the girls he admires by being a story teller and photographer acquiring maternal permission to get romanticized pictures of their unclad daughters.

Juvenilism not coupled with pedophilia, should it prove to be an independent entity, may well be more prevalent in female than male adults. There is a stereotype of the baby doll girlfriend or wife that strongly appeals to some men. Correspondingly, the stereotype of the helpless male boytoy appeals to some women.

There is no vernacular term for adolescentism. The Greek derived term is *ephebism* (from Greek, *ephebicos*, pertaining to puberty). The paraphilic counterpart of ephebism is not pedophilia but *ephebophilia*. Its lesser used synonym is *hebephilia* (from Greek, *hebe*, youth). Ephebism has not been given official diagnostic status independently of ephebophilia.

The dividing line between pedophilia and ephebophilia is set by two incompatible criteria, one legal and the other developmental. The legal definition of the end of childhood and the beginning of the age of consent to a sexual relationship is transculturally variable. It ranges from age eighteen in the United States to age twelve in Spain. Thus the criterion of what constitutes pedophilia is a legal or customary one, irrespective of the biomedical stage of individual development and consensuality.

Regardless of the legal age of childhood, developmentally it is puberty that separates childhood from adolescence and fertility. Puberty may be completed by age nine, if not earlier, at one extreme, and not until age nineteen, at the other extreme.

The nomenclature of the chronophilias leaps from ephebophilia to *gerontophilia* (from Greek, *geras*, old age). Gerontophilia may raise the eyebrows of envy or avariciousness, especially if a much younger second spouse threatens to rob the grown offspring of the first marriage of their patrimony. Regardless of the age disparity, gerontophilia is not, per se, illegal. Some gerontophiles may also be serial impostors who combine sexual attraction to their elderly partners with exploitation. For example, they have themselves made heir to their estates and possibly bring about their deaths prematurely. Others are genuinely turned on in response only to a partner equivalent in age to their parent or grandparent.

In between ephebophilia and gerontophilia, there may well be unnamed chronophilias representing the ages of twenty, thirty, forty and so on. In some cases of separation and divorce, no explanation may be needed other than that the wife or husband has aged in appearance and no longer matches in age the idealized image of a younger partner still persisting in the spouse's lovemap. The spouse who breaks away may have or may look for a much younger partner as if to begin life all over again in youthful adulthood.

Such a discrepancy between the representation of the image of the idealized partner in the lovemap and the image of the actual partner is explicitly evident in pedophilia. When the juvenile partner undergoes the visible, olfactory, and hirsute changes of puberty, his/her sexual attractant value for the pedophile comes to an end. The relationship does not necessarily terminate. The older partner may become a sponsor and benefactor of the younger one's career. The younger partner's lovemap development progresses through an age concordant adolescence (Money and Weinrich 1983). In ephebophilia, the history of the relationship may parallel that of pedophilia.

Such a benign history necessitates an absence of coercion, absolutely no sadistic violence or injury, a contractual understanding that the relationship can be discontinued upon request at any time, and freedom from reprisals from peers or family should the nature of the relationship become suspected or known.

For boys, reprisals are not a big worry if they live in a subculture in which everyone knows that for three, four, or five generations, it has been known that boys between the ages of eleven and fifteen may be financially supported by a pedophilic patron or patrons.

Secrecy and the burden of reprisals if the secret of a forbidden relationship leaks out is the source of the Catch-22 dilemma that in many instances is more traumatizing than pedophilic sexual activity, per se. This is the dilemma of being damned if you do and damned if you don't admit what is happening. For the child, admitting the relationship is the equivalent of betrayal and the grief of losing a friend never to be seen again. Not admitting it means living under the constant threat of being unable alone to cease the relationship before it is discovered. The pathos of this dilemma is intense when the older person is a beloved parent or sibling, and the reprisal is deconstruction and destitution of the family, including foster home placement of the child and imprisonment of the beloved partner.

The phylismic underpinning of pedophilia is pairbondship in which parental-child bonding and lover-lover bonding, both of which manifest much in common, overlap too extensively and too one-sidedly in the pedophile, irrespective of whether or not the younger partner is fully ready for complete lover-lover bonding. This same formulation applies certainly to infantophilia. To a lesser extent, it may apply also to ephebophilia, especially if the age discrepancy between the two partners is extreme.

It is usually presumed that infantophiles, pedophiles, and ephebophiles are males, but females are not exempt. Whether or not they are less prevalent or simply less reported is not known.

Solicitation and Allure

In the design of experiments to test the sexual responses of male laboratory animals, the female in heat (estrus) is often defined as a lure. In four legged mammals, the allurative signal is transmitted as an odor or pheromone secreted from within the vagina in synchrony with estrus which itself is in synchrony with ovulation (see also chap. 1). In seasonal breeders, the male becomes hormonally prepared for breeding in seasonal synchrony with the female. In other species, the male is hormonally ready to respond to the pheromonal signal of an estrual female at any time.

In primate species, as already mentioned (see chap. 1), the eyes take over where the nose leaves off, so that allure as well as solicitation is more visual than olfactory (vomeronasal). In some subhuman primate species, the female signals her state of ovulation midway between two menstrual periods by swelling and vivid coloration of the external genital organs. She may invite an indolent male to pay attention by thrusting her genitals in his face. Conversely, a male may display his erect penis as a sign of invitation. In the great apes, except for the bonobo, solicitation and allure are cyclical, in synchrony with the ovulatory phase of the female's menstrual cycle. The bonobo is the subhuman primate that most resembles the human species in that the female accepts the solicitation of the male 75 percent of the nonovulatory days of the menstrual cycle. In women there are idiosyncratic fluctuations in the relationship between the phase of the menstrual cycle and taking the initiative in the solicitation of the male. Fluctuations occur in the frequency of solicitation of the female by the male also, though not with cyclic regularity.

In human beings the phylismic underpinnings of the paraphilias of solicitation and allure are, perhaps in a residual evolutionary way, vomeronasal, i.e., by way of the bilateral vomeronasal organs (see chap. 1) which may register the presence of pheromonal molecular stimuli without registering them in conscious recognition.

The phylism of grooming also plays a part in solicitation and allure and their paraphilias, insofar as touch and the contrectative senses facilitate not only troopbondship but pairbondship as well. Grooming, in the form of massage, is one of the components of foreplay and a signal of anticipated sexual union. It may also be climactic in and of itself.

The predominant phylismic underpinning of human solicitation and allure is, however, neither vomeronasal nor contrectative, but visual. It is a peculiarity of the human primate species that visual solicitation and allure are not tied to the hormonal sequences of the menstrual cycle, nor to seasonal cyclicity. Also, human solicitation and allure is not narrowly confined to display of the genital anatomy. They involve an extensive repertory of body language to which vocal language is added.

Among men and women, genital exhibitionism as a manifestation of solicitation and allure is not the same as theatrical exhibitionism. Theatricality is a form of entertainment which is not generically sexual, although it is compatible with explicitly genital solicitation and allure, as in live shows and so-called adult movies, videotapes, and web sites on the Internet.

The paraphilias of solicitation and allure are paraphilias of displacement as compared with paraphilias of inclusion. The inclusion paraphilias are those that include a practice that is typically extraneous to mating and breeding, per se. By contrast, the displacement paraphilias relocate a preliminary practice, like genital display, from the proceptive perimeter of a sexual encounter to the orgasmic center of the acceptive phase.

The paraphilic versions of solicitation and allure subdivide tripartitely into showing and looking, touching and being touched, and narrating and listening or reading. In all three categories, solicitation and allure may be manifested as a so-called normal variant of sexuality, or it may be morbidly pathological and legally criminalized.

The morbidly pathological versions of the paraphilias of showing and looking are exhibitionism and voyeurism. To avoid confusion with theatrical or sartorial exhibitionism, paraphilic exhibitionism of the genitals in males (see chap. 6) is specifically named *peodeikophilia* (from Greek *peos*, penis + *deiknunain*, to show). The corresponding female term is *Baubophilia*, named for the mythical Baubo, who exposed her genitals to the goddess, Demeter, as a distraction to cheer her up while searching for her wandering daughter, Persephone, who had been abducted by Hades, god of the underworld. As compared with peodeikophilia in men, Baubophilia in women is either less prevalent or less reported. It is less of an affront to males to see a woman's pudenda exposed by a skirt hitched too high as she sits in a subway car or hotel lobby than it is for females to see a man's penis hanging out of his unzipped pants.

The converse of genital exhibitionism is *voyeurism* (from French, *voir*, to see) or the peeping Tom syndrome. The typical stereotype of the voyeur is that of a night prowler who stalks a neighborhood in search of lighted bedroom windows through which there is a chance of seeing a woman disrobing or naked. Another stereotype is that of a teenaged neighbor looking through the window of his own bedroom to get a sexually stimulating glance of the girls next door undressing for bed.

An apparently harmless variant of voyeurism turned out to be less than benign when its disclosure cost a man a very prestigious job promotion. Voyeurism, in his case, was restricted to the stealth of ascertaining whether a woman was wearing underpants made of white cotton and not some other fabric. His fixation was exclusively on the white cotton type. It burdened him with so much guilt that he confessed it during his promotion interview. His guilt also provided an explanation of why he had never had sexual intercourse and had not married, even though his steady girlfriend of eight years wanted to get married. White cotton underpants usurped all of his sexual attention.

As in exhibitionism, so also in voyeurism, either the prevalence of the syndromes or the frequency of reporting is greater in males than females. In both syndromes, the paraphilic scenario may include concurrent masturbation, with or without climax. The alternative, delayed scenario is to replay the event mentally, at home, while masturbating alone or performing intercourse with a partner.

The stereotypic response to either an exhibitionist or a voyeur is to call the police and have the intruder arrested. The musician and exhibitionist who described his paraphilic fugue state (see chap. 6) recommended a different approach to a woman medical student when he addressed the class. He told the story of how he had exposed his penis to three young women at a suburban bus stop. One of them asked him, disdainfully, if he didn't know that he was supposed to keep that thing in his pants. That query broke the spell. He put his penis away and, until the bus came, carried on a nonsexual conversation with the young ladies.

The paraphilic scenario of either an exhibitionist or a voyeur may include the possibility of getting a positive response from the recipient of his exposure or peeping. To illustrate: the paraphilic ritual in one case of an exhibitionist with a juvenile history of enuresis was as follows. He would go into a downtown Roman Catholic church where he could count on finding a few elderly women in silent daytime worship. As a mark of disrespect for the church and for the foster mother under whose disciplinary rearing he grew up alienated, he would expose his penis to the old ladies sitting in the pews. Then, after urinating on the floor, he would leave. After dark, he would go to a nearby downtown alley lined by the backyards of mansion houses converted into apartments. Through one third floor back window, he knew he could expect to see the occupant disrobing at bed time. He had convinced himself that she expected to be spied on and to see him below, spying on her as he masturbated. His paraphilic fantasy did not include personal contact with her. His wife did not know about his paraphilic excursions until, eventually, he was arrested and lost his job as a steel worker.

A variant of voyeurism is *somnophilia* (from Greek, *somnus*, sleep), the sleeping princess syndrome. The scenario of this paraphilia is that a male voyeur stalks a neighborhood in search of a female asleep in a dwelling easy to break into. Having gained entry, the next part of the scenario is to awaken the woman to the joy of foreplay, including oral sex, followed by penial vaginal penetration. The outcome is most likely to be getting arrested for attempted rape.

Another variant of voyeurism is watching people copulate: *mixoscopia* (from Greek, *mixis*, sexual intercourse + *skopein*, to view), also known as *skopophilia* or *scoptophilia* (from Greek, *skopein*, to view). The watching may be clandestine, as in peeping through a keyhole, or in public, as at a live show on stage, or at a group sex party.

The exhibitionistic counterpart of mixoscopia is *autagonistophilia* (from Greek, *autos*, self + *agonistes*, principal dramatic actor).

This form of exhibitionism was morbidly self-sabotaging in the case of an executive administrator who spent his lunchbreaks with a girl-friend on the roof garden of his office building. There, under the gaze of occupants of tall surrounding skyscrapers, they would engage in sexual intercourse. His inability to take action to change this behavior cost him his job, his pension, his marriage, and his family.

The morbidly pathological versions of paraphilias of touching and being touched are named by the borrowed French term *toucherism* or if the touching is more in the nature of pressing and rubbing by another borrowed French term, *frotteurism*. Public transportation in crowded and enclosed spaces, such as subway cars, buses, or elevators, with standing room only, provide a ready made venue for the frotteur. This is another of the paraphilias that is usually attributed to the harassment of females by males rather than the harassment of males by females. This disparity may be otherwise explained, namely by the fact that males regard being rubbed by a stranger not as an effrontery, unless the frotteur is another male. The frotteur positions himself so that rubbing and pressing is a sexual signal, not coincidental to the swaying of a moving vehicle. The male, for example, may have an erection and perhaps even an ejaculation. Most recipients of frotteurism, however, do not reciprocate the frotteur's behavior. In addition, anonymity of the encounter is intrinsic to the paraphilic separation of lust and love in the frotteur.

The touching of toucherism is less dependent on crowding than is frotteurism. It incorporates an element of surprise, and so it may be directed at a stranger who becomes scared lest it represent a prelude to rape. In one case, a boy in early adolescence pestered girls of his own age group and surprised them by touching their breasts. He also reiteratively drew sketches of girls' breasts. The school authorities were apprehensive that he would progress to sexual molestation. By contrast, what he did progress to was a fixation on developing breasts of his own and undergoing sex reassignment. His problem was identification with females, to which harassment of them was only coincidental.

The morbidly pathological versions of the paraphilias of narrating and listening or reading are subsumed under the name of *narratophilia*. Narratophiles are those whose sexuoerotic arousal is fixated on the process of reciting or hearing erotic material, or else of writing or reading it. The closer the concordance between content of narrative erotic material and the personal sexuoerotic imagery and ideation of the listener or reader, the higher the degree of sexuoerotic arousal.

An illustrative example is that of a married couple whose marriage fell irrevocably apart after the husband's name was published in the county newspaper along with the names of dozens of others who had been arrested for homosexual solicitation in the men's room of a highway rest stop. Up until that time, the couple and their children had been considered by the local citizenry to constitute an idealized example of the moral American family, responsibly participating in church, school, and community affairs. They alone knew that they were not so ideally perfect everyday of the week.

On Saturday nights, when the children were asleep, they shut themselves in their bedroom and became carnal transgressors. The formula for his coital performance required her to listen while he narrated pornographic stories of what, in military life, he had watched soldiers do to themselves and to other men, sexually, and of what he had heard of their fantasies. He narrated silently to himself alone his account of his own involvement, this being essential to his getting and keeping an erection while performing with his wife. After his name and offense appeared in the newspaper, she could not cope with his having betrayed her own sense of sexual righteousness, nor could she make a compromise on behalf of the children who were deprived of a devoted father they could ill afford to lose.

The visual counterpart of narratophilia is *pictophilia*, i.e., being paraphilically dependent on sexually explicit pictures, books, movies, or videotapes for sexual arousal and performance, either alone as an essential antecedent to sex with a partner or on the Internet.

Whereas solicitation and allure are able to become paraphilically morbid, as in the foregoing, for the public at large they are the nonmorbid mainstay of sexually explicit visual and narrative entertainments. In both the print and the electronic media, including the Internet, if sexually explicit material gets a bad name it is called *pornography*. Otherwise, it is called *erotica*. Pornography (from Greek, *porne*, prostitute + *graphein*, to write) originally meant to write about harlotry. In a society that bans or imposes censorship on sexual explicitness, it is condemned simply on the basis of being sexually explicit. Transculturally, the criteria of pornography are not consistent. Historically, in Asian cultures, for example, French deep kissing has been cut from American made movies as being pornographic and equivalent in explicitness to the depiction of copulation which is banned in American movie houses.

The dividing line between what is pornographic and what is not is set by those members of society who collectively have the power to constitute the sex police. The extremists among them would ban all sexually explicit material, including videos of normal sexual activities that normal people might use as a substitute for Viagra to stimulate sexual arousal and the performance of normal sexual intercourse.

As an incentive to one's own performance, watching the copulation of others is not limited to the human species: sexually sluggish chimpanzees at Britain's Chesington Zoo were shown explicit movies of other chimpanzees mating. That activated their own lovemaps and they began copulating (Chicago Tribune, May 30, 1973), with resultant pregnancy.

Pornographic movies or writings activate what is already in the lovemap. Paraphilic ideation and imagery does not get implanted in the lovemap de novo by viewing, hearing, or reading paraphilic pornography. For example, hours of viewing videotapes of *coprophilia* (from Greek, *kopros*, dung) or *urophilia* (from Greek, *ouron*, urine) will not convert the viewer into a coprophile or urophile. On the contrary, unless the viewer has these paraphilias represented at least incipiently in the lovemap, seeing the movies will induce either indifference or revulsion. Correspondingly, viewing heterosexual movies will not convert homosexual into heterosexual lovemaps, nor will exposure to homosexual ideation and imagery recruit people with heterosexual lovemaps into the ranks of homosexuality.

Pornography has always kept pace with technological advance. Pornographic "French" postcards, for example, were among the early commercial products of pornography after the invention of the camera in the mid-nineteenth century. The telephone ushered in the era of interactive pornography, namely phone sex, in which two people talk "dirty" to one another, while one or both masturbate to orgasm. Most phone sex is consensual, even between strangers, but some is an imposture. In one case of serial impostoring, an unidentified man artfully convinced several women, including a college professor, a psychiatric nurse, and a retired social worker, that he had a sex hormone deficiency, and that he desperately needed someone in whom to confide. He cleverly led them on until they were disclosing details of the size and functionality of their husbands' penises, the length and color of their own pubic hair, and the frequency of their sexual intercourse and the strength of their orgasms. His paraphilia (telephone scatologia or *telephonicophilia*) could have passed undetected, except that he supported his self-diagnosis with the false claim that he was a patient of Dr. John Money in the psychohormonal clinic at Johns Hopkins. Dismayed that they had been so easily hoaxed, several of the women, or their husbands, phoned me for verification. In this case, the impostor was not threatening, whereas others are stalkers by telephone. They know more than would a complete stranger about the past history and present work schedule of the women whom they phone, while maintaining themselves in complete anonymity. They may threaten the possibility of abduction and rape, but scaring the women is more important grist to the mill of their paraphilia than is the actuality of carrying out the threat.

Phone sex has been commercialized (Anthony 1998). Incoming calls are prepaid by credit card. They are predominantly from men who engage in interactive, sexually explicit talk while they masturbate to orgasm. To be effective, the talk must be congruous with the ideation and imagery of the caller's lovemap. From subtle cues, the skilled phone worker recognizes the configuration of the lovemap which, in some cases, is paraphilically morbid. Phone sex provides the anonymity without which the caller is unable to make what amounts to a confession of sexual practices that he finds both shameful and orgasmically rewarding. Some callers make repeat calls on a regular basis to the same phone sex worker and engage in what amounts to sexological therapy in which phone sex substitutes for dangerous, furtive, or illicit paraphilic practices.

It was by way of phone sex that a popular performance artist was enabled to write, and to be quoted with permission:

> No one knows of my fantasies. They have remained a secret of very many years. This is the very first time that I have admitted to them. Thank you. . . . In my fantasy, I always appear as Slave Girl Ramona, always submissive, and always dominated and abused by women. I never have a fantasy of being made a slave or being dominated by men. . . . I am always well dressed, forced

to strip, sometimes my clothing is ripped to shreds and torn from by body . . . I am forced to be a sex slave. I must serve drinks to imaginary guests who always throw the drinks all over me. Sometimes they throw food over me. I actually do these things to myself. Then all the mess has to be cleaned up. I am whipped for errors during this time. I am always placed in bondage. This can include ropes, chains, with padlocks, wrist and ankle leather cuffs. Quite often when in bondage, I will put out all the lights, place myself into a small space, i.e., in an imaginary dungeon. I then put lights onto a time switch, say 15–20 minutes ahead. I then remain in bondage, struggling in vain until the lights snap suddenly on, and my tormentors come to reclaim their victim. . . . I am always ordered to masturbate to a climax for their entertainment. I, of course, refuse to do this and am whipped (I do this to myself) until I scream for mercy and beg to be allowed to masturbate for the enraged women. . . . I don't always reach this stage. Sometimes I have climaxed far too soon. . . . My first sexual intercourse took place with a married woman who seduced me at a professional conference. I was thirty-two years old then. With my wife I have remained practically celibate, although we do have two children.

The most up-to-date source of interactive pornography is the Internet. Like noncommercial telephone sex, it provides the possibility of anonymity and impostoring, but not of harassment and surprise: people who log into the same chat room know in advance that they share the same paraphilic interest. If and when two people agree to meet in person, that may be the moment of surprise or disillusion and also of paraphilic danger. The Internet is a still untapped source of prime information concerning the paraphilias that are not ascertained in either the clinic or the courtroom. For example, the Internet has provided a forum for "squishers" whose paraphilia is to squash bugs and small slippery creatures.

Protectorship and Rescue

SOCIAL SPECIES OF animals and birds that live in flocks, families, or troops in many instances sound a warning call if danger threatens. Several such species provide an early warning system by having scouts stationed at strategic vantage points. Some species do more than issue warnings. They respond to cries of distress from group members and come to the aid of those who utter them. Among the great apes, an orphan infant survives only if adopted by a surrogate parent, as commonly is the case. Also, an aunt or other troop member might "borrow" an infant and watch out for its safety.

In a case that drew world wide attention in the media (Chicago Tribune, August 18, 1996, C1), a three-year-old boy clambered over a barrier and fell twenty-four feet onto the concrete of the lowland gorilla enclosure at Chicago's Brookfield Zoo. Binti-Jua, an eight-year-old mother with her own baby clinging to her back, gently picked up the unconscious boy and carried him to the gatekeepers' entry where the gorilla's keeper completed the rescue. Like adoption, this rescue exemplifies the stratagem of protectorship and rescue, namely, the provision of a missing service or the replacement of an absentee by a substitute or subrogate.

The phyletic underpinning of protectorship and rescue is subrogation. It is conjunctive with the phylisms of pairbondship and troopbondship. In the human species, it is an underpinning of the altruistic performance of care giving and supportive services.

Historically, the grand stratagem of subrogation—that is, of protectorship and rescue—has been overlooked as one of the seven grand stratagems of the lovemap. One of its paraphilic manifestations, *hetairaphilia* (from Greek, *hetaira*, fem. of *hetairos*, companion), has been condemned as a social evil rather than examined as a paraphilia. Yet, there are both men and women whose erotosexual role, with or without payment, is to be a Good Samaritan who rescues.

The history of prostitution has been written mostly as the history of the social evil of indentured sexual servitude and of children sold into sexual slavery, all of which is correct. There is no corresponding history, however, of prostitution as a paraphilic fixation which, indeed, it sometimes is: witness the case of the masochistic prostitute in chapter 5.

For the paraphilic prostitute or hustler, the risks and dangers of physical injury, sexually transmitted disease, and police entrapment are an integral part of hetairaphilia. So also is the plurality and anonymity of clients and the satisfaction of being able to supply them, maybe, with the special services such as oral sex, sadistic beating and humiliation, or cross dressing that they cannot obtain at home. The prostitute's most virtuoso performances are those in which the paraphilic imagery and ideation in her own lovemap and in the lovemap of her client are cross matched. For a masochistic client, for instance, a dominatrix who is not faking hetairaphilic sadism in her dungeon is far more satisfactory than one who is a perfunctory performer (Stoller 1985). A dominatrix may specialize in *klismaphikia* (giving enemas), *catheterophilia* (inserting a catheter into the urethra and bladder), in injecting saline solution so as to inflate the scrotum, and in piercing the genitals or other organs. The same procedures may be practiced in homosexual sadomasochism.

Whereas prostitution is generally institutionalized primarily as an entertainment for the sex deprived and for tourists and other transients in town, it caters also to clients whose lovemaps dictate an extended alliance only with a person who earns a living as a prostitute. Financially and otherwise, such a client may be a highly supportive Good Samaritan. One case of the Good Samaritan syndrome was that of a man with a severely deformed penis and pubertal hormonal deficiency. He reached the point of setting up suburban housekeeping with one of his prostitute friends. She drove her car to work every morning, and home in the evening, as did many other women in the neighborhood. In view of his sexual handicap, it appeared that their cooperative arrangement was ideal, since as a sex worker she did not lack a sufficiency of full sized penises. With him, she was satisfied with what work did not provide, namely, intimate cuddling and hugging. He could not tolerate the guilt of success, however, nor the lie of suburban normality. Logic notwithstanding, he deserted his partner and went back to the city streets of anonymity.

Women prostitutes perform lesbian acts for male clients whose response is enhanced by seeing a stimulus in duplicate and by the fantasy of one penis rescuing both of the women from themselves. Some prostitutes may have a lesbian predisposition; but, through lack of demand, they do not cater to a lesbian clientele. By contrast, male prostitutes or hustlers, although they may be gigolos with a female clientele, are likely also to have a male clientele, some exclusively so. A hustler may adopt the party line that he is in the trade of catering to males strictly for the money, and he may prove to be correct. By history, however, he is either bisexual or homosexual in practice. Similarly, the men whom he services may be, by history, either homosexual only, or bisexual and perhaps married with offspring. The hustler who lays a claim to being straight does so on the basis of the stereotype that his penis is invariably inserted into a receptive orifice, whereas his own orifices are off limits to a client's penis.

A defining characteristic of the client-prostitute sexual relationship is that it is a contract entered into with informed consent. The client expects and agrees to experience explicit erotic stimulation of the genitalia. In other professions, for example, in the medical specialties of urology and gynecology, the patient expects genital exposure, but not explicit erotic stimulation. That spells doom for any health care personnel with a paraphilic fixation on repetitiously and unilaterally changing the doctor-patient contract by introducing explicit erotic stimulation into the relationship. There was a time, half a century ago, when the word of the doctor was more likely to be given credence over that of the patient. Then, the pendulum swung the other way. In part, it swung in response to the demands of militant feminism and in part as a manifestation of the late twentieth-century counterrevolutionary antisexual assault on the sexual revolution of the 1960s and 1970s. False accusations of sexual harassment, molestation, and abuse have become a money making specialty for some attorneys and their clients.

Not all accusations are false. When they are recurrent, then it is likely that the role of protectorship and rescue has become pathologized as a fixated paraphilia. For instance, the case of a young doctor in training as a pediatric psychiatrist has been in the news of late (Bruni 1998). Despite professional reprimands, and a period of imprisonment, he has not been able to fulfill his resolution to abstain from getting sexually involved with male juveniles under his care. Pedophilia and ephebophilia haunt the protectorship and rescue professions, for example, those of priests, coaches of juvenile recreations and sports, and teachers. Some pedophiles are given to hypergraphia. In other words, they write extensive essays on the philosophy and justification of pedophilia. This phenomenon is worth mentioning insofar as hypergraphia is a characteristic of temporal lobe epilepsy (Lambert 1999) and deserves further investigation.

In addition to the phylism of subrogation, protectorship and rescue may rest also on the disparity between the phylisms of copulatory bonding and parental bonding. In a great many avian species, for example, nesting couples bond for life, each year sharing the building of a nest, incubating the young, and feeding them. In the absence of any conclusive test of paternity, it was assumed that the two parents copulated exclusively with one another. Following the recent arrival of DNA testing, that was discovered not to be so. Gowarty (quoted by Morell 1998) found that 15 percent to 20 percent of the chicks of Eastern bluebirds were sired not by the nesting father but another male. DNA tests of 180 species in which pairs bonded in providing parental care showed that in only 10 percent of species did the nesting pairs mate exclusively and monogamously with one another.

Among mammals, the avian system of pairbonding as parents, with or without copulatory fidelity, is rare. The California mouse is one species that exhibits both parental pairbonding and pairbonded fidelity. These mice and those of related species that practice infidelity have different receptor sites in their brains for the uptake of the neuropeptide hormones, oxytocin and vasopressin (Sue Carter, quoted by Morell 1998).

Infidelity is a logical non sequitur if applied to barnyard animals that breed opportunistically and indiscriminately, for there is no one to whom to be unfaithful. By contrast, fidelity is possible in species that live in extended families or troops, as do the majority of higher primates. Within the troop, a male and a female do not pairbond as parental caregivers. An infant's mother is its primary caregiver, with some assistance from other members of the troop. She does not become permanently pairbonded with the baby's father as a copulatory mate. However, if he commands sufficient authority in the dominance hierarchy of the troop, he may monopolize the right to copulate with her at the estrual or ovulatory stage of her menstrual cycle. If interested in another male, she may find a clandestine way to copulate with him, too. One maneuver is to wait until the dominant male is challenged by a competitor and to take advantage of his distraction by going off and copulating furtively with a second competitor. It is also possible that several females form an alliance which provides them with increased opportunity for adultery. Of course, adultery works both ways in giving an increased variety of sexual partners to both the males and the females, without destroying the communal parenting of the troop.

Like the majority of the primate species, we human beings are a troopbonding species. We are also a pairbonding species. A primate minority, which includes gibbons and South American marmosets and tamarins, are pairbonders. Human pairbondship combines the copulatory bond of preferential mating on the one hand, with the bond of parenting together on the other. The copulatory and the parenting components of a pairbond do not necessarily have the same lifespan. More often than not, the copulatory bond destabilizes first, and adultery promises to effect a compromise.

Sometimes adultery is consensual, as when a couple admits a third person and becomes a threesome (troilism), engages in wife swapping, or attends group sex parties. Sometimes adultery is tolerated, provided it is casual, so that the couple is able to retain the bond of parenting together.

One, if not both of the partners in adultery, may be regarded as a stand-in for the officially or legally recognized spouse. In this scenario, the adulterer may be on a rescue mission that, if repeated serially and without let up, amounts to a paraphilia of protectorship and rescue. An etymologically suitable term might be derived from *sotero*, savior: *soterophilia*. The same term might be used also for the particular scenario of incest. There was no generic word for incest in ancient Greek.

In one version of incest, a daughter is coerced into rescuing her mother from an abhorrent sexual relationship with her father. She takes on the role of little wife. If she complains to her mother, she is either ignored or condemned as a liar. If she complains to her father, she is threatened with reprisals. She is caught in a Catch-22 dilemma of having nowhere to turn. If she does not seek outside help, she lives under the cloud of unforeseen consequences, including possible pregnancy. If she does seek outside help, she is condemned to the probable break up of her family and the imprisonment of her father with whom she may be affectionately, albeit ambivalently, attached. The father's paraphilia is one of being persistently fixated on an untenable relationship and on rationalizing it.

In the case of an older stepdaughter with a new stepfather, the scenario of incest may be complicated by the girl's rivalry with her mother. If the girl is explicitly seductive toward her stepfather, he may prove to be too vulnerable.

Incestuous adultery may involve a father and son. An example is that of a paraphilic transvestite father whose wife could not respond to him sexually while he was cross dressed. His compromise took the form of a "television game" in which he would cross dress himself and his son to impersonate a mother and daughter. The game culminated in fellation of the son. In another case, a grandfather became involved with fondling a grandson when they both had to share a bed together after the grandfather, following his wife's death, moved into the crowded household of his married daughter. The counterpart of the father-daughter or stepfather-stepdaughter scenario is that of mother-son or stepmother-stepson.

The human species is a nest-sleeping species, and children like to nestle in bed with a parent where they are sheltered and out of harm's way. There is no clearcut transition from nestling as creature comfort and cuddling as a precursor to sexual arousal. After the onset of puberty, if not sooner, should a son continue to share his mother's bed, his proximity to her body, even without genital contact, is likely to be experienced as more erotically arousing than with which he can cope. For the mother, the son is a substitute for a missing husband or one with whom she is on the outs. In the clinic, this is the version of mother-son incest that one encounters more often than that of actual copulation. It registers as paraphilic and morbid in degree insofar as the mother's role is fixated and the son is caught in a Catch-22, without escape. The extent to which mother-son or mother-stepson incest goes unreported has not been ascertained. The same applies to paternal incest.

Juvenile sexual rehearsal play between siblings or other relatives of similar age is not paraphilic. Siblings and nonsiblings who grow up in close proximity in infancy and the early juvenile years, as in an Israeli kibbutz (Shepher 1971; see also Spiro 1958; Brown 1991), and whose sex education and play are not restricted are protected from incest in postpuberty. They do not experience adolescent romantic and erotic yearnings toward one another and do not marry one another. This erotic neutrality, the Westermarck effect, is named after the Finnish sociologist, Edward Westermarck (1922) (see also pp. 172–73). When the Westermarck effect fails, the greater the age discrepancy between the two participants, the greater the likelihood of paraphilic morbidity in the older of the two and, subsequently, in the younger one as well. The greater also the likelihood of a history of gross sexual dysfunctionality, including homicide, in the household of origin (Miccio-Fonseca 1996).

8

Intervention

Misfits in the Troop

L ong before the advent of the civilizations of our forebears, we human beings were troop-living primates as we still are. Continuity of the troop, whatever its size, from remote hamlet to nation state, is contingent on the conformity of individuals to their given or achieved position in the troop's power hierarchy.

Logically, there have always been three ways of dealing with non-conformity. One way is to provide a social niche within which it can be tolerated. The second way is not to tolerate nonconformity but to criminalize it and to quarantine, expel, incarcerate, or execute nonconformists. The third way is to attempt to change nonconformity into conformity. Historically and transculturally, each of these three ways of dealing with nonconformity has been diversely applied to unorthodox lovemaps. Societary tolerance of unorthodoxy in the lovemap is a sophisticated and relatively recent occurrence. Societary condemnation and eradication of lovemap unorthodoxy is globally of very ancient vintage. It is institutionalized in religious and secular legal doctrine. Societary policy on converting lovemap unorthodoxy to orthodoxy is contingent on the perceived efficacy of the methodology available at any given time. For example, the methodology of exorcism lost its perceived efficacy after demon possession theory was supplanted by germ theory at the end of the nineteenth century, even though germ theory had little of specific relevance to lovemap pathology itself, except for lovemap pathology as a tertiary symptom of syphilis.

An example of societary intolerance becoming tolerance is provided by the history of the rehabilitation of masturbation in the lovemap in the late twentieth century (Money 1985; 1999, chap. 15). For the preceding two centuries, intolerance of masturbation had been based on the revival and extension of the ancient theory of semen depletion, namely, that loss of semen from the secret vice of self-abuse brought on the same array of symptoms as did its loss from the social vice of promiscuity with whores. It required the discovery of germ theory to show that the diseases of promiscuity were caused by the microorganisms of syphilis and gonorrhea. Those organisms were transmitted by infected partners. The symptoms they produced had nothing to do with masturbation.

In contemporary Europe, America, and elsewhere, intolerance of the lovemaps of homosexuality is giving way to tolerance, though not without heavy political and religious counterattack. In the absence of an equivalent of germ theory with which to explain the origin of homosexuality, people take sides on whether homosexuality is a developmental condition that cannot be deconditioned or a voluntarily chosen sin against God's moral law.

Oral sex in the lovemap is a third example of intolerance giving way to tolerance. In the United States and many foreign states, fellatio and cunnilingus are purely private matters. Elsewhere, they are condemned as crimes against nature. In the United States, the states of Texas, Oklahoma, Arkansas, Missouri, and Kansas, at the close of the twentieth century, oral sex is a crime only if performed by two men, not a man and a woman, nor by two women.

The epidemic of bubonic plague, the Black Death, that devastated Europe in 1347, killed up to an estimated one third of all the population of Europe—75 percent or more of the population in some places. With the knowledge of twentieth-century hindsight, it is known to have been caused by the bacterium *Yersinia pestis*, transmitted by the bite of a flea living on an infected rat. Superstition of the middle ages attributed the plague in part to the presence of Jews in a Christian community. So Jews were sealed in their houses and incinerated or left to starve to death (Mee 1990). Today, bubonic plague can be prevented by immunization and cured with antibiotics.

Six and a half centuries since the Black Death, there still are no equivalents of immunizations or antibiotics with which to allay people's anxieties and superstitions regarding lovemaps that they define as being too quirky, bizarre, or hazardous. Public policy is to nullify unorthodox lovemaps by criminalizing them and by sequestering or disposing of their owner. Medically, this policy is the equivalent of dealing with hypertension by getting rid of all patients with high blood pressure before they die with a heart attack. Execution of an offender with a paraphilic lovemap deprives biomedical science of the possibility of discovering the cause, prevention, and cure of the offending type of paraphilia. It eliminates repeat offenses by the same offender, but it does nothing to eliminate the recurrence of the same paraphilia in the oncoming generation. The more heinous the paraphilic offense, as in serial lust rape and murder, the greater the research need in society to find a way of preventing the paraphilia from developing in a child in the first place. Permanent quarantine of a paraphile protects society. It also permits new research discoveries, which the death penalty does not. Moreover, the possibility of participating in a scientific breakthrough into the cause of their condition is something that intrigues a number of paraphiles. They would give signed and informed consent to volunteer as experimental subjects, for they are as mystified as are the rest of us by the pathology of their lovemaps, its automaticity, and its resistance to change by voluntary effort.

The ethical principle of the law on execution or a lifetime of incarceration is not forthrightly stated as vengeance, nor as societary protection. Instead, it is upheld with the principles of the corrective value of punishment in modifying behavior and in setting an example that will discourage future offenders. These principles are so enshrined in the philosophy of the criminal justice system that to question them is heresy. However, the fact is that they are not scientifically supported with empirical data. They are, as they have been for centuries, invincible dogmas. The law is always right. It needs no proof, only precedent, which may be factually outdated and moribund.

Modalities of Intervention

THE THIRD METHOD of dealing with sexological nonconformity is to intervene with a view to bringing about change. In contemporary medicine, there are three targets of intervention: the lab results, the organ system, or the whole person. Each of the three is effective if tailored to time and place. Treating the lab results is effective as a public health measure. To prevent the spread of an infectious or toxic epidemic, it may be necessary to identify asymptomatic carriers by laboratory testing so as to protect the uninfected population from exposure to the infectious or toxic agent. Compulsory immunizations are also a method of preventive control of the spread of disease, as are likewise compulsory additives to the water or food supply, like antibacterial chlorination of the water supply, fluoridization of water to inhibit dental decay, and iodization of salt to prevent endemic cretinism.

Some people are resistant to protective epidemiologic procedures, and some are indifferent to the logic of being treated for symptoms that they do not yet have. This, no doubt, accounts for the failure of many whose lovemaps put them at risk for hepatitis B to get themselves immunized against the virus.

Targeting the organ system is the veterinary way of medicine, since the animal cannot speak. For many patients, it fulfills their expectation of a pill or a potion that will fix up whatever is wrong with them. One of the newest triumphs in targeting the organ system is the treatment of penial impotence with the pill Viagra (sildenafil). Its efficacy, at around 70 percent, is independent of whether or not the lovemap is to some degree paraphilic.

Lovemaps themselves have not, up until now, yielded any lab results that have proved to be efficacious targets of intervention; nor have even the most morbidly paraphilic lovemaps yielded a clue as to their clandestine organ system (undoubtedly in the brain) that might prove to be a suitable target for therapeutic intervention. In consequence, there is no alternative but to target any attempt at treatment or rehabilitation at the whole person (Cawte 1996).

In the holistic approach to health, it is axiomatic that patient compliancy is prerequisite. Then, incomplete compliancy, such as having insufficient faith, repentance, remorse, abstinence, obedience, or whatever is sufficient to explain failure to improve. In this way, the power and authority of the healer has been upheld since the earliest era of the witch doctor or the shaman until the present day.

When the interventions of modern laboratory and organ-system medicine fail in the treatment of paraphilic lovemap morbidity, then, apart from permanent incarceration or execution, there is no alternative but to revert to the ancient principles of witch-doctor medicine as transformed into contemporary practices. Altogether, there are six principles.

The first is to provide a supportive convalescent environment and to be ready to take rehabilitative advantage of a spontaneous remission, should it occur.

The second is to provide somesthetic, massage therapy with the healing hands, perhaps in combination with acupuncture for pain relief, relaxation and meditation therapy, exercise and fitness therapy, and sensate-focus homework assignments in sex therapy.

The third is to prescribe dietetic rules of what to eat and what to avoid eating and drinking, together with rules of fresh air, special clothing, hard bedding, and avoidance of sexual stimulation.

The fourth is to provide the patient (or client) with the possibility of troopbonding in group therapy for social skills, sex education, or sobriety from so-called sexual addiction. Group therapy is a two edged sword. Its members may form a covert network that endorses rather than repudiates their shared paraphilia.

The fifth is to provide training therapy, generically known as behavior-modification therapy. Training therapy is adapted from the method of reward and punishment long known to animal trainers. Theoretically, it is derived from principles of conditional reflexology and operant conditioning. When applied in conjunction with electronic instrumentation that displays the degree of the subject's response to a stimulus, it goes under the name of biofeedback.

The sixth practice is to provide talktime therapy sessions modeled after the confessional and the unburdening of personal confidences in dialogues with trusted kith or kin. *Psychotherapy* is the gentrified name of talking therapy. Some call it insight therapy. There are many schools and doctrines of psychotherapy and counseling, all of which trace their ancestry back to the application of hypnosis to psychiatry in the nineteenth century, and its eventual metamorphosis into Freudian psychoanalysis by the end of the century. One of the newest schools is cognitive-behavioral.

The convergence of all six of these methods of intervention is that they assist the individual to cope in the best way possible with the morbidity of a pathological lovemap that cannot yet be effectively depathologized. Moreover, the assistance is nonjudgmental, without which the paraphile is not helped but alienated.

Androgen Depletion

THERE IS NO historical record of the discovery of the demasculinizing effect of the castration of domesticated animals, nor of when demasculinization was applied to human males either punitively or to render them more docile as slaves. By contrast, it is known that eugenics, the theory of the purification of the human race by castration of the genetically unfit to breed, followed closely on the heels of Darwin's *Origin of Species* in 1859. Those considered unfit to breed included the mentally retarded, the insane, the epileptic, and the sexually deviant. Castration as a eugenic policy, which reached its apogee in Hitler's Germany, is not far removed from castration as a punishment for sex offenders.

In Europe after World War II, castration for sexual deviancy was retained in the forensic law of the former West Germany, though now on a voluntary basis only. It has continued to be legal, though seldom performed, in several other European countries like Switzerland. By contrast, it was not legalized in Canada and the United States. On the contrary, in San Diego, California, two forty-five-year-old pedophiles who had been found guilty of "exciting the lust of a child" were sentenced to life imprisonment after pleading to be castrated instead (*New York Times*, October 25, 1975; February 15, 1976). The judge had agreed to put the men on probation postoperatively but, after a year of waiting, no surgeon could be found who was willing to run the risk of a malpractice suit.

Two decades later, a sixty-year-old British pedophilic offender with a history of multiple offenses and a total of seventeen years in prison was, after six years of pleading to be castrated, the first sex offender in Britain to receive the operation (*The Sunday Times*, October 23, 1994). A year later, he befriended an eleven-year-old boy with whom he became infatuated.

Castration for the prevention of sex offending or reoffending is based on the premise that the lower the level of male hormone, testosterone, in the bloodstream, the lower the level of sex drive or libido. Since the testicles are the main source of testosterone, a eunuch should, like the gelded male of many though not all animal species, manifest no sex driven behavior. That, however, is not the case, for castration returns a postpubertal human male to the status of a prepubertal boy, and prepubertal males are capable of some manifestations of sexuality, including penile erection. Moreover, in the present day and age, the blood level of testosterone can easily be brought up to par by means of synthetic testosterone taken daily by mouth or monthly by injection. The only irreversible effect of castration that can be guaranteed with certainty is sterility. Individual diversity after castration is exemplified by Wille and Beier (1989) in their extensive study here excerpted:

> All castrates showed reduced sexual interest and activity, reduced erotic fantasies, and reduced capability of spontaneous or stimulated erections. In most cases, the amount of intercourse and number of ejaculations were also reduced within 6 months after the operation. A more careful exploration, however, revealed important individual differences. In some cases, libido and erection returned to the preoperational level within 6 months after surgery but ejaculation naturally was not restored. One-third of the castrated men still sometimes had spontaneous morning erections, but not as often as in the past. Approximately 25% of all castrated men were still capable of intercourse after 3 years and 20% still after 5 years; admittedly at greater intervals and only after intensive stimulation. There was an increased new need for skin contact and petting without coitus. As subjective experience, the loss of the testicles was the gravest impairment to masculinity. The castrated men felt stigmatized by their empty scrota. For this reason, the operation was kept secret to a circle of acquaintances and only the wife or female partner was informed. All men involved reported surprise at the understanding shown by their female sex partners.

Wille and Beier quote one case in particular that shows the danger of assuming that castration will cure morbid lovemap pathologies.

> This one case is in several ways, exceptional and made spectacular criminal case history in West Germany. This applicant of average intelligence (IQ=93) was burdened by divorce and chaotic family life as a child. After completing an apprenticeship as a butcher and military service, he abused alcohol and had an unsteady work history. He was involved in minor delinquency, but also carried out a violent pedophilic assault on a girl. After a suspended sentence, he underwent psychotherapeutic treatment which he soon discontinued because he did not think it was working. Three years later, at the age of 30, a pedophilic offence followed and then he was committed to a psychiatric hospital. At that time he was castrated and he was soon released into the community and he returned to his fiancée. After 1 1/2 years, he achieved legal permission for hormone substitution therapy employing androgens with the aim of improving his severely diminished libido and his erection/cohabitation difficulties. This was accompanied by a revival of his pedophilic inclinations. Following sexual contact with a 7-year-old girl, he ended up killing her. During the period of detention, two follow-up interviews took place. A few weeks later in court, under the eyes of the interviewer, he was shot dead by the mother of the murdered girl.

The steroid hormones from the gonads, estrogen and progesterone (female hormones) from the ovaries, and testosterone (male hormone) from the testes were isolated in the 1920s, synthesized in the 1930s, and marketed in the 1940s. As well as feminization, one of the properties of estrogen proved to be antiandrogenic and demasculinizing. Consequently, for a period of time, estrogen became popular for its ability to mimic the effects of surgical castration in the treatment of male sex offenders. Its effects, unlike those of surgical castration, could be reversed upon cessation of treatment, except for enlargement of the breasts (gynecomastia) which could be flattened only by surgery (mastectomy). The long term outcome of estrogen therapy on sex offending paraphilias proved to be, in general, idiosyncratic and unpredictable with respect to success or failure.

The way the body works in producing the steroid hormones is to begin with cholesterol from which, in progression, it synthesizes progesterone from which it synthesizes testosterone from which finally it synthesizes estrogen. Historically, the commercial synthesis of progesterone and related progestinic hormones began with a soapy substance (saponin) found in Mexican tropical plants by Russell Marker (summarized in Money 1997b, 162). It made possible the development of the contraceptive Pill. It also made feasible the use of artificially synthesized steroidal, progestinic hormones as antiandrogens for the treatment of paraphilic sex offenders.

Cyproterone acetate (CPA), now marketed under the trade name of Androcur in Europe, was the antiandrogen that was first used for the treatment of paraphilias, it was developed and tested as an antiandrogen on rats by Friedmund Neumann (1966) at the Schering A. G. Laboratories in West Berlin. Its first human use was under Hans Giese at the sex research institute of Hamburg University in West Germany. I learned about it when I visited there in July 1966. The first patient was a severely mentally retarded boy whose education had come to a halt as he masturbated so constantly that he could not appear in public. The second patient was a farmer who had been arrested for molestation of young girls. The boy became able to refrain from masturbating in public, and the farmer, still under observation, was perhaps improving.

Very soon after I returned to Baltimore, I was confronted with a case of pedophilic incest between a transvestitic father and his six-year-old son. After a brief period of resistance, the father volunteered for any form of treatment, including aversion therapy, but none could be found. Then, as now, cyproterone acetate could not be prescribed for use in the United States, as it had not been cleared by the Food and Drug Administration. I consulted with two endocrine specialist colleagues, Claude Migeon and Marco Rivarola. They suggested an alternative antiandrogenic treatment, namely, with the hormone, medroxyprogesterone acetate (MPA) marketed as Depo-Provera (Upjohn). Together with joint family counseling (Money 1968, 1970), MPA allowed pedophilic incest to desist.

The significance of the foregoing historical fragments is not that antiandrogenic hormones have become a panacea for the treatment of all paraphilic pathology, which they have not, but that they represent the thin edge of the wedge that opens the way for the transfer of paraphilic pathology from demonology and criminology to the realm of biomedical science. There is no evidence, as yet, of a straight line of hormonal cause and paraphilic effect (see reviews by Bradford

1990; Hucker and Bain 1990; Lehne 1994; Gijs and Gooren 1996; Kravitz et al. 1996; Bradford 1997; Balon 1998).

In molecular structure, MPA and CPA are both steroidal hormones. Flutamide (trade named Eulexia) is a nonsteroidal antiandrogen taken orally. It is a 5α-reductase inhibitor, which prevents the intracellular conversion of testosterone to 5α-dihydrotestosterone, the active metabolite of testosterone essential for some target cells. It has been used clinically for the treatment of prostate cancer, but has not been tested systemically for its antiandrogenic effect on paraphilias.

Although MPA and CPA are both antiandrogenic, their pathways of action differ from that of flutamide and from one another. Androcur suppresses the production of androgen by inhibiting an enzyme prerequisite to the synthesis of all steroids bilaterally in the gonads and also in the adrenocortical glands. MPA does so by suppressing release of the pituitary gonadotropic hormones, LH (luteinizing hormone) and FSH (follicle stimulating hormone), without which the gonads cannot make their own hormones. For the duration of treatment, MPA and CPA both reduce the frequency of erection and the amount of the ejaculate. Both effects are reversible.

Although MPA has seldom been offered to female paraphiles, preliminary evidence indicates that it may help them, too. The level of testosterone in the normal female is very low in comparison with the male, but sufficient to qualify it as a so-called libido hormone for women (Money 1961; Sherwin 1988). By reducing even a low level of testosterone still lower, MPA may have the same effect as in male paraphiles, as well as having the same effect on the female as the male hypothalamus.

A direct action of MPA on the hypothalamus may be conjectured from the rapidity of its effect in suppressing the floridly delusional and hallucinatory symptoms of the periodic psychosis of puberty (Berlin et al. 1982; Abe and Ohta 1992). Its diagnosis is often missed, and this psychosis fluctuates in synchrony with the menstrual cycle and is at its worst in the high estrogen phase of the cycle. It improves as the progesterone phase takes over. Exogenous estrogen has a toxic effect and exaggerates the psychotic symptoms. Another conjecture of a direct action of MPA on hypothalamic cells is derived from the known antianxiety, hypnotic, and anesthetic effects of progesterone (Freeman et al. 1993; Meyerson 1967).

The hypothalamus, a small organ of the brain situated bilaterally deeply behind the bridge of the nose, is an important part of the still unfolding story of sex and the brain. From its posterior region, hypothalamic cells produce releasing hormones that instruct the adjacent pituitary gland to release its own hormones, two of which are the gonadotropins, LH and FSH. They are released by GnRH (gonadotropin releasing hormone) which is also referred to as LHRH. According to the evidence of animal studies, the posterior region of the hypothalamus mediates the hormones of reproduction, whereas the anterior region mediates the behavior.

MPA reaches the hypothalamus rapidly after being intramuscularly injected. In male monkeys, in as short a time as fifteen minutes following injection, molecules of MPA were found to have been taken up by receptors attached to neurons in sexual nuclei of the preoptic area of the anterior hypothalamus, but not elsewhere in the brain (Rees et al. 1986; Michael and Zumpe 1993).

Hypothetically, in human beings the anterior hypothalamus might mediate not only the behavior of mating, but also the imagery and ideation that instigates this behavior—hence the clinical interest in molecular analogues, also referred to as agonists, or antagonists, of LHRH. One of the LHRH analogues—leuprolide acetate, trade named Lupron—is a synthetic nonapeptide that possesses greater potency than naturally occurring LHRH (GnRH). Lupron was first used to suppress gonadotropin and hence testicular androgen in the treatment of prostate cancer. Eventually, it was discovered to have a peculiar and novel property of pulsatility—namely, that if released in pulses, it would induce and maintain puberty, whereas if released continuously from a long-acting injection it would suppress puberty that had begun precociously at age six or younger. It is intriguing to speculate that pulsatility may in some way mediate the development or else the suppression of a paraphilia, but that possibility has not yet been investigated. In the meantime, Lupron has been used for its antiandrogenic effect in the treatment of paraphilias. It has not yet been systematically compared with MPA, nor with other GnRH analogues, of which one is goserelin acetate, trade named Zoladex. Zoladex is used as a long-acting implant. In Britain, it has proved successful in some cases of paraphilia that were resistant to CPA and MPA (Russell Reid personal communication).

Another GnRH analogue, triptorelin, manufactured in Sweden, has recently been used for the treatment of paraphilic sex offenders in France (Cordier et al. 1996; Thibaut et al. 1996) and in Israel (Rosler and Witzum 1998). Like Lupron and goserelin, triptorelin was successful in reducing testosterone in the bloodstream to a prepubertal level and in reducing paraphilic expression. Both of these reductions were contingent on compliancy.

Serotonergics

FROM THE LATE 1950s onward, in addition to the androgen-depleting medications, two quite unrelated sets of new drugs opened a window of opportunity from which to view the pharmacology of sexual functions. One set, like guanethidine monosulphate (Ismelin), was for the control of hypertension. The other set, the psychotropics, like thioridazine (Mellaril), a major tranquilizer, was for the control of psychotic symptoms and moods. Initially, there was no mention of sexual side effects of these drugs in clinical publications. Then sporadic reports of a possible negative side effect on male libido began to appear namely, a dry-run orgasm usually with erectile and ejaculatory insufficiency. Initially, the corresponding diminution of libido in women received no mention.

In an Ismelin study of hypertensive patients, one of the volunteer control subjects wrote an exceptionally lucid self-report:

> Even more disturbing than these side effects was my general attitude while taking the larger amounts of Ismelin. I was physically immobilized. Towards the end of the second week I had become increasingly depressed and unable to pursue any of my usual academic or social activities. I just didn't seem to care about anything. This was especially disturbing since I had never experienced such extreme languor. Normally I'm energetic with a positive, aggressive attitude. It was this change that led me to decide to stop taking the drug. About three days after I stopped, life began to return to normal.

> I suppose that it was worthwhile to experience what a depression must be like. Now I can appreciate the dilemma of those unfortunates whose lives amount to little because they just don't care what happens. In retrospect, I am surprised that I did not blame the drug but rather sought elsewhere in my daily experience for a

rationalization of this novel and alien change of self. (Money and
Yankowitz 1967)

According to the data of this study, the effect of the drug was
dose responsive. In sequence, it lowered the blood pressure, then
with dosage increase brought on sexual anhedonia, and finally induced severe apathy and depression. This sequence reversed the commonly held assumption that sexual anhedonia is a symptom of
depression, not a precursor of it.

The drug induced diminution of libido by psychotropic drugs led
to occasional speculation regarding the possible use of these drugs to
control a presumptive excess of libido in repetitious sex offending.
However, nothing came of these early speculations, probably because
libido reduction was a side effect of the drugs that could not be predicted or controlled. However, as new psychotropics were synthesized and increasingly used, so did the evidence of their sexual side
effects accumulate (Gitlin 1994).

The side effects of antidepressants were to some extent paradoxi-
cally inconsistent. Libido, for example, was reported to be either decreased or increased, and orgasm as either spontaneous, delayed,
anhedonic, or absent (anorgasmia). Erection either failed or persisted
as priapism which affected the clitoris as well as the penis. In some
men ejaculation was delayed or suppressed, and in some women
vaginal lubrication was insufficient. Genital numbness or anesthesia
was also reported. These various side effects were published as clinical observations, not as prevalence statistics. Regardless of whether
they were regarded as suppressors or enhancers, their significance
was, like that of the androgen depleters, that they demonstrated a direct pharmacologic action on sexual function.

One trailblazing report (Fedoroff 1988) was of a man with a severe problem of generalized anxiety. It could be relieved by alcohol
or by masturbating while cross dressed, which occurred approxi-
mately four times a month. Sexual intercourse, only once every two
or three months with his wife, required a concurrent fantasy of being
cross dressed. In addition to psychotherapy, he was treated with al-
prazolam (Xanax), one of the benzodiazepine class of central nervous system drugs. The drug was ineffectual. If he stopped drinking,
anxiety worsened. Therefore, he was started on buspirone (BuSpar),
an antidepressant, which had the unforeseen effect of abolishing
cross dressing. He had intercourse with his wife, weekly, without

being dependent on cross dressing, in actuality or fantasy, in order to get an erection and to ejaculate. When buspirone was withdrawn for a trial period, the symptoms returned.

One of the characteristics of buspirone is that, by mimicking the neurotransmitter serotonin, it blocks the synaptic reuptake of serotonin by receptors in brain neurons. Medications that disrupt the normal uptake serotonin, collectively known as serotonergics (Borne 1994), are most widely used for the treatment of depression.

The most popular serotonergic medication is fluoxetine (Prozac), a selective serotonin reuptake inhibitor (SSRI). It first became commercially available in the early 1990s. Despite its great popularity as a positive mood enhancer, Prozac had a major drawback, namely that it has a sporadic inhibiting effect on sexual function. Men complained of having difficulty in getting an erection and in being able to reach orgasm. Some complained also of less frequent sexual arousal. Though disadvantageous for most users of Prozac and the other SSRIs, this sexually inhibiting side effect could be taken advantage of as a sexual suppressant effect in the treatment of paraphilic sex offenders.

Nearly twenty years before the Prozac era, one of Prozac's serotonergic predecessors, clomipramine (Anafranil), while being prescribed as an antidepressant, had been recognized as being beneficial also for the treatment of obsessive compulsive disorder (OCD) in at least some cases, such as *trichotillomania* (depilation from compulsive hair pulling) (Rapoport 1989; Cooper 1996).

The ideation and imagery of paraphilia is often characterized by paraphiles of all ages, male and female, as an obsession, and its translation into action as a compulsion. Sooner or later, therefore, the serotonergic treatment of OCD would be applied to paraphilia (Kafka and Prentky 1992; Kruesi et al. 1992; Fedoroff 1995). The outcome of treatment was not consistent, but variable according to individual idiosyncracy and type and dosage of medication. Nonetheless, the serotonergics have opened another new window of opportunity for the treatment of paraphilias, as well as for understanding the brain neurochemistry that sustains them.

Lithium Carbonate

ALTHOUGH IT IS not classified as a selective serotonin uptake inhibitor, lithium carbonate increases the body's supply of serotonin by stimulating the conversion of the precursor substance, L-tryptophan, to serotonin. Although it has been used in the treatment of manic-depressive bipolarity for half a century (see review by Jefferson 1998), lithium carbonate has been prescribed for the treatment of paraphilic disorders only in the century's final decade. Clinically, it has proved to be ameliorative. Examples are the treatment of two cases of autoerotic self-strangulation (asphyxiophilia) (Cesnik and Coleman 1989); one case of the skoptic syndrome of fixation on becoming a eunuch (Coleman and Cesnik 1990); and one case of self-exposure and assault with extreme social phobia (Veenhuizen et al. 1992). Besides being a treatment option, lithium carbonate adds to what the antiandrogens and SSRIs contribute to the basic neuroscience of the sexology of paraphilias.

Cognitive-Behavioral

THE PHARMACEUTICAL revolution of the mid-1950s in psychiatry bypassed the paraphilias which were still officially classified as crimes, perversions, or deviancies.

For the most part, the paraphilias have been relegated to the criminal justice system and not to medicine and science. One early and brief exception pertained to psychosurgery. It entailed surgically deconnecting sexual pathways in the hypothalamus from their projections to cognitional relays elsewhere in the cerebral cortex. This was a procedure based on animal experimental data and on prefrontal lobotomy for the treatment of schizophrenia and obsessive compulsive disorder. The outcome was unsatisfying and, on the basis of ethical criticism, the practice of psychosurgery did not survive.

In the aftermath of World War II, Freudian psychiatry became increasingly Americanized. Orthodox psychoanalytic theory became broadened and known as psychodynamic theory. The search for the psychodynamic origins of the sexual perversions or deviations (they were not yet known as paraphilias) became a challenge that was pursued by American neo-Freudians. Homosexuality, even though Freud himself had declared it not to be an illness, was targeted as a perversion to be treated, not as a legitimate sexual orientation to be tolerated. Although no one recognized it at the time, homosexuals were in the vanguard of decriminalizing sexual unorthodoxy by bringing it into the realm of medicine, science, and health.

Another move away from criminalization toward medicalization came from within the criminal justice system itself. It was brought into effect by the Supreme Bench of Baltimore on the recommendation of its Chief Medical Officer, Manfred S. Guttmacher. He referred a select group of nonviolent sex offenders to a Johns Hopkins psychiatrist, Jacob E. Conn (1949; 1954), for a psychodynamic brand of therapy to which Conn gave the name *hypnosynthesis*. In concordance with John C. Whitehorn, the chairman of his department, Conn differentiated the meaning of a symptom from its cause. He emphasized not the sexual offending, but its interpersonal correlation with, for example, insufficiency of self-esteem or of self-assertion. Conn's therapy sessions combined talking with the patient in quasi-hypnotic relaxation and were directed toward attainment of insight. They lasted for half an hour, initially weekly and then biweekly. They were maintained for six months to as long as five years. A probation officer interviewed the men on a monthly basis. They were on probation for child molestation, indecent exposure, homosexuality, obscene mail or phone calls, and arson. Of twenty-three cases, nineteen were rated as "socially adjusted" at followup which ranged from six months to nine years.

Contemporaneously with the development of psychodynamic therapy for sex offenders, behavior modification therapy was imported into American psychiatry from South Africa by Joseph Wolpe and Arnold Lazarus (Wolpe 1969). Behavior modification theory was derived from the Pavlovian conditional reflex paradigm and John B. Watson's behaviorism (Watson 1930) in combination with B. F. Skinner's operant conditional paradigm (Skinner 1953).

The advent of the psychopharmaceutic revolution attracted the oncoming generation of psychiatrists away from the time-consuming and costly practice of psychodynamic and behavioral modification forms of therapy. That opened a new discount market for the services of certified practitioners in clinical psychology, marriage counseling, and social work. All told, these newcomers began and continue to practice either some form of psychodynamic (talking) therapy, or of behavioral modification therapy, or the combination of both that has become known as cognitive-behavioral therapy.

In all talking therapy, the technology is uncomplicated, namely talking and listening, with or without audiotape or videotape recording.

The differences between talking therapies are differences in ideology. In style they may be interrogatory, confrontational, accusatory, authoritarian, and didactic; or they may be versus nondirective, open-ended, nonjudgmental, and collaborative. Talking therapy may be combined with quasi-hypnotic relaxation or, more rarely, with induction of a full hypnotic trance.

Although not normally classified as cognitive therapy, self-cures are closely related. Getting married is one example. It is commonly undertaken by cross dressers. Resorting to alcohol or other drugs is another form of an attempted self-cure. There are some who also turn to churches or cults for religious cures. Self-cures are typically of no avail.

The behavioral part of cognitive behavioral therapy is not the same as veterinary behavioral modification, for its involves instructions conveyed in words. It resembles animal training, however, in being based on reward and punishment. For example, it was formerly fashionable to treat homosexuality by harnessing the penis to a plethysmograph, an apparatus that detected any degree of erectile enlargement in response to visual stimuli. If pictures of naked males produced a response, then the homosexual subject was punished with either an electric shock or a stinking odor. The aversive stimulus would be avoided only by pressing the button for heterosexual stimuli. The outcome was not conversion of the lovemap to heterosexuality. In some cases it was experimental panic; and in some, it was impotence in response to any erotic stimulus.

Another version of avoidance therapy that proved futile was to require masturbation to the point of orgasm and then to enforce continuous masturbation far beyond the point of penile satiation and aversive painfulness.

A more benign treatment design would have been the positive one of rewarding a series of masturbatory exercises to a series of heterosexual stimuli with an orgasm from a sexy homosexual stimulus; and to require an ever increasing number of heterosexual stimuli in order to earn the reward of a sexy homosexual stimulus.

To prove itself valid, behavior modification to convert homosexuals into heterosexuals should, of course, prove itself valid to convert heterosexuals to homosexuals, which it does not do, unless the person has a bisexual disposition with which to begin. By the same token, behavior modification should be able to convert anyone into a pedophile, which is not possible. In fact, it is not possible to produce any type of paraphilia by behavior modification of a lovemap which lacks the necessary predisposition.

Surrogacy

ONE OF THE deficiencies of behavior modification in the treatment of any type of sexual offence, dysfunction, or disability is that treatment must, because of societal prudishness and taboo, be done at one remove from observed behavior. For example, a pedophile incarcerated for having sex with underaged girls cannot undergo reward training for engaging in sexual intercourse with consenting adult females if the prison where he is held is sex segregated. Prison is an unreal world.

If Masters and Johnson (1966) had taken on sex therapy with prisoners, they might have circumvented the impediment of sex segregation by introducing surrogate sexual partners for the treatment of sex offenders who had also a problem of impotence or other sexual inadequacy.

Some upper echelon call-girls have always known that, among their regular male clients, some were as much in need of talking therapy as of copulatory relief. There is, for example, the case of a congenitally intersexed man with an embarrassingly small micropenis that had responded poorly to multiple attempts at corrective surgery. His wife, a chronically impaired invalid was unable to cope with sexual intercourse. He found salvation in the person of a masseuse, in the days when sexual massage parlors were still legal. This lady worked there as a masseuse so as to finance her two children through college. Helping people had always been her line of work. She helped her intersexual client by not remarking on his deformed genitalia, by always bringing him to a "delightful" orgasm, and by listening to his work and home related tales. After the parlor closed, they maintained nonsexual, social contact.

The first generation of surrogate sex therapists included some with a history of having been a prostitute by profession. Others were volunteers. To supplement the talking treatment of the primary sex and marital therapist, surrogates were trained in how and when to use nongenital sensate focus for excessively shy and inhibited clients or for those with performance anxiety. For clients with premature ejaculation, they were trained in the squeeze technique. They gave explicit demonstration of the female genital anatomy to those who had never had a sexual partner. When clients are suitably screened, surrogate therapy has had its fair share of success, but it does not work for everyone—not for pedophiles, for example, whether heterosexually or homosexually oriented.

One of the deficits of surrogate therapy is that it shortchanges the proceptive phase of a sexualized and romantic encounter, even if the surrogate and a socially inept client do some socializing, like going out to dinner and the theater. By the rules of the game, pairbonding in a love affair and a therapeutic dependency relationship are also ruled out.

Among the helping professions, surrogate sex therapy is unconventional. However, being unconventional is a far cry from being morbidly paraphilic. That does not rule out the possibility that some surrogates and some of their clients might happen to be paraphilic in some degree.

The heyday of surrogate sex therapy was in the 1970s. It extended into the 1980s, until the delayed recognition of the full impact of the HIV/AIDS epidemic hit home. Surrogacy then entered an era of dormancy and is still waiting for the epidemic to be brought under control.

Support and Therapy Groups

THE ECONOMICS OF one-on-one sexological intervention of any type, even if it is brief, puts it beyond the reach of all but a select few. This economic limitation has worsened under the present system of managed care that limits long-term insurance reimbursements for the treatment of psychiatric disabilities, overall, not only for sexological pathologies. One response to this economic limitation has been the formation of self-help support groups modeled on the twelve-step system of Alcoholics Anonymous, even down to the name, Sexoholics Anonymous. There is, however, no exact parallel between the two. An alcoholic may give up alcohol entirely, but there is no substance equivalent to alcohol that all members of an S. A. group may give up entirely. Total abstinence from sex would be the equivalence of total abstinence from drinking all fluids, not just alcohol. S. A. groups often splinter on whether masturbation is permitted or not.

The exact counterpart of an A. A. group in sexology would be an S. A. group comprised of individuals with the same clinical manifestation.

Cross-dressing is a good example, as the cross-dressing transgender people, as they now call themselves, already have a national and international network of self-help support groups. However, they are ideologically committed to self-help in cross-genderism, not in abstaining from it. Their membership includes professionally qualified surgeons, physicians, and counselors who specialize in transgender care, including sex reassignment.

People who assemble in self-help groups may be at ideological cross purposes. This is what happens sometimes in the group therapy that is provided as part of the follow-up of sex offenders after they have been started on individual treatment with medication. Professionally supervised group therapy is, like self-help support groups, economical. In addition, it allows members of the group to compare themselves with one another and to impose peer constraints on evasiveness or prevarication. On the negative side, it allows the too reticent to yield to the voluble and also allows for the formation of collusions among members who say one thing, and after the group meeting, socialize and do another. Information from family members or other sources is necessary though not always available. It may also be slanted by collusional pathology. There are no easy ways in the treatment of paraphilic sex offenders.

Megan's Law

THE NONMEDICAL, NONSCIENTIFIC approach of the criminal-justice system to the problem of paraphilic violence and murder produced both state and federal laws that commemorate the name of Megan Kanka, a seven-year-old girl who was paraphilically abducted and murdered in New Jersey, in 1994. Her abductor, having already completed a term of imprisonment as a repeat sex offender had been released to return to the neighborhood in which the girl had been abducted.

One of the dogmas of law is that the punishment of a perpetrator of child sexual abuse by imprisonment will act as a deterrent against future victimization. Despite the amount of prison based research given over to the statistics of recidivism, there is no proof of the correctness of this ancient dogma, nor is there any way of prophesying who will be a future recidivist and who will not. Megan's law makes the assumption that all convicted perpetrators of child sexual abuse are at risk to perpetrate again and should, therefore, be registered after release from prison as sex offenders publicly identifiable by name and address in the communities in which they live.

Legislators, not being social scientists, are not required to submit any evidence that a new law will be effective. Thus, there is at present no evidence of what will happen to the community in which the identified former offender lives. One possibile scenario is that panicky property owners will sell out at a loss and relocate. Their community and its surroundings may then degenerate and act as a magnet that attracts exconvicts. Moreover, for those property owners who relocate, there is no guarantee that their new neighborhoods, or even their own households will be free of pedophilic or of any other type of offender including ostensibly normal school children who ambush their classmates and teachers and kill them, as has happened in 1998 and 1999.

Megan's law is not restricted to New Jersey, but has been legislated in other states also. D. J. West (1998) has written lucidly of the confusion and illogicality that encompasses the issue of child abuse and protection in the United Kingdom. The possibility of vigilantism has already materialized in far away Wellington, New Zealand, as reported in the *Evening Post*, November 18, 1998. Neighbors circulated flyers identifying the name and address of the wife of a twenty-five-year-old man who, three years earlier, had been arrested and convicted on two charges of indecent assault and two charges of performing indecent acts on an eleven-year-old girl. As a condition of parole, he was banned from living with his wife, because she had children. Nonetheless, her landlord evicted her, alleging that her house would become a target for people upset that she was married to a molester. She had nowhere to go, except to live in her car with her children. She had been born and reared in the small community where she lived.

Commentary

IN FRENCH, ONE says "Plus ça change, plus c'est la même chose," or in English, "The more things change, the more they stay the same." That is what Jean Gerson (1363–1429) would have to say were he able to compare the sexology of our own era with that of his own when Europe was reeling from the Black Death. Sex as theological, moral, or legal doctrine is the bridge between Gerson's medieval era and our own. In the intervening six centuries of scholarship, most of it in the last century or so, although there has been the beginning of a scientific sexology, human scientific sexology remains pitifully neglected. In the matter of treatment of sexual dissidence, we really are not much further ahead than was Gerson with his faith in punishment and penance, cold baths, flagellation, prayer, monitors, informants, and wholesome company (Gerson 1706/1987).

At the close of the twentieth century, masturbation phobia no longer holds the preeminence it had held since Gerson's day, but sexual phobia flourishes with respect to homosexuality, explicit sex education in schools, pornography, teenaged pregnancy, sexual harassment, and sexual abuse. Sexual phobia reached an acme on December 19, 1998, when the President of the United States was impeached by the House of Representatives, ostensibly for perjury about sex, but actually for infidelity and receiving fellation, about which he had been less than forthright.

To glance now on the brighter side: a small scientific beginning has been made with sexological pharmacology. The most dramatic and newest discovery is that impotence can be reversed by direct injection into the spongy corpora cavernosa of the penis. The drugs that bring on the erection are alpha adrenergic nerve blocking agents. They prevent the minute smooth muscles of the spongy tissue of the corpora cavernosa of the penis from contracting and squeezing out the blood that holds the penis firm and erect. The substance that relaxes the smooth muscle cells to produce the erection is itself released from their endothelial lining. It is the gas nitric oxide (NO) (Burnett et al. 1992) and is the first discovered example of a gas that acts as a neurotransmitter. It is released and used extremely rapidly, within ten seconds.

The first drug discovered (in 1982) to be an erectile agent was papaverine hydrochloride, a non-narcotic alkaloid from the opium poppy (Wagner and Kaplan 1993, 78). It was prescribed either alone or combined with phentolamine. In 1986 it was more or less supplanted by prostaglandin E1 (PGE1), a hormone that occurs naturally throughout the human body. It induces vasodilation.

The most talked about and most widely used erection inducing drug is Viagra, first marketed in April 1998. It is a pill, taken orally, in anticipation of a sexually stimulating encounter. In the corpora cavernosa of the penis, Viagra potentiates smooth muscle relaxation and erection by inhibiting the intracellular level of the enzyme phosphodiesterase (PDE) type 5, thus enhancing the effect of nitric oxide (Moreland et al. 1998).

These new findings on the neuropharmacology of reversing erectile deficiency in the lovemap have not yet been shown to bear any relationship to their counterpart, namely the neuropharmacology of treatment for the sex offending lovemaps of the paraphilias. There are only two forms of treatment, both previously examined in this chapter. One is to deplete the supply of androgen in the male. The other is to increase the supply of serotonin, which is an inhibitor of sexuality in the male.

The oldest method of depleting the body of its supply of androgen is by means of surgical castration. Surgical castration was without rival until the so-called chemical castrators, the synthetic hormones MPA (medroxyprogesterone acetate) and CPA (cyproterone acetate) appeared in the mid-1960s (see pp. 214–15). These synthetic hormones are not genuine castrating agents as their antiandrogenic action is reversible upon cessation of treatment. The primary target of these and other antiandrogenic agents are variously the gonads, producers of progesterone, testosterone, and estrogen, differentially in males and females; the pituitary, producer of gonadotropic hormones; and the anterior hypothalamus, producer of GnRH (gonadotropin releasing hormone). The final common pathway of these different agents is the depletion of androgen, regardless of other side effects. However, in no single instance does an androgen depletor guarantee a paraphilic suppression in all suitable subjects, regardless of the route of suppression. Nonetheless, the covert assumption, still unproved, on which all the androgen depleting agents depend is a quantitative one, namely that androgen is the cause of all male sexuality—and hence the less androgen, the less sexuality; and, conversely, the more androgen the more sexuality.

The history of the advent of each new androgen suppressant tends to have followed the same course. Initially, there is a report on the outcome of treatment in a single case, or a very small sample of cases selected for successful treatment. Data on the incidence of the outcome of unsuccessful treatment have tended not to be accepted for publication. It is more or less covertly assured that an androgen depleting agent will unmask a normophilic lovemap of male/female copulation in pairs. This assumption does not hold up against the criterion of absolute androgen loss by means of surgical castration. Moreoever, it is statistically impossible to get a randomly selected normophilic control group, since many putatively normophilic controls do not disclose data that may be self-incriminating. Instead, it is necessary to replace a randomly selected control group with a randomly selected clinical comparison or contrast group—which is rarely done.

All the foregoing misgivings notwithstanding, it does appear that the androgen depleting agents, namely the hormonal antiandrogens and the SSRI (selective serotonin reuptake inhibitors), have tapped into different parts of the still undeciphered cascade of events that regulate different sexual expressions and lovemap pathologies. We know more than did our nineteenth-century forebears, but still not enough. Except by trial and error, we do not know how to match efficacy of treatment with the agent of treatment and the individual patient. We lack a unifying theory that accommodates the action within the brain of both the androgen-depleting hormones and the selective serotonin reuptake inhibitors (SSRIs).

The androgen depletion agents were provided with an empirically tested, age old theory from animal husbandry, namely that castration depletes testosterone which, in turn, increases the docility of domesticated farm and household male animals. Increased docility applies specifically to dominance and mating rivalry. There is no animal model for the paraphilias and, therefore, no animal model on which to test the efficacy of androgen depleting agents on paraphilias in human beings.

As compared with the castration-docility theory, there was no theory with which to explain the serotonergic neuropharmacology of paraphilias and their treatment with SSRIs and lithium. Their efficacy, which is sporadic and not predictably regular, was discovered serendipitously in the course of treating patients with two diagnosed syndromes, namely, depression and obsessive compulsive disorder (OCD). The coexistent, paraphilic syndrome proved to respond favorably to the medication prescribed for the primary complaint.

The connection between paraphilia and OCD is that paraphilic ideation and imagery is obsessionally fixated and its enactment is compulsive. The connection of paraphilia with depression is that both syndromes are prone to periodicity, with nonsymptomatic periods alternating with symptomatic ones.

Prozac (fluoxetine), the widely acclaimed antidepressant SSRI, was the first to bring to attention a sexually suppressant side effect, namely prolonged delay in achieving orgasm and ejaculation in males. This side effect is, at least on the surface, potentially a plus in the treatment of premature ejaculation. In cases of paraphilia, however, it is outweighed by another side effect, namely vividly eidetic Prozac dreams (Nelson Cooper personal report; Money et al. 1991) in which horrifying paraphilic ideation and imagery are unmasked in night terrors.

Whenever periodicity is a feature of any diagnosable condition, there is always the possibility that in the nonsymptomatic period, the condition will appear to have gone into remission. A spontaneous remission may thus be misconstrued as a successful effect of treatment. This possibility is overlooked in most of the literature, presumably as there is no concomitant measurable effect of spontaneous remission.

Periodicity wreaks havoc among sexologists who, working within the criminal justice system, do not use the medical concept of relapse, but the legal concept of recidivism. They publish voluminously on the prediction of recidivism. This is the equivalent of predicting death from a heart attack, in that it is possible to construct actuarial tables, but not to make a prophecy that a particular individual will die from a heart attack on a specified occasion.

For sexologists in the criminal justice system, notably those whose primary qualification is in psychology or social work, there is a theory behind their attempts to predict and prevent recidivism. It is the theory of behavior modification. The metaphysical assumption behind prison controlled behavior modification is that all individuals are responsible for all of their behavior. If they fail to exercise this responsibility, then a program of reward and punishment will nudge them into doing so. The sexological ramifications of a sex-segregated prison life are not taken into account. An imprisoned heterosexual or homosexual male or female adult pedophile will have no real-life test of potential recidivism, except at second hand, in imagination.

Imagination may turn behavior modification end up, as it is possible to become addicted to deprivation and abuse—as in the case of a prisoner who was an exhibitionist, and a recidivist while still incarcerated for life. Deprived of all contact with female prison personnel, he arranged for a fellow inmate to stab his bladder through the abdominal wall. The wound necessitated female nursing care, and the chance to exhibit his penis to a female.

Recidivism has led to the application of behavior modification to a new clinical practice, namely, relapse prevention. It assumes that a paraphile can be trained, by behavior modification procedures, not to have a relapse—which is equivalent to assuming that a temporal lobe epileptic can be trained not to have another seizure. The split between exclusively pro or con behavior modificationists in sexology is the same as the split between exclusively pro or con social constructionists. It does much harm to the credibility of sexology as a scientific discipline.

Perhaps the next wave in understanding the etiology and natural history of the paraphilias and their treatment will come from genetically engineered animal studies, knocking out some genes or splicing in others, to ascertain what happens to sexuality in behavior and in the brain (see also chap. 4, above). Then normophilic sexuality will be better understood, also. The study of animals cloned so that they have the same genome promises to open up entirely new vistas on the effect of contrived experimental differences in the prenatal intrauterine environment as well as in the postnatal extrauterine environment. Although the technology is not yet in place, it should eventually be possible to correlate changes engineered in the genome with corresponding changes in brain functioning that can be identified by brain imaging technology. In the science fictional future, through informative science and technology, it may become possible to read out paraphilic ideation and imagery directly from the neuronal pathways and centers in the brain.

The most serious handicap to the advancement of human sexological research in the third millennium might very well be dubbed the Gerson handicap, in recognition of his affirmation of the theological, moral, and legal ideology of all expressions of sexuality both normal and abnormal. The persistence of these ideologies into the present means that illegal forms of sexuality cannot be studied preventively and without the prejudice of self-incrimination, unless the subject has already been convicted. Hence the skewed preponderance of paraphilic research toward those who have been accused or who are already in detention. The exception is for those whose paraphilia is not illegal but who constitute a skewed sample of the total population of paraphiles. This is hardly a heritage to boast about next century!

There are two American ideological codes of sex that third millennium sexologists will inherit from their predecessors. One is puritanical and the other sportive. The former prescribes total abstinence and chastity from childhood through puberty and adolescence, virginity until marriage, and monogamous fidelity after marriage. Total abstinence includes abstinence from masturbation. Sportive sex is allowable, if at all, only within the bounds of monogamy.

The sportive ideology, although ostensibly applicable to females as well as to males, allows husbands more leeway than it does wives. This ideology is recognized variously in folk sexological adages as "sowing your wild oats while young," as the postmarital "seven year itch," and as in the adage "life begins at forty." Within the population of the United States, there are local class and ethnic variations as to what constitutes sportive sex. For many American young men between the ages of adolescence and marriage, sportive sex is a measure of manhood. Rivalries arise as a sequel to the relative scarcity of sex-sportive women. They issue in violence, false charges of rape, and, among those already married, legal action for divorce or other penalties. For younger people, the protocol of sportive sex is to engage in it and to protest a disavowal if the news leaks out onto the grapevine. If you are young enough and your mother doesn't believe you, then you get your mouth washed out with soapy water. This is the American way which gets many people into trouble, accused on grounds of sportive sex.

Do what you do sexually, but be sure to keep it hidden from the sex police. The price of arrest is the price America pays for having a Janus-faced ideology of sex. It inflates the cost of self-incrimination beyond the reach of sportive sex research in the millennium ahead.

The two great engines that propel change in the way people relate morally to one another are demographics and technological innovation or borrowing. Demographically, this is the era of the HIV/AIDS pandemic which is wreaking havoc with the young adult and infantile population everywhere, but most notably in Africa, India, and southeast Asia. HIV/AIDS changes the age ratio of a population.

One way in which a population's sex ratio is altered is by selective abortion of female fetuses, as happens in regions of the planet where population density is excessive and where male heirs are valued more than females are. Very soon in those regions there will be a shortage of nubile females and an excess of young men for whom a traditional marriage will be unattainable. Young marriage and pregnancy, prior to the mother's exposure to the HIV epidemic, may become the new ideal.

The most far-reaching technological innovation on the present moral horizon is in genetics—mapping and sequencing the human genome, genetic engineering, cloning, and who knows what next? Exploration of space and Internet informatics are both close followups.

Technological innovations and demographic shifts will surely leave their imprint on the lovemaps of human sexuality. No one, however, has the lenses of clairvoyance to see what these imprints will be.

Paraphilic lovemap pathologies must, in the meantime, be conceptualized as chronic conditions that cannot yet be eradicated. They can, however, be monitored and brought under control with the help of medication and nonjudgmental talking therapy. Treatment necessitates compliancy when symptoms are brought under control. It is easy for the paraphile to be self-convinced that his/her symptoms will never come back. Also, the cost of treatment may become too expensive to pay. Compliancy then falls by the wayside, for which society has only the institution of costly reimprisonment, if the paraphilia is criminalized.

Epilogue

After having been sealed and unseen for thirty-two thousand years in the caverns of the Grotte Chauvet in south-central France, the immense paleolithic drawings of the last ice age were revealed to modern eyes for the first time at the end of 1994 (Balter 1999). It is impressive enough to see reproductions of the great totemic beasts outlined and shaded in charcoal and red ochre, but one needs to stand within the caves to get the full impact of their artistic achievement. This I was lucky enough to do forty years ago at Altamira in northwestern Spain, before those caves were climatized and closed to sightseers in order to prevent deterioration of the paintings. The impact of this stone-age imagery on me was more indelible than I would know at the time, for my mind has kept returning to the artists and their art.

In my mind's eye, I look up to the ceiling of the cave and I see a Michelangelo on a scaffolding, lying on his back, drawing with his arm stretched upward, foreshortening the features of the animal and making allowances for the bumpy surfaces and angles of the cave surface. He sees what he has drawn either by the glowing embers of a fire or by the candlepower of an oil or grease-burning lamp.

On the basis of technical virtuosity alone, there is no doubt that the paleolithic ice-age painters of Altamira, Lascaux, and Chauvet of ten to thirty-odd-thousand years ago were intellectually as well endowed as we, their descendants, are today. How else did they apply their intellects? There is no answer to this question except in science fictional history.

My own essay into science fictional history is that the great painted caverns of the paleolithic were sacred places. In the course of subsequent millennia, they gave rise to other underground sacred places, as in the burial places of ancient Egyptian kings, even up to the twentieth century in Spain's basilica in the Valley of the Fallen, which is really General Franco's self-monument in the interior of a mountain.

Today's basilicas, cathedrals, and temples are designed by their very grandiloquence to be awe inspiring. The painted caverns of the paleolithic still have that same power. We are today awe stricken. No doubt those to whom they were first revealed were awe stricken, too. Their awe was enhanced, maybe, by some paleolithic Timothy Leary's discovery of the hallucinogenic power of magic mushrooms. Those with sufficient charisma, claimed divine power as priestly rulers and ceremonial officers of the caverns and were acclaimed by an enchanted congregation.

As in religions everywhere, ruler priests of the paleolithic doubtless knew that the source of their power lay in their understanding of what, indeed, they may lay claim to have discovered: namely, the psychology of behavior modification. The principles of behavior modification are to reward conformity and punish nonconformity, both here and, especially, in the hereafter.

Paleolithic ruler priests imbued with the psychological principle of behavior modification would know as ruler priests still know today that the years of childhood are the sure fire years for imprinting the principles of reward and punishment. Presumably, they knew also that some manifestations of human behavior are more malleable than others. For example, fasting and the menu are malleable, but not the total abolition of food intake. Sexual behavior is particularly susceptible to behavior modification restrictions since total abstinence is not totally incompatible with existence.

There is no technology presently available by which to ascertain whether or not the great paleolithic cave paintings did or did not have anything to do with either sexual celebration or sexual regulation and taboo. If it is correct that in the course of human evolution the great principles of religion evolved only once, then the religious sexual taboo was invented only once. Sexual taboo maintained a very firm foothold in European and Asiatic religious systems. In Amazonia and New Guinea, the sexual taboo either did not penetrate, or it was lost. In Polynesia, the big taboo was not sexual but on sacrilege of the dead and their burial places.

In pre-Christendom and Christendom, antisexualism and the sexual taboo maintained very firm roots that might very well have paleolithic origins dating back to twenty thousand or more years ago. Small wonder, then, that the sexual taboo not only resists uprooting today, but also severely hinders the investigations of sexology as science. The sexual taboo also gets a politician in trouble for what everyone knows in colloquial speech as getting oral sex whereas officially it is referred to chastely as perjury or obstruction of justice. How did paleolithic ruler priests talk about it twenty thousand years ago? Did they too use only evasions and circumlocutions? Is it possible that the sexual taboo is so ancient and so powerful that there is no foreseeable way of making human sexological research respectable? That constitutes a major scientific challenge for the third millennium.

Terminology of the Paraphilias

The purpose of this terminology list is to allow the reader to recognize each paraphilia by name and by a short definition of the type of sexuoerotic fixation for which the name stands. For the sake of brevity, sexuoerotic is shortened to erotic, but it is understood that genital sexual performance and the achievement of orgasm in paraphilia is contingent on the ideation and imagery of the erotic fixation. It is understood also that in paraphilia affectionate love is of the spirit and is deconnected from carnal lust which is of the flesh, even to the point of having different partners for love and lust.

The number of paraphilias varies as an artifact of diagnosis. For example, a foot fetish and a rubber fetish may be diagnosed not as two simplex paraphilias but as a single multiplex paraphilia. Multiplex paraphilias are named by their most inclusive manifestation, e.g., asphyxiophilia even though asphyxiation is clustered with transvestism, masochism, and klismaphilia (Boglioli et al., 1991).

In Greek, according to the *Oxford English Dictionary (OED)*, *para* means "beside, beyond, past, to one side, amiss, irregular, subsidiary, or altered." Etymologically, paraphilia means altered love. In Greek, *philia* means, friendship, fondness, affinity for, tendency toward, and love of or liking for (frequently excessive or abnormal). The OED definition of paraphilia is "a condition characterized by abnormal sexual desires." Paraphiliac is both the noun and the adjective for the person with a paraphilia. Paraphile and paraphilic are shorter alternatives.

The OED has no entry for paralagnia, nor is this term listed in medical dictionaries. In Greek, *lagnos* means salacious or lustful. It appears in such terms as urolagnia (urophilia) and scopolagnia (scopophilia) terms which have fallen into disuse. Lagnesis is an obsolete term for erotomania; and lagnosis is obsolete for excessive sexual desire, especially in the male, and in *Dorland's Medical Dictionary* (26th ed.) for satyriasis. Etymologically, *philia* has completely won out over *lagnia*.

Names that may appear to be missing from this list are those that apply to finger and hand fetishism. The omission is not an oversight. It reflects the fact that, unlike foot fetishism, hand fetishism is not commonly seen. The explanation may be in part that the hands are not covered as the feet so often are, and they do not carry a distinctive smell.

It is also not an oversight that this list of the paraphilias does not contain names for food paraphilias. Despite the fact that many foods have a popular reputation of being aphrodisiacs, paraphilic fixation on food stuffs is seldom reported. In part, the explanation may be that eating in public is not forbidden. Quite to the contrary, it is societally endorsed as a prelude to having sex. Thus, the developmental dynamic of paraphilic formation is absent. One exception is token cannibalism which, though only with great rarity, may be revealed in the practices and confessions of serial lust murderers. It then serves the symbolic function of mystically imbuing the cannibal with the spirit of the deceased lover. For the most part, however, eating paraphilias appear to be nonexistent. Rather, it would appear that the orgiastic build up of binge eating, as encountered in bulimia, is a substitute for sexuoerotic orgasm; whereas anorectic fasting represents renunciation of the carnality which a paraphilia endorses. It remains to be ascertained whether food paraphilias are manifested in cultures in which some foodstuffs are classified as for women only, or for men only. Yet another omission that is not an oversight pertains to the sexuoerotic ideation and imagery, with or without paraphilia, of those who were at birth either totally blind and totally deaf. In both of these conditions, the absence of explicit sexuoerotic research data leaves one with nothing to say.

The seven grand stratagems of the paraphilias (see chap. 8) are, to recapitulate, sacrifice and expiation; marauding and predation; mercantilism and venality; fetishes and talismans; stigma and eligibility; solicitation and allure; and protectorship and rescue.

The definition of all seven stratagems employs the concept of the absence of propinquity between the spiritual purity of love, on the one hand, and the sinful carnality of lust, on the other hand. Although this duality may have a religious sound of causality, it has absolutely nothing to do with the cause of an individual's particular paraphilia. It simply reflects the fact that we all grow up in a society that spiritualizes love and carnalizes lust, and the fact that some individuals are more caught up in the split than others are. The seven grand stratagems are seven ready-made paleodigms that can be applied to solving the cognitive dissonance between love and lust. They may provide temporal sequences in an individual's paraphilic development, but they do not provide causal explanations. They are cast in religious and moral terminology, because that is the way sexuality is cast in the society in which our children grow up and live.

* * * * *

abasiophilia: erotic fixation on having a partner who is disabled and requires a wheel chair or other support. From Greek, *a*, not + *basis*, step.

acrotomophilia: erotic fixation on amputees and prostheses. From Greek, *akron*, extremity + *tomé*, a cutting.

adolescentism: erotic fixation on behaving like and being treated as an adolescent. From Latin, *adolescentia*, growing up from childhood.

agalmatophilia: erotic fixation on nude statues (archaic) and, hence, on pliable or inflatable life-sized mannequins. From Greek, *agalma*, image.

amelotasis: synonym for apotemnophilia used chiefly in apotemnophile groups. From Greek, *an*, not + *melos*, limb + *tasis*, attraction.

anal sex: penetration of the anus by a penis or dildo.

andromimesis: erotic fixation on living as a man with breasts and female genitalia and impersonating a male. *See also* gynemimesis.

andromimetophilia: erotic fixation on having an andromimetic partner, i.e., one who is a natal female who mimes or impersonates a man. From Greek, *andros*, man + *mimos*, mime.

apotemnophilia: erotic fixation on becoming an amputee. From Greek, *apo*, from + *temnein*, to cut.

asphyxiophilia: erotic fixation on self-strangulation or self-suffocation. From Greek, *asphuxia*, without pulsation.

autoagonistophilia: erotic fixation on being observed or being on stage or on camera doing live sex performances. From Greek, *autos*, self + *agonistes*, principal dramatic actor or contestant.

autoassassinophilia: erotic fixation on arranging the possibility of one's own masochistic death by homicide. From Greek, *autos*, self, + from French, *assassin*, originally from Arabic, *hasisi*, hashish-eater.

autoerotic death: inadvertent death as a side effect of risky erotic practices; *see* asphyxiophilia; hypoxiophilia.

autonepiophilia: erotic fixation on wearing diapers and being treated as an infant. From Greek, *autos*, self + *nepon*, infant.

Baubophilia: exhibitionism, specifically of the female genitalia. From Baubo, a mythical figure who exposed her genitalia to the Greek goddess Demeter in order to distract her from melancholy while searching for her daughter Persephone, who had been abducted by Hades, god of the underworld.

bestiality: synonym for zoophilia.

biastophilia: erotic fixation on violent and assaultive male or female rape, as compared with sporadic nonviolent, nonconsensual coitus, date rape, or statutory rape. From Greek, *biastes*, rape or forced violation. Synonym, raptophilia.

blow job: vernacular for fellatio.

bondage and discipline: popular name for a form of sadomasochism in which one of the partners (the bottom) is bound and chastized by the other (the top).

catheterophilia: erotic fixation on having a catheter inserted into the urethra. From Greek, *katheter*, a thing let down or put in, from *kata*, down + *hienai*, to send.

chrematistophilia: erotic fixation on arranging to be forced to pay for sex or to be robbed. From Greek, *chremistes*, money dealer.

chronophilia: one of a group of paraphilias involving erotic fixation on a significant age discrepancy between the self and partner. From Greek, *chronos*, time.

Clérambault-Kandinsky syndrome: irrational fixation on unrequited love; erotomania.

cocksucking: vernacular term for fellatio or blow job, which may take place between male and female or male and male, and is illegal in some jurisdictions, but legal in others.

coprolagnia: seldom used synonym for coprophilia.

coprophilia: erotic fixation for eating or smearing feces. From Greek, *kopros*, dung.

cunnilingus: oral sex performed on a vulva, rarely fixated as a paraphilia. *See also* eating pussy; giving head.

date rape: coitus without explicit consent or with consent subsequently withdrawn; possibly attributed to alcohol or other drugs.

death row groupie: slang for erotic fixation on a condemned criminal; hybristophilia.

dominance and submission: vernacular synonyms for respectively, sadism and masochism.

dominatrix: a female in the sadomasochistic professional role of total domination and disciplinary control.

drag queen: colloquialism for a gynemimetic cross dresser who may be also a preoperative transexual.

eating pussy: vernacular for oral sex performed on a female by either a male or a female partner.

ectomorphophilia: erotic fixation on lean body build. From Greek, *ektos*, external + *morphe*, form.

endomorphophilia: erotic fixation on round body build. From Greek, *endon*, internal + *morphe*, form. *See also* ectomorphophilia; mesomorphophilia.

ephebophilia: a chronophilia in which an older person's eroticism is fixated on having a partner of adolescent age only. From Greek, *ephebos*, postpubertal young person. *See also* hebephilia.

erotomania: synonym, seldom used, for the Clérambault-Kandinsky syndrome.

erotophonophilia: erotic fixation on lust murder or serial lust murder. From Greek, *eros*, love, + *phonein*, to murder.

exhibitionism: erotic fixation on explicit, uninvited sexual display of the genitalia to a stranger. From Latin, *exhibere*, to exhibit. *See also* peodeikophilia; Baubophilia.

fellatio: oral sex performed on a penis, rarely fixated as a paraphilia. *See also* cocksucking; giving head.

feminoid: feminine but not female.

fetishism: erotic fixation on some particular talisman or fetish object, substance, or part of the body belonging to the partner. *See also* partialism.

fetishistic and talismanic: one of a group of paraphilias characterized by triumph wrested developmentally from sexuoerotic tragedy by means of a strategy that incorporates sinful lust into the lovemap on the condition that a token, fetish, or talisman be substituted for the lover, since lust irrevocably defiles saintly love.

fetishistic transvestism: erotic fixation on cross dressing as a contingency of masturbation and/or homosexual or heterosexual intercourse.

fisting: erotic fixation on anal intromission, usually homosexual and unilateral, with the partner's hand and arm.

formicophilia: erotic fixation on small creatures like snails, frogs, and insects crawling on the genitalia. From Greek, *formica*, ant.

frotteurism: erotic fixation on sexually close body contact with and rubbing against a stranger in a crowd. From French, *frotter*, to rub.

gerontophilia: a chronophilia in which a younger person's eroticism is fixated on having a partner of parental or grandparental age only. From Greek, *geras*, old age.

gigantophilia: erotic fixation on extreme tallness in the size of a partner. From Greek, *gigas*, superhuman in size.

giving head: vernacular for oral sex between people, either sex male or female; a synonym for either fellatio or cunnilingus.

golden shower: vernacular synonym for urophilia.

group sex: multipartnered sex, but not a paraphilia if sportive and nonfixated.

gynemimesis: erotic fixation on impersonating a female and living as a women with a penis. *See also* andromimesis.

gynemimetophilia: erotic fixation on a gynemimetic partner, i.e., one who is a natal male who mimes or impersonates a woman. From Greek, *gyne*, woman + *mimos*, mime.

hebephilia: synonym, rarely used, for ephebophilia. From Greek, *hebe*, age of manhood and military service, from age eighteen to twenty.

heterophobia: pathological aversion to or fear of heterosexuality. From Greek, *heteros*, other + *phobos*, fear.

homophobia: pathological aversion to or fear of homosexuality. From Greek, *homos*, same + *phobos*, fear.

hybristophilia: erotic fixation on a partner known to have committed an outrage or crime, such as rape, murder, or armed robbery. From Greek, *hybridzein*, to commit an outrage against someone.

hyperphilia: the category of copulatory disorders often associated with paraphilias and characterized by functioning of the genital organs that is above and beyond par.

hyphephilia: a paraphilia of the fetishistic, touchie-feelie type pertaining to textures associated with the human body like skin and hair, hence to leather, feathers, hair, fur, rubber, plastic, and such like. From Greek, *hyphe*, web. *See also* olfactophilia.

hypophilia: the category of copulatory disorders seldom associated with paraphilias and characterized by functioning of the genital organs that is not up to par.

hypoxiophilia: erotic fixation on oxygen deprivation by, for example, strangulation or inhalation which may inadvertently produce death. From Greek, *hypo*, under + oxygen.

infantilism: erotic fixation on acting like and being treated as an infant.

infantophilia: a chronophilia in which an older person's eroticism is fixated on having an infant partner at the diaper age. From Latin, *infans*, child. Synonym, nepiophilia.

isosexual: of the same natal sex; consistently either masculine or feminine in development; bonding between two natal males or two natal females with or without a homoerotic component. From Greek, *isos*, same.

juvenilism: erotic fixation on behaving like and being treated as a juvenile. From Latin, *juvenis*, young person.

kleptophilia: erotic fixation on irrational stealing as prerequisite to erotic arousal. From Greek, *kleptein*, to steal.

klismaphilia: erotic fixation on receiving an enema for sexual arousal. From Greek, *klisma*, enema.

masculinoid: masculine but not male

masochism: erotic fixation on being the recipient of abuse, torture, punishment, humiliation, discipline, bondage and domination, variously mixed. From Leopold von Sacher-Masoch, 1836–95, Austrian author and masochist. *See also* sadism.

master and slave: a variety of sadomasochism in which the subservient partner is abused and deprived if not totally obedient to the dominant partner.

marauding and predatory: one of a group of paraphilias characterized by triumph wrested developmentally from sexuoerotic tragedy by means of a strategy that incorporates sinful lust into the lovemap on the condition that it be stolen, abducted, or imposed by force, since it irrevocably defiles saintly love.

mercantile and venal: one of a group of paraphilias characterized by triumph wrested developmentally from sexuoerotic tragedy by means of a strategy that incorporates sinful lust into the lovemap on the condition that it be traded, bartered, or purchased and paid for, not freely exchanged, since it irrevocably defiles saintly love.

mesomorphophilia: erotic fixation on powerful, compact and muscular body build. From Greek, *mesos*, middle + *morphe*, form. *See also* ectomorphophilia; endomorphophilia.

mixophilia: synonym for scoptophilia. From Greek, *mixos*, intercourse.

mixoscopia: synonym for scoptophilia. From Greek, *mixos*, intercourse + *skopein*, to examine.

morphophilia: a paraphilia involving erotic fixation on a major discrepancy in bodily appearance, size, color, or shape between the partners. From Greek, *morphe*, form.

mysophilia: erotic fixation on self-defilement by smelling, chewing, or otherwise utilizing sweaty or soiled clothing or articles of menstrual hygiene. From Greek, *mysos*, uncleanness.

nanophilia: erotic fixation on extreme smallness in the size of the partner. From Greek, *nanos*, dwarf.

narratophilia: erotic fixation on using words and telling stories commonly classified as dirty, pornographic, or obscene, in the presence of a sexual partner. From Latin, *narrare*, to narrate.

necrophilia: erotic fixation involving not a living partner but a corpse. From Greek, *nekros*, dead.

nepiophilia: a chronophilia in which an older person's eroticism is fixated on infant aged children. From Greek, *nepon*, infant. *See also* autonepiophilia.

normophilia: the category of genital or copulatory function that is either statistically average or, more likely, is ideologically, and possibly arbitrarily, prescribed societally as normal.

nymphomania: in popular usage, an excessive and unrelenting fixation on pursuit of sexuality in a female. From Greek, *nymphe*, nymph + *mania*, madness. *See also* satyromania.

obesophilia: erotic fixation on having a partner of extreme girth. From Latin, *obesus*, having eaten oneself fat.

olfactophilia: a paraphilia of the fetishistic smelly-tasty type pertaining to smells or odors associated with the human body and its functions. From Latin, *olfacere*, to smell. *See also* hyphephilia.

oral sex: stimulation of a partner's genitalia with the mouth.

paraphilia: the biomedical term for the category of sexual and erotic function popularly recognized as kinky and legally classified as perversion. From Greek, *para*, altered + *philia*, love.

partialism: a fetishism in which erotic fixation is on a part of the partner's body, e.g., hair, breasts, legs, buttocks, wrinkles, dental configuration, genital morphology, and so on.

pederasty (pedication): the custom, tracing back to classical Greece, of postadolescent men having younger adolescent male lovers as the recipients of anal intercourse. From Greek, *pais*, boy + *erastes*, lover.

pedophilia: a chronophilia in which an older person's eroticism is fixated on postinfantile juveniles. From Greek, *paidos*, child.

peeping Tom: a voyeur.

peodeikophilia: exhibitionism, specifically of the male genitalia. From Greek, *peos*, penis + *deiknunain*, to show.

petticoat punishment: a vernacular term for a masochistic transvestite practice in which a male, dressed as a school girl or servant girl, gets spanked or otherwise punished.

pictophilia: erotic fixation on viewing pictures, movies, videotapes, or live shows of activities commonly classified as dirty, pornographic, or obscene, alone, in the presence of a sexual partner or as a member of a larger audience. From Latin, *pictus*, painted.

protectorship and rescue: one of a group of paraphilias characterized by triumph wrested developmentally from sexuoerotic tragedy by means of a strategy that incorporates sinful lust into the lovemap, though only on the condition that it serves to protect or rescue someone else's saintly love from being defiled by unwanted carnal attention.

raptophilia: synonym for biastophilia. From Latin, *rapere*, to seize.

renifleurism: erotic stimulation from the odor of urine. From French, *ren*, kidney + *fleur*, flower.

riding bareback: vernacular for an erotic fixation on having sex with multiple partners in defiance of protection against the transmission of sexually transmitted disease (STD) especially HIV/AIDS.

sacrificial and expiatory: one of a group of paraphilias characterized by triumph wrested developmentally from sexuoerotic tragedy by means of a strategy that incorporates sinful lust into the lovemap on the condition that it requires reparation and atonement by way of penance and sacrifice, since it irrevocably defiles saintly love.

sadism: erotic fixation on being the dominant partner in inflicting injury, pain, punishment, discipline, chastisement, humiliation, abuse, and deprivation, variously mixed, either consensually or brutally. From the Marquis de Sade, 1740–1814, French author and sadist.

sadomasochism: combination term for sadism and masochism (S/M) with or without alternation of roles.

satyriasis: satyromania.

satyromania: in popular usage, an excessive and unrelenting fixation on pursuit of sexuality in a male. From Greek, *satyros*, satyr + *mania*, madness. *See also* nymphomania.

scarfing: paraphilic vernacular for self-asphyxiophilia.

scat: paraphilic vernacular term for coprophilia. From Greek, *skatos*, dung.

scopophilia, scoptophilia: erotic fixation on watching others engage in sexual activity, sexual intercourse included. From Greek, *skopein*, to view or examine.

serial lust murder: erotic fixation on serial abduction and murder of partners, usually always males or always females, over an extended period of time.

shrimping: erotic fixation on toe sucking; otherwise an optional act of foreplay.

size queen: male homosexual slang for one who is erotically fixated on very large penises.

skopophilia, skoptophilia: alternative spellings of scopophilia and scoptophilia.

Skoptic syndrome: a fixation on becoming erotically anhedonic and anatomically castrated.

skoptolagnia: *see* scopophilia.

sleepsexing: by analogy with sleepwalking, engaging in sexual activity without waking up.

sodomy: any form of sexual intercourse with a person of the same or the other sex, except penial vaginal copulation; specifically anal intercourse; also bestiality. From the Biblical town of Sodom. Except in legal use, archaic.

solicitational and allurative: one of a group of paraphilias characterized by triumph wrested developmentally from sexuoerotic tragedy by means of a strategy that incorporates sinful lust into the lovemap on the condition that an invitatory act belonging to the preliminary or proceptive phase be substituted for the copulatory act of the central or acceptive phase, thus ensuring that saintly love be not defiled by the sinful lust of penial vaginal penetration.

somnophilia: erotic fixation on intruding upon and awakening a sleeping stranger with erotic caresses, including oral sex, and not involving force or violence. From Latin, *somnus*, sleep.

statutory rape: sexual engagement with a person younger than the juridical age of consent.

stigmatic and eligibilic: one of a group of paraphilias characterized by triumph wrested developmentally from sexuoerotic tragedy by means of a strategy that incorporates sinful lust into the lovemap on the condition that the partner be, like a pagan infidel, ethnically or by religion, unqualified or ineligible to be a saint defiled.

stigmatophilia: erotic fixation on a partner who has been tattooed, scarified, or pierced for the wearing of gold jewelry (bars or rings), especially in the genital region. From Greek, *stigma*, mark.

symphorophilia: erotic fixation on stage managing the possibility of a disaster, such as a conflagration (arson) or traffic accident, and watching it happen. From Greek, *symphora*, disaster.

telephonicophilia: erotic fixation on deceiving or luring a telephone respondent, known or unknown, into listening to and making personally explicit conversation in the sexuoerotic vernacular.

Telephone sex may also be normophilic. From Greek, *tele*, far + *phone*, sound.

top and bottom: vernacular terms for, respectively, sadist and masochist.

toucheurism: erotic fixation on surreptitiously touching a stranger, usually in a crowd, on an erotic part of the body, particularly the breasts, buttocks, or crotch. From French, *toucher*, to touch.

transexualism: transposition of gender identity and role (G-I/R) socially, hormonally, and surgically which is not itself a paraphilia but may be preceded by fetishistic transvestism. The term is used as a diagnosis and as the name of a method of rehabilitation by sex reassignment. From Latin, *trans*, across, + *sexus*, sex.

transgenderism: the newly popular term that comprises all manifestations of gender crossing, including transexualism, transvestism, gynemimesis, and andromimesis.

transvestism: cross dressing but not as as a contingency of masturbation and/or homosexual or heterosexual intercourse and orgasm.

transvestophilia: erotic fixation on cross-dressing as a prerequisite to genitosexual performance. From Latin, *trans*, across + *vestis*, garment.

troilism: three-partnered sex, but not a paraphilia if sportive and nonfixated. Also known as ménage à trois, French for household of three.

uncut: vernacular for males who have not been circumcised, attraction to whom may be an erotic fixation.

urolagnia: synonym for urophilia.

urophilia: erotic fixation on drinking urine, or being urinated upon, or listening to someone urinating. From Greek, *ouron*, urine. Synonyms, Undinism (German), Ondinisme (French), water sports, and golden shower.

vomeronasal organ: a small organ inside the nose and attached to the nasal septum in mammals; it has cells that respond to pheromonal scent molecules that are mating smells.

voyeurism: erotic fixation on surreptitious sexual spying, the spy being popularly known as a peeping Tom. From French, *voir*, to look at. *See also* exhibitionism.

water sports: vernacular synonym for urophilia.

zoophilia: erotic fixation on cross-species sexual interaction, one being human. From Greek, *zoon*, animal.

Annotated Bibilography of Select Reference Sources

Cornog, M., and T. Perper. *For Sex Education, See Librarian: A Guide to Issues and Resources*. Westport, Conn.: Greenwood Press, 1996.
This volume is a thematically systematic and annotated bibliography of books related to sex and sexology.

Francoeur, R.T., ed. *The International Encyclopedia of Sexuality*. New York: Continuum, 1997.
This three-volume encyclopedia is international and transcultural in scope and will be useful for those who want comparative information on various issues of general sexological interest. The section on the United States has been expanded into a fourth volume: *Sexuality in America: Understanding Our Sexual Values and Behavior* (R. T. Francoeur, general ed.; P. B. Koch and D. L. Weis, eds.). New York: Continuum, 1998; Continuum paperback edition, 1999.

Francoeur, R. T., M. Cornog, T. Perper, and N. A. Scherzer. *The Complete Dictionary of Sexology*. New York: Continuum, 1995 (paperback).
Sexological terminology across the board, not restricted to just unusual practices, is broadly covered in this new and expanded edition of an earlier dictionary of sexology.

Frayser, S. G., and T. J. Whitby. *Studies in Human Sexuality: A Selected Guide*. Englewood, Colo.: Libraries Unlimited, 1995.
For easy access to hundreds of systematically collated and annotated journal articles one should consult this second edition.

Heidenry, J. *What Wild Ecstasy: The Rise and Fall of the Sexual Revolution*. New York: Simon and Schuster, 1997.
The title is taken from John Keats's "Ode to a Grecian Urn." The book takes the reader behind the scenes of history with a view from above as well. No other sexological history of our era is so comprehensive.

Love, B. *The Encyclopedia of Unusual Sex Practices*. New York: Barricade Books, 1992.
Love has compiled an expansive lexicon of "more than 750 entries and 150 original illustrations on the world's strange sex activities." These activities are not restricted to paraphilias. They include practices that, even though odd and bizarre by everyday standards, are not rated as pathological provided they are engaged in sporadically and sportively, and are not compulsively fixated.

Bibliography

Abe, K., and M. Ohta. Periodic psychosis of puberty: A review on near-monthly episodes. *Psychopathology,* 25:218–28, 1992.

Abramovich, D. R., L. A. Davidson, A. Longstaff, and C. R. Pearson. Sexual differentiation of the human midtrimester brain. *European Journal of Obstetrics, Gynecology, and Reproductive Biology,* 25:7–14, 1987.

Albert, D. J., M. L. Walsh, and R. H. Jonik. Aggression in humans: What is its biological foundation? *Neuroscience and Biobehavioral Reviews,* 17:405–25, 1993.

American Psychiatric Association. *Diagnostic and Statistical Manual of Mental Disorders,* 3rd ed. Washington, D.C.: American Psychiatric Association Press, 1980.

———. *Diagnostic and Statistical Manual of Mental Disorders,* rev. 3rd ed. Washington, D.C.: American Psychiatric Association Press, 1987.

———. *Diagnostic and Statistical Manual of Mental Disorders,* 4th ed. Washington, D.C.: American Psychiatric Association Press, 1994.

Anderson, L. T., M. Ernst, and S. V. Davis. Cognitive abilities of patients with Lesch-Nyhan disease. *Journal of Autism and Developmental Disorders,* 22:189–203, 1992.

Anthony, G., with R. Bennett. *Dirty Talk: Diary of a Phone Sex "Mistress."* Amherst, N.Y.: Prometheus Books, 1998.

Ariès, P. *Centuries of Childhood: A Social History of Family Life.* New York: Vintage Books, 1962.

Aveling, J. H. *The Chamberlens and the Midwifery Forceps.* London: J. and A. Churchill, 1882/1977.

Balon, R. Pharmacological treatment of paraphilias with a focus on antidepressants. *Journal of Sex and Marital Therapy,* 24:241–54, 1998.

Balter, M. New light on the oldest art. *Science,* 283:920–22, 1999.

Basham, A. L. *The Glory That Was India: A Survey of the Culture of the Indian Sub-Continent before the Coming of the Muslims.* New York: Grove Press, 1959.

Bass, E., and L. Davis. *The Courage to Heal: A Guide for Women Survivors of Child Sexual Abuse.* New York: Harper Perennial, 1988.

Bauman, N. Panic over falling sperm counts may be premature. *New Scientist,* 150(2029):10, 1996.

Beach, F. A. Sexual attractivity, proceptivity, and receptivity in female mammals. *Hormones and Behavior,* 7:105–38, 1976.

Behrman, R. E., R. M. Kliegman, and N. M. Arvin. *Nelson Textbook of Pediatrics,* 15th ed. Philadelphia: Saunders, 1996.

Benjamin, H. *The Transsexual Phenomenon.* New York: Julian Press, 1966.

Benton, D. Hormones and human aggression. In *Of Mice and Women: Aspects of Female Aggression* (K. Bjoerkqvist and P. Niemelae, eds.). San Diego: Academic Press, 1992.

Berlin, F. S., G. K. Bergey, and J. Money. Periodic psychosis of puberty: A case report. *American Journal of Psychiatry*, 139:119–20, 1982.

Berezin, M. A. Masturbation and old age. In *Masturbation: From Infancy to Senescence* (I. M. Marcus and J. J. Francis, eds.). New York: International Universities Press, 1975.

Bick, D., B. Franco, R. J. Sherins, B. Heye, L. Pike, J. Crawford, A. Maddalena, B. Incerti, A. Pragliola, T. Meitinger, and A. Ballabio. Intragenic deletion of the *KALIG-1* gene in Kallmann's syndrome. *New England Journal of Medicine*, 326:1752–55, 1992.

Birkin, A. *J. M. Barrie and the Lost Boys: The Love Story that Gave Birth to Peter Pan*. New York: Clarkson N. Potter, 1979.

Blacker, C. *The Catalpa Bow: A Study of Shamanistic Practices in Japan*. London: George Allen and Unwin, 1975.

Blanchard, R., and P. Klassen. H-Y antigen and homosexuality in men. *Journal of Theoretical Biology*, 185:373–78, 1997.

Blanchard, R., K. J. Zucker, R. D. Siegelman, and P. Klassen. The relation of birth order to sexual orientation in men and women. *Journal of Biosocial Science*, 30:511–19, 1998.

Bobrow, N. A., J. Money, and V. G. Lewis. Delayed puberty, eroticism, and sense of smell: A psychological study of hypogonadotropinism, osmatic, and anosmatic (Kallmann's syndrome). *Archives of Sexual Behavior*, 1:329–44, 1971.

Boglioli, L. R., M. L. Taff, P. J. Stephens, and J. Money. A case of autoerotic asphyxia associated with multiplex paraphilia. *American Journal of Forensic Medicine and Pathology*, 12:64–73, 1991.

Borne, R. F. Serotonin: The neurotransmitter for the '90s. *Drug Topics*, 138(19):108, 1994.

Bradford, J. M. W. The antiandrogen and hormonal treatment of sex offenders. In *Handbook of Sexual Assault: Issues, Theories, and Treatment of the Offender* (W. L. Marshall, D. R. Laws et al., eds.). New York: Plenum Press, 1990.

Bradford, J. Medical interventions in sexual deviance. In *Sexual Deviance: Theory, Assessment, and Treatment* (D. R. Laws and W. O'Donohue, eds.). New York: Guilford Press, 1997.

Brown, D. E. *Human Universals*. New York: McGraw-Hill, 1991.

Bruni, F. Child psychiatrist and pedophile: His therapist knew but didn't tell; a victim is suing. *New York Times*, April 19, 1998, 34.

Bullough, V. *Sexual Variance in Society and History*. New York: John Wiley and Sons, 1976.

Burnett, A. L., C. J. Lowenstein, D. S. Bredt, T. S. K. Chang, and S. H. Snyder. Nitric oxide: A physiologic mediator of penile erection. *Science*, 257:401–3, 1992.

Caher, J. M. *King of the Mountain: The Rise, Fall, and Redemption of Chief Judge Sol Wachtler*. Amherst, N.Y.: Prometheus Books, 1998.

Cairns, F. J., and S. P. Rainer. Death from electrocution during auto-erotic procedures. *New Zealand Medical Journal*, 94:259–60, 1981.

Capellanus, A. *The Art of Courtly Love*. (J. J. Parry, trans.; Frederick W. Locke, ed.). New York: Ungar Publishing, 1978.

Carballo-Diéguez, A. The sexual identity and behavior of Puerto Rican men who have sex with men. In *AIDS, Identity, and Community: The HIV Epidemic and Lesbians and Gay Men* (G. M. Herek and B. Greene, eds.). Thousand Oaks, Calif.: Sage Publications, 1995.

Carlsen, E., A. Giwercman, N. Keiding, and N. E. Skakkebaek. Evidence for decreasing quality of semen during past 50 years. *British Medical Journal*, 305:609–13, 1992.

Carnes, P. *The Sexual Addiction*. Minneapolis, Minn.: CompCare Publications, 1983.

Carrier, J. *De los Otros: Intimacy and Homosexuality among Mexican Men*. New York: Columbia University Press, 1995.

———. Gay liberation and coming out in Mexico. In *Gay and Lesbian Youth* (G. Herdt, ed.). Binghamton, N.Y.: Haworth Press, 1989.

Carter, C. S., I. I. Lederhendler, and B. Kirkpatrick, eds. *The Integrative Neurobiology of Affiliation*. Annals of the New York Academy of Sciences, Vol. 807. New York: New York Academy of Sciences, 1997.

Cauldwell, D. O. Psychopathia transexualis. *Sexology*, 16:247–80, 1949.

Cawte, J. *Healers of Arnhem Land*. Sydney: University of New South Wales Press, 1996.

Cesnik, J., and E. Coleman. Use of lithium carbonate in the treatment of autoerotic asphyxia. *American Journal of Psychotherapy*, 43:277–86, 1989.

Charlifue, S. W., K. A. Gerhart, R. R. Menter, G. G. Whiteneck, and G. S. Manley. Sexual issues of women with spinal cord injuries. *Paraplegia*, 30:192–99, 1992.

Christensen, F. M. *Pornography: The Other Side*. New York: Praeger, 1990.

Clarke, J. W. *On Being Mad or Merely Angry: John W. Hinckley, Jr. and Other Dangerous People*. Princeton, N.J.: Princeton University Press, 1990.

Cohen, M. N. *Lewis Carroll, Photographer of Children: Four Nude Studies*. New York: Clarkson N. Potter, 1978.

Coleman, E., and J. Cesnik. Skoptic syndrome: The treatment of an obsessional gender dysphoria with lithium carbonate and psychotherapy. *American Journal of Psychotherapy*, 44:204–17, 1990.

Coleman, E., P. Colgan, and L. Gooren. Male cross-gender behavior in Myanmar (Burma): A description of the Acault. *Archives of Sexual Behavior*, 21:313–21, 1992.

Comarr, A. E., J. M. Cressy, and M. Letch. Sleep dreams of sex among traumatic paraplegics and quadriplegics. *Sexuality and Disability*, 6:25–29, 1983.

Conn, J. H. Brief psychotherapy of the sex offender: A report of a liaison service between a court and a private psychiatrist. *Journal of Clinical Psychopathology*, 10:347–72, 1949.

———. Hypno-synthesis: Hypnotherapy of the sex offender. *Journal of Clinical and Experimental Hypnosis*, 2:13–26, 1954.

Connolly, J. L. *John Gerson: Reformer and Mystic*. Louvain: Libraire Universitaire, 1928.

Cooper, A. J. Auto-erotic asphyxiation: Three case reports. *Journal of Sex and Marital Therapy*, 22:47–53, 1996.

Cordier, B., F. Thibaut, J. M. Kuhn, and P. Deniker. Traitements hormonaux des troubles des conduites sexuelles. *Bulletin de l'Academie Nationale de Medecine*, 180:599–605, 1996.

Crews, D., ed. *Psychobiology of Reproductive Behavior: An Evolutionary Perspective*. Englewood Cliffs, N.J.: Prentice-Hall, 1987.

————. Unisexual organisms in the behavioral neurosciences. In *Evolution and Ecology of Unisexual Vertebrates* (R. M. Dawley and J. P. Bogart, eds.), Bulletin 466. Albany: New York State Museum, 1989.

Crews, D., and K. T. Fitzgerald. "Sexual" behavior in parthenogenic lizards. *Proceedings of the National Academy of Sciences USA*, 77:499–502, 1980.

Danielsson, B. *Love in the South Seas*. New York: Reynal, 1956.

Denny, D., ed. *Current Concepts in Transgender Identity*. New York: Garland, 1998.

Dewaraja, R., and J. Money. Transcultural sexology: Formicophilia, a newly named paraphilia in a young Buddhist male. *Journal of Sex and Marital Therapy*, 12:139–45, 1986.

Dittmann, R. W., M. E. Kappes, and M. H. Kappes. Sexual behavior in adolescent and adult females with congenital adrenal hyperplasia. *Psychoneuroendocrinology*, 17:153–70, 1992.

Ellis, H. *Studies in the Psychology of Sex*, Vols. 1–6 (copyrighted 1900–1910). Philadelphia: F. A. Davis, 1920.

Evans, E. P. *The Criminal Prosecution and Capital Punishment of Animals*. London: Faber and Faber, 1987.

Everaerd, W. A. A case of apotemnophilia: A handicap as sexual preference. *American Journal of Psychotherapy*, 37:285–93, 1983.

Fedoroff, J. P. Buspirone in the treatment of transvestic fetishism. *Journal of Clinical Psychiatry*, 49:408–9, 1988.

————. Antiandrogens vs. serotonergic medications in the treatment of sex offenders: A preliminary compliance study. *Canadian Journal of Human Sexuality*, 4:111–22, 1995.

Fedoroff, J. P. and I. C. Fedoroff. Buspirone and paraphilic sexual behavior. *Journal of Offender Rehabilitation*, 18(3/4):89–108, 1992.

Fedoroff, J. P., C. Peyser, M. L. Franz, and S. E. Folstein. Sexual disorders in Huntington's disease. *Journal of Neuropsychiatry and Clinical Neurosciences*, 6:147–53, 1994.

Fedoroff, J. P., A. Brunet, V. Woods, C. Granger, E. Chow, P. Collins, and C. M. Shapiro. A case-controlled study of men who sexually assault sleeping victims. In *Forensic Aspects of Sleep* (C. M. Shapiro and A. McCall Smith, eds.). New York: John Wiley, 1997.

Fenwick, P. Sleep and sexual offending. *Medicine, Science, and the Law*, 36:122–34, 1996.

Field, T. M. Massage therapy for infants and children. *Journal of Developmental and Behavioral Pediatrics*, 16:105–19, 1995.

————. Massage therapy effects. *American Psychologist*, 53:1270–81, 1998.

Field, T. M., S. M. Schanberg, F. Scafidi, C. R. Bauer, N. Vega Lahr, R. Garcia, J. Nystrom, and C. M. Kuhn. Effects of tactile/kinesthetic stimulation on preterm neonates. *Pediatrics*, 77:654–58, 1986.

Foucault, M. *The History of Sexuality*. Vol. 1, *An Introduction*. New York: Pantheon Books, 1978.

Foulkes, D. Dream ontogeny and dream psychophysiology. In *Sleep Disorders: Basic and Clinical Research* (M. Chase and E. D. Weitzman, eds.). New York: SP Medical and Scientific Books, 1983.

Franks, L. To catch a judge: How the F.B.I. tracked Sol Wachtler. *The New Yorker*, December, 21, 1992, 58–66.

Freeman, E. W., R. H. Purdy, C. Coutifaris, K. Rickels, S. M. Paul. Anxiolytic metabolites of progesterone: Correlation with mood and performance measures following oral progesterone administration to healthy female volunteers. *Clinical Neuroendocrinology*, 58:478–84, 1993.

Freund, K., H. Scher, and S. Hucker. The courtship disorders. *Archives of Sexual Behavior*, 12:369–79, 1983.

———. The courtship disorders: A further investigation. *Archives of Sexual Behavior*, 13:133–39, 1984.

Frock, J., and J. Money. Sexuality and menopause. *Psychotherapy and Psychosomatics*, 57:29–33, 1992.

Gainer, H., and S. Wray. Oxytocin and vasopressin: From genes to peptides. In *Oxytocin in Maternal, Sexual, and Social Behaviors* (C. A. Pedersen, J. D. Caldwell, G. F. Jirikowski, and T. R. Insel, eds.). New York: New York Academy of Sciences, 1992.

Gastaut, H., and H. Collomb. Etude du comportement sexuel chez les épileptiques psychomoteurs. *Annales Medico-Psychologiques*, 112: 657–96, 1954.

Gerson, J. *De Pollutione Nocturna*. Cologne: Johann Guldenschaff, 1466.

———. *De Confessione Mollicei*. Vol. 2 of *Opera Omnia*, 309 (Louis E. Du Pin, ed.). Hildesheim/New York: Georg Olms, 1987. Reprint of Paris/Antwerp, 1706 edition.

Gijs, K., and L. Gooren. Hormonal and psychopharmacological interventions in the treatment of paraphilias: An update. *Journal of Sex Research*, 33:273–90, 1996.

Gilmartin, B. G. Shyness and Love: Causes, Consequences, and Treatment. New York: Lanham, 1987.

Ginsburg, J. Tackling environmental endocrine disrupters. *Lancet*, 347: 1501–2, 1996.

Gitlin, M. J. Psychotropic medications and their effects on sexual function: Diagnosis, biology, and treatment approaches. *Journal of Clinical Psychiatry*, 55:406–13, 1994.

Green, R. *"The Sissy Boy Syndrome" and the Development of Homosexuality*. New Haven: Yale University Press, 1987.

———. *Sexual Science and the Law*. Cambridge: Harvard University Press, 1992.

Green, R., and J. Money. Incongruous gender role in boys: Nongenital manifestations in prepubertal boys. *Journal of Nervous and Mental Disease*, 130:160–68, 1960.

———, eds. *Transexualism and Sex Reassignment*. Baltimore: Johns Hopkins University Press, 1969.

Guo, Y. L., G. H. Lambert, and C. C. Hsu. Growth abnormalities in the population exposed *in utero* and early postnatally to polychlorinated biphenyls and dibenzofurans. *Environmental Health Perspectives*, 103(Suppl 6):117–22, 1995.

Hamer, D. H., S. Hu, V. L. Magnuson, N. Hu, and A. M. L. Pattatucci. A linkage between DNA markers on the X chromosome and male sexual orientation. *Science*, 261:321–27, 1993.

Hampson, J. G., and J. Money. Idiopathic sexual precocity in the female. *Psychosomatic Medicine*, 17:16–35, 1955.

Harrison, W., J. Stewart, P. J. McGrath, and F. Quitkin. Unusual side effects of clomipramine associated with yawning. Letter to the editor. *Canadian Journal of Psychiatry*, 29:546, 1984.

Hazelwood, R. R., P. E. Dietz, and A. W. Burgess. *Autoerotic Fatalities*. Lexington, Mass.: Lexington Books, 1983.

Hendricks, S. E., D. F. Fitzpatrick, K. Hartmann, M. A. Quaife, R. A. Stratbucker, and B. Graber. Brain structure and function in sexual molesters of children and adolescents. *Journal of Clinical Psychiatry*, 49:103–12, 1988.

Henican, E. Judge's ties survived her three marriages. *New York Newsday*, November 10, 1992, 3 ff.

Herdt, G. H. *Guardians of the Flutes: Idioms of Masculinity*. New York: McGraw-Hill, 1981.

———, ed. *Ritualized Homosexuality in Melanesia*. Berkeley and Los Angeles: University of California Press, 1984.

———. *The Sambia: Ritual and Gender in New Guinea*. New York: Holt, Rinehart, and Winston, 1987.

Hertoft, P. Nordic traditions of marriage: The betrothal system. In *Handbook of Sexology* (J. Money and H. Musaph, eds.). Amsterdam: Elsevier/Excerpta Medica, 1977.

Hirschfeld, M. *Die Transvestiten: Eine Untersuchung uber den erotischen Verkleidungstrieb*. Berlin: Pulvermacher, 1910.

———. *Transvestites: The Erotic Drive to Cross-Dress* (M. Lombardi-Nash, trans.). Amherst, N.Y.: Prometheus Books, 1991.

Hoenig, J. The development of sexology during the second half of the 19th century. In *Handbook of Sexology* (J. Money and H. Musaph, eds.). Amsterdam: Elsevier/Excerpta Medica, 1977.

Holmgren, B., R. Urba-Holmgren, M. Aguiar, and R. Rodriguez. Sex hormone influences on yawning behavior. *Acta Neurobiologiae Experimentalis*, 40:515–19, 1980.

Hopp, D. H. A new concept of evolution. Abstract. Presented at the U.S. Army Medical Institute of Infectious Diseases, Fort Detrick, Md., May 2, 1980.

Hu, S., A. M. L. Pattatucci, C. Patterson, L. Li, D. W. Fulker, S. S. Cherny, L. Kruglyak, and D. H. Hamer. Linkage between sexual orientation and chromosome Xq28 in males but not in females. *Nature Genetics*, 11:248–57, 1995.

Hucker, S. J., and J. Bain. Androgenic hormones and sexual assault. In *Handbook of Sexual Assault: Issues, Theories, and Treatment of the Offender* (W. L. Marshall, D. R. Laws et al., eds.). New York: Plenum Press, 1990.

Hunter, J. A., and R. Mathews. Sexual deviance in females. In *Sexual Deviance: Theory, Assessment, and Treatment* (D. R. Laws and W. O'Donohue, eds.). New York: Guilford Press, 1997.

Huws, R., A. P. Shubsachs, and P .J. Taylor. Hypersexuality, fetishism, and multiple sclerosis. *British Journal of Psychiatry*, 158:280–81, 1991.

Ignarro, L. J. Nitric oxide as the physiological mediator of penile erection. *Journal of NIH Research*, 4(5):59–61, 1992.

Jay, M. *Gerald/ine: For the Love of A Transvestite: An Autobiographical Episode*. Sandnes, Norway: OutPost Press, 1995.

Jefferson, J. W. Lithium: Still effective despite its detractors. *British Medical Journal*, 316:1330, 1998.

Jones, M. B., and R. Blanchard. Birth order and male homosexuality: Extension of Slater's index. *Human Biology*, 70:775–87, 1998.

Joshi, V. N., and J. Money. Dhat syndrome and dream in transcultural sexology. *Journal of Psychology and Human Sexuality*, 7(3):95–99, 1995.

Kafka, M. P., and R. Prentky. Fluoxetine treatment of nonparaphilic sexual addiction and paraphilias in men. *Journal of Clinical Psychiatry*, 53:351–58, 1992.

Kano, Y. *The Last Ape: Pygmy Chimp Behavior and Ecology* (E. O. Vineberg, trans.). Stanford: Stanford University Press, 1992.

Kaplan, H. S. *Disorders of Sexual Desire and Other New Concepts and Techniques in Sex Therapy*. New York: Brunner/Mazel, 1979.

Karpman, B. *The Sexual Offender and His Offenses*. New York: Julian Press, 1954.

Kendall, S. Well-tuned brains. *Harvard Magazine*, 98(2):19–20, 1996.

Keyes, R. W., and J. Money. *The Armed Robbery Orgasm: A Lovemap Autobiography of Masochism*. Amherst, N.Y.: Prometheus Books, 1993.

Kinsey, A. C., W. B. Pomeroy, and C. E. Martin. *Sexual Behavior in the Human Male*. Philadelphia: Saunders, 1948.

Kline, P. Sexual deviation: Psychoanalytic research and theory. In *Variant Sexuality: Research and Theory* (G. D. Wilson, ed.). Baltimore: Johns Hopkins University Press, 1987.

Komisaruk, B. R., C. A. Gerdes, and B. Whipple. "Complete" spinal cord injury does not block perceptual responses to genital self-stimulation in women. *Archives of Neurology*, 54:1513–20, 1997.

Krafft-Ebing, R. von. *Psychopathia Sexualis with Especial Reference to Contrary Sexual Instinct: A Medical Legal Study*, 12th ed. (F. J. Rebman, trans.). Chicago: Logan Brothers, 1931.

Kravitz, H. M., T. W. Haywood, J. Kelly, S. Liles, J. L. Cavanaugh Jr. Medroxyprogesterone and paraphilias: Do testosterone levels matter? *Bulletin of the American Academy of Psychiatry and Law*, 24:73–83, 1996.

Kreusi, M. J. P., S. Fine, L. Valladares, R. A. Phillips, and J. L. Rapoport. Paraphilias: A double-blind crossover comparison of clomipramine versus desipramine. *Archives of Sexual Behavior*, 21:587–93, 1992.

Kreuter, M., M. Sullivan, and A. Siosteen. Sexual adjustment and quality of relationship in spinal paraplegia: A controlled study. *Archives of Physical Medicine and Rehabilitation*, 77:541–48, 1996.

Lambert, C. Van Gogh's malady. *Harvard Magazine*, 101(3):23–24, 1999.

Langevin, R., J. Bain, G. Wortzman, S. Hucker, R. Dickey, and P. Wright. Sexual sadism: Brain, blood, and behavior. *Annals of the New York Academy of Sciences*, 528:163–71, 1988.

Langfeldt, T. Childhood masturbation: Individual and social organization. In *Children and Sex: New Findings, New Perspectives* (L. L. Constantine and F. M. Martinson, eds.). Boston: Little, Brown, 1981.

Lehne, G. K. Brain damage and paraphilia: Treated with medroxyprogesterone acetate. *Sexuality and Disability*, 7:145–58, 1984–86.

———. Case management and prognosis of the sex offender. In *Handbook of Forensic Sexology* (J. J. Krivacska and J. Money, eds.). Amherst, N.Y.: Prometheus Books, 1994.

Leibowitz, M. R. *The Chemistry of Love*. Boston: Little, Brown, 1982.

Liliequist, J. Peasants against nature: Crossing the boundaries between man and animal in 17th and 18th century Sweden. In *Forbidden History: The State, Society, and the Regulation of Sexuality in Modern Europe* (J. C. Fout, ed.). Chicago: University of Chicago, 1992.

LoLordo, V. M., and M. E. P. Seligman. Richard Lester Solomon (1918–95). *American Psychologist*, 52:567–68, 1997.

Lombroso, C. *Criminal Man*. Montclair, N.J.: Patterson Smith, 1972.

Lorefice, L. S. Fluoxetine treatment of a fetish. *Journal of Clinical Psychiatry*, 52:41, 1991.

Lorenz, K. *King Solomon's Ring*. New York: Thomas Y. Crowell. 1952.

Malin, M. A preliminary report of a case of necrophilia. Paper presented at the 8th World Congress of Sexology, Heidelberg, June 14–20, 1987.

Maple, T. Unusual sexual behavior of nonhuman primates. In *Handbook of Sexology* (J. Money and H. Musaph, eds.). Amsterdam: Elsevier, 1977.

Margulis, L., and M. F. Dolan. Swimming against the current. *The Sciences*, 37(1):20–25, 1997.

Marshall, D. S., and R. C. Suggs, eds. *Human Sexual Behavior: Variations in the Ethnographic Spectrum*. New York: Basic Books, 1971.

Masson, J. *The Assault on Truth: Freud's Suppression of the Seduction Theory*. New York: Farrar, Straus, and Giroux, 1984.

Masters, W. H., and V. E. Johnson. *Human Sexual Response*. Boston: Little, Brown, 1966.

———. *Human Sexual Inadequacy*. Boston: Little, Brown, 1970.

Matthews, M. *The Horseman: Obsessions of a Zoophile*. Amherst, N.Y.: Prometheus Books, 1994.

McClintock, M. K. Menstrual synchrony and suppression. *Nature*, 229:244–45, 1971.

McLean, J. D., R. G. Forsythe, and I. A. Kapkin. Unusual side effects of clomipramine associated with yawning. *Canadian Journal of Psychiatry*, 28:569–70, 1983.

Medlicott, R. W. Paranoia of the exalted type in a setting of folie à deux: A study of two adolescent homicides. *British Journal of Medical Psychology*, 28:205–23, 1955.

Mee, C. L. How a mysterious disease laid low Europe's masses. *Smithsonian*, 20(11):66, 1990.

Meyer-Bahlburg, H. F. L., R. S. Gruen, M. I. New, J. J. Bell, A. Morishim, M. Shimshi, Y. Bueno, I. Vargas, and S. W. Baker. Gender change from female to male in classical congenital adrenal hyperplasia. *Hormones and Behavior*, 30:319–32, 1996.

Meyerson, B. J. Relationship between the anesthetic and gestagenic action and estrous behavior-inducing activity of different progestins. *Endocrinology*, 81:369–74, 1967.

Miccio-Fonseca, L. C. Comparative differences in the psychological histories of sex offenders, victims, and their families. *Journal of Offender Rehabilitation*, 23(3/4):71–83, 1996.

———. *Personal Sentence Completion Inventory*. Burlington, Vt.: Safer Society Press, 1997.

Michael, R. P., and D. Zumpe. 1993. Medroxyprogesterone acetate decreases the sexual activity of male cynomolgus monkeys (*Macaca fascicularis*): An action on the brain? *Physiology and Behavior*, 53:783–88.

Migeon, C. J., and M. G. Forest. Androgens in biological fluids. In *Nuclear Medicine in Vitro* (B. Rothfield, ed.). Philadelphia: J. B. Lippincott, 1983.

Migeon, C. J., G. Berkovitz, and T. Brown. Sexual differentiation and ambiguity. In *Wilkins: The Diagnosis and Treatment of Endocrine Disorders in Childhood and Adolescence*, 4th ed. (M. S. Kappy, R. M. Blizzard, and C. J. Migeon, eds.). Springfield, Ill.: Charles C. Thomas, 1994.

Mistress Jacqueline. *Whips and Kisses: Parting the Leather Curtain*. (As told to C. Tavel and R. H. Rimmer). Amherst, N.Y.: Prometheus Books, 1991.

Moll, A. *The Sexual Life of the Child.* New York: Macmillan, 1912.

Moltz, H. Of rats and infants and necrotizing enterocolitis. *Perspectives in Biology and Medicine,* 27:327–35, 1984.

Moltz, H., and T. M. Lee. The coordinate roles of mother and young in establishing and maintaining pheromonal symbiosis in the rat. In *Symbiosis in Parent-Offspring Interactions* (L. A. Rosenblum and H. Moltz, eds.). New York: Plenum Press, 1983.

Money, J. Phantom orgasm in the dreams of paraplegic men and women. *Archives of General Psychiatry,* 3:373–82, 1960.

———. Sex hormones and other variables in human eroticism. In *Sex and Internal Secretions* (W. C. Young, ed.). Baltimore: Williams and Wilkins, 1961.

———. Discussion on hormonal inhibition of libido in male sex offenders. In *Endocrinology and Human Behavior* (R. P. Michael, ed.). London: Oxford University Press, 1968.

———. Use of an androgen-depleting hormone in the treatment of sex offenders. *Journal of Sex Research,* 6:165–72, 1970.

———. Two names, two wardrobes, two personalities. *Journal of Homosexuality,* 1:65–70, 1974.

———. *Love and Love Sickness: The Science of Sex, Gender Difference, and Pairbonding.* Baltimore: Johns Hopkins University Press, 1980.

———. Paraphilia and abuse-martyrdom: Exhibitionism as a paradigm for reciprocal couple counseling combined with anti-androgen. *Journal of Sex and Marital Therapy,* 7:115–23, 1981.

———. New phylism theory and autism: Pathognomonic impairment of troopbonding. *Medical Hypotheses,* 11:245–50, 1983.

———. Gender transposition theory and homosexual genesis. *Journal of Sex and Marital Therapy,* 10:75–82, 1984.

———. *The Destroying Angel: Sex, Fitness, and Food in the Legacy of Degeneracy Theory, Graham Crackers, Kellogg's Corn Flakes, and American Health History.* Amherst, N.Y.: Prometheus Books, 1985.

———. *Lovemaps: Clinical Concepts of Sexual/Erotic Health and Pathology, Paraphilia, and Gender Transposition in Childhood, Adolescence, and Maturity.* New York: Irvington, 1986. [Paperback, Amherst, N.Y.: Prometheus Books, 1988.]

———. The Skoptic syndrome: Castration and genital self-mutilation. *Journal of Psychology and Human Sexuality,* 1(1):113–21, 1988.

———. Forensic sexology: Paraphilic serial rape (biastophilia) and lust murder (erotophonophilia). *American Journal of Psychotherapy,* 44:26–36, 1990a.

———. Homosexual/heterosexual gender research: From sin to science to secret police. In *Sexology: An Independent Field.* Proceedings of the 9th World Congress of Sexology, Caracas, December 3–8, 1989 (F. J. Bianco and R. Hernandez Serrano, eds.). Amsterdam: Excerpta Medica, 1990b.

———. Paraphilia in females: Fixation on amputation and lameness; two personal accounts. *Journal of Psychology and Human Sexuality,* 3(2):165–72, 1990c.

———. *Biographies of Gender and Hermaphroditism in Paired Comparisons: Clinical Supplement to the Handbook of Sexology.* Amsterdam: Elsevier, 1991a.

———. Semen-conservation theory vs. semen-investment theory, antisexualism, and the return of Freud's seduction theory. *Journal of Psychology and Human Sexuality,* 4(4):31–46, 1991b.

———. *The Kaspar Hauser Syndrome of "Psychosocial Dwarfism": Deficient Statural, Intellectual, and Social Growth Induced by Child Abuse.* Amherst, N.Y.: Prometheus Books, 1992.

———. *The Adam Principle: Genes, Genitals, Hormones, and Gender — Selected Readings in Sexology.* Amherst, N.Y.: Prometheus Books, 1993.

———. Body-image syndromes in sexology: Phenomenology and classification. *Journal of Psychology and Human Sexuality,* 6(3):31–48, 1994a.

———. *Reinterpreting the Unspeakable: Human Sexuality 2000; The Complete Interviewer and Clinical Biographer, Exigency Theory, and Sexology for the Third Millennium.* New York: Continuum, 1994b.

———. *Sex Errors of the Body and Related Syndromes: A Guide to Counseling Children, Adolescents, and Their Families,* 2nd ed. Baltimore: Paul H. Brookes, 1994c.

———. *Gendermaps: Social Constructionism, Feminism, and Sexosophical History.* New York: Continuum, 1995.

———. Evolutionary sexology: The hypothesis of song and sex. *Medical Hypotheses,* 48:399–402, 1997a.

———. *Principles of Developmental Sexology.* New York: Continuum, 1997b.

———. Homosexuality: Bipotentiality, terminology, and history. In *Bisexualities: The Ideology and Practice of Sexual Contact with Both Men and Women* (E. J. Haeberle and R. Gindorf, eds.). New York: Continuum, 1998a.

———. Speechmaps, songmaps, and lovemaps in evolutionary sexology. *Current Psychology of Cognition,* 17:1229–35, 1998b.

———. *Sin, Science, and the Sex Police: Essays in Sexology and Sexosophy.* Amherst, N.Y.: Prometheus Books, 1999.

Money, J., and D. Alexander. Psychosexual development and absence of homosexuality in males with precocious puberty: Review of 18 cases. *Journal of Nervous and Mental Disease,* 148:111–23, 1969.

Money, J., and R. G. Bennett. Postadolescent paraphilic sex offenders: Antiandrogenic and counseling therapy follow-up. *International Journal of Mental Health,* 10:122–33, 1981.

Money, J., and C. Bohmer. Prison sexology: Two personal accounts of masturbation, homosexuality, and rape. *Journal of Sex Research,* 16:258–66, 1980.

Money, J., and J. G. Hampson. Idiopathic sexual precocity in the male. *Psychosomatic Medicine,* 17:1–15, 1955.

Money, J., and M. Lamacz. *Vandalized Lovemaps: Paraphilic Outcome of Seven Cases in Pediatric Sexology.* Amherst, N.Y.: Prometheus Books, 1989.

Money, J., and Pruce, G. Psychomotor epilepsy and sexual function. In *Handbook of Sexology* (J. Money and H. Musaph, eds.). Amsterdam: Elsevier/Excerpta Medica, 1977.

Money, J., and A. J. Russo. Homosexual outcome of discordant gender identity/role in childhood: Longitudinal follow-up. *Journal of Pediatric Psychology,* 4:29–41, 1979.

———. Homosexual vs. transvestite or transexual gender-identity/role: Outcome study in boys. *International Journal of Family Psychiatry,* 2:139–45, 1981.

Money, J., and K. W. Simcoe. Acrotomophilia, sex and disability: New concepts and case report. *Sexuality and Disability,* 7:43–50, 1984–86.

Money, J., and J. D. Weinrich. Juvenile, pedophile, heterophile: Hermeneutics of science, medicine and law in two outcome studies. *Medicine and Law,* 2:39–54, 1983.

Money, J., and J. Werlwas. Folie à deux in the parents of psychosocial dwarfs: Two cases. *Bulletin of the American Academy of Psychiatry and the Law*, 4:351–62, 1976.

Money, J., and R. Yankowitz. The sympathetic-inhibiting effects of the drug Ismelin on human male eroticism, with a note on Mellaril. *Journal of Sex Research*, 3:69–82, 1967.

Money, J., C. Wiedeking, P. Walker, C. Migeon, W. Meyer, and D. Borgaonkar. 47, XYY and 46, XY males with antisocial and/or sex-offending behavior: Antiandrogen therapy plus counseling. *Psychoneuroendocrinology*, 1:165–78, 1975.

Money, J., C. Wiedeking, P. Walker, and D. Gain. Combined antiandrogenic and counseling program for the treatment of 46, XY and 47, XYY sex offenders. In *Hormones, Behavior and Psychopathology* (E. J. Sachar, ed.). New York: Raven Press, 1976.

Money, J., J. E. Cawte, G. N. Bianchi, and B. Nurcombe. Sex training and traditions in Arnhem Land. *British Journal of Medical Psychology*, 43:383–99, 1970. Reprinted in J. Money and H. Musaph, eds. *Handbook of Sexology*. Amsterdam: Elsevier/Excerpta Medica, 1977.

Money, J., R. Jobaris, and G. Furth. Apotemnophilia: Two cases of self-demand amputation as a paraphilia. *Journal of Sex Research*, 13:115–25, 1977.

Money, J., M. Schwartz, and V. G. Lewis. Adult erotosexual status and fetal hormonal masculinization and demasculinization: 46, XX congenital virilizing adrenal hyperplasia and 46, XY androgen-insensitivity syndrome compared. *Psychoneuroendocrinology*, 9:405–14, 1984.

Money, J., C. Annecillo, and C. Lobato. Paraphilic and other sexological anomalies as a sequel to the syndrome of child-abuse (psychosocial) dwarfism. *Journal of Psychology and Human Sexuality*, 3(1):117–50, 1990.

Money, J., G. Wainwright, and D. Hingsburger. *The Breathless Orgasm: A Lovemap Biography of Asphyxiophilia*. Amherst, N.Y.: Prometheus Books, 1991.

Monga, T. N., M. Monga, M. S. Raina, and M. Hardjasudarma. Hypersexuality in stroke. *Archives of Physical Medicine and Rehabilitation*, 67:415–17, 1986.

Moreland, R. B., I. Goldstein, and A. Traish. Sildenafil: A novel inhibitor of phosphodiesterase type 5 in human corpus cavernosum smooth muscle cells. *Life Sciences*, 62:309–18, 1998.

Morell, V. A new look at monogamy. *Science*, 281:1982–83, 1998.

Moritz, C. Parthenogenesis in the endemic Australian lizard *Heteronotia binoei* (Gekkonidae). *Science*, 220:735–37, 1983.

Moser, C. S/M (sadomasochistic) interactions in semi-public settings. *Journal of Homsexuality*, 36 (2):19–29, 1998.

Moser, C., and J. J. Madeson. *Bound to Be Free: The SM Experience*. New York: Continuum, 1996.

Mulaikal, R. M., C. J. Migeon, and J. A. Rock. Fertility rates in female patients with congenital adrenal hyperplasia due to a 21-hydroxylase deficiency. *New England Journal of Medicine*, 316:178–82, 1987.

Nanda, S. *Neither Man Nor Woman: The Hijras of India*. Belmont, Calif.: Wadsworth, 1990.

National Guidelines Task Force. *Guidelines for Comprehensive Sexuality Education*. New York: Sex Information and Education Council of the U.S., 1991.

Nelson, R. J., G. E. Demas, P. L. Huang, M. C. Fishman, V. L. Dawson, and S. H. Snyder, Behavioral abnormalities in male mice lacking neuronal nitric oxide synthase. *Nature*, 378:383–86, 1995.

Neumann, F. Permanent changes in gonadal function and sexual behaviour as a result of early feminization of male rats by treatment with an antiandrogenic steroid. *Endokrinologie*, 50:209–25, 1966.

Niedermeyer, E. *Compendium of the Epilepsies*. Springfield, Ill.: Charles C. Thomas, 1974.

Niragu, J. O. Tale told in lead. *Science*, 281:1622–23, 1998.

Noel, B., and D. Revil. Some personality perspectives of XYY individuals taken from the general population. *Journal of Sex Research*, 10: 219–25, 1974.

O'Halloran, R. L., and P. E. Dietz. Autoerotic fatalities with power hydraulics. *Journal of Forensic Sciences*, 38:359–64, 1993.

Parker, R. Youth, identity, and homosexuality: The changing shape of sexual life in contemporary Brazil. In *Gay and Lesbian Youth* (G. Herdt, ed.). Binghamton, N.Y.: Haworth Press, 1989.

Peele, S., with A. Brodsky. *Love and Addiction*. New York: Taplinger, 1975.

Perkins, A., and J. A. Fitzgerald. Luteinizing hormone, testosterone, and behavioral response of male-oriented rams to estrous ewes and rams. *Journal of Animal Science*, 70:1787–94, 1992.

Perkins, A., J. A. Fitzgerald, and G. E. Moss. A comparison of LH secretion and brain estradiol receptors in heterosexual and homosexual rams and female sheep. *Hormones and Behavior*, 29:31–41, 1995.

Poasa, K. The Samoan fa'afafine: One case study and discussion of transsexualism. *Journal of Psychology and Human Sexuality*, 5(3):39–51, 1992.

Ramachandran, V. S., and S. Blakeslee. *Phantoms in the Brain*. New York: William Morrow, 1998.

Rapoport, J. L. *The Boy Who Couldn't Stop Washing: The Experience and Treatment of Obsessive-Compulsive Disorder*. New York: Dutton, 1989.

Rees, H. D., R. W. Bonsall, and R. P. Michael. Preoptic and hypothalamic neurons accumulate [^{3}H] medroxyprogesterone acetate in male cynomolgus monkeys. *Life Sciences*, 39:1353–59, 1986.

Rey, R., and N. Josso. Regulation of testicular anti-Mullerian hormone secretion. *European Journal of Endocrinology*, 135:144–52, 1996.

Rice, G., C. Anderson, N. Risch., and G. Ebers. Male homosexuality: Absence of linkage to microsatellite markers Xq28. *Science*, 284:571, 1999.

Riddle, G. C. *Amputees and Devotees*. New York: Irvington Books, 1989.

Roes, F. An interview with Sarah Blaffer Hrdy. *Human Ethology Bulletin*, 13(2):9–14, 1998.

Rosenfeld, D. S., and A. J. Elhajjar. Sleepsex: A variant of sleepwalking. *Archives of Sexual Behavior*, 27:269–78, 1998.

Rosler, A., and E. Witzum. Treatment of men with paraphilia with a long-acting analogue of gonadotropin releasing hormone. *New England Journal of Medicine*, 338:416–22, 1998.

Schanberg, S. M., and C. M. Kuhn. The biochemical effect of tactile deprivation in neonate rats. In *Neuroendocrine Control and Behavior: Perspectives in Behavioral Medicine*, Vol. 2 (R. B. Williams Jr., ed.). New York: Academic Press, 1985.

Schanberg, S. M., and T. M. Field. Sensory deprivation stress and supplemental stimulation in the rat pup and preterm human neonate. *Child Development*, 58:1431–47, 1987.

Schlaug, G., L. Jancke, Y. Huang, and H. Steinmetz. In vivo evidence of structural brain asymmetry in musicians. *Science*, 267:699–701, 1995.

Schwartz, A. E. *The Man Who Could Not Kill Enough: The Secret Murders of Milwaukee's Jeffrey Dahmer*. New York: Birch Lane Press, 1992.

Siegel, A., and M. K. Demetrikopoulos. Hormones and aggression. In *Hormonally Induced Changes in Mind and Brain* (J. Schulkin et al., eds.). San Diego: Academic Press, 1993.

Sheldon, W. H. *Atlas of Men: A Guide for Somatotyping the Adult Image for All Ages*. New York: Macmillan, 1970.

Shepher, J. Mate selection among second generation kibbutz adolescents and adults: Incest avoidance and negative imprinting. *Archives of Sexual Behavior*, 1:293–307, 1971.

Sherer, D. M., P. C. Eggers, and J. R. Woods Jr. In-utero fetal penile erection. *Journal of Ultrasound in Medicine*, 9:371, 1990.

Sherwin, B. B. A comparative analysis of the role of androgen in human male and female sexual behavior: Behavioral specificity, critical thresholds, and sensitivity. *Psychobiology*, 16:416–25, 1988.

Shirozu, H., T. Koyanagi, T. Takashima, N. Horimoto, K. Akazawa, and H. Nakano. Penile tumescence in the human fetus at term: A preliminary report. *Early Human Development*, 41:159–66, 1995.

Skinner, B. F. *Science and Human Behavior*. New York: Macmillan, 1953.

Smith, E. M., and D. R. Bodner. Sexual dysfunction after spinal cord injury. *Urologic Clinics of North America*, 20:535–42, 1993.

Snyder, S. H. Nitric oxide: First in a new class of neurotransmitters? *Science*, 257:494–96, 1992.

Solomon, R. The opponent-process theory of acquired motivation. *American Psychologist*, 35:691–712, 1980.

Spiro, M. *Children of the Kibbutz*. Cambridge: Harvard University Press, 1958.

Stiles, H. R. *Bundling: Its Origin, Progress, and Decline in America*. Facsimile edition. Chester, Conn.: Applewood Books/Globe Pequot Press, n. d.

Stoller, R. J. *Perversion: The Erotic Form of Hatred*. New York: Pantheon, 1975.

———. *Observing the Erotic Imagination*. New Haven: Yale University Press, 1985.

Suggs, R. C. *Marquesan Sexual Behavior*. New York: Harcourt, Brace, and World, 1966.

Sulloway, F. J. *Freud, Biologist of the Mind: Beyond the Psychoanalytic Legend*. New York: Basic Books, 1979.

Tennov, D. *Love and Limerence: The Experience of Being in Love*. New York: Stein and Day, 1979.

Thibaut, F., B. Cordier, and J. M. Kuhn. Gonadotrophin hormone releasing hormone agonist in cases of severe paraphilia: A lifetime treatment? *Psychoneuroendocrinology*, 21:411–19, 1996.

Tissot, S. A. *A Treatise on the Diseases Produced by Onanism*. Translated from a new edition of the French, with notes and appendix by an American physician. New York: Private, 1832. [Facsimile reprint edition in *The Secret Vice Exposed! Some Arguments Against Masturbation* (C. Rosenberg and C. Smith-Rosenberg, eds.). New York: Arno Press, 1974.]

Tomkins, S. *Affect, Imagery, Consciousness, Cognition: Duplication and Transformation of Information*, Vol. 4. New York: Springer, 1992.

Veenhuizen, A. M., D. C. Van Strien, and P. T. Cohen-Kettenis. The combined psychotherapeutic and lithium carbonate treatment of an adolescent with exhibitionism and indecent assault. *Journal of Psychology and Human Sexuality*, 5(3):53–80, 1992.

Waal, F. B. M. de. *Good Natured*. Cambridge: Harvard University Press, 1996.

Waal, F. B. M. de., and F. Lanting. *Bonobo: The Forgotten Ape*. Berkeley and Los Angeles: University of California Press, 1997.

Wachtler, S. *After the Madness: A Judge's Own Prison Memoir*. New York: Random House, 1997.

Wagner, G., and H. S. Kaplan. *The New Injection Treatments for Impotence: Medical and Psychological Aspects*. New York: Brunner/Mazel, 1993.

Ward, I. L. Sexual behavior: The product of perinatal hormonal and prepubertal social factors. In *Handbook of Behavioral Neurobiology, Volume 11 Sexual Differentiation* (A. A. Gerall, H. Moltz, and I. L. Ward, eds.). New York: Plenum Press, 1992a.

Ward, O. B. Fetal drug exposure and sexual differentiation of males. In *Handbook of Behavioral Neurobiology*. Vol. 11, *Sexual Differentiation* (A. A. Gerall, H. Moltz, and I. L. Ward, eds.). New York: Plenum Press, 1992b.

Watson, J. B. *Behaviorism*. New York: W. W. Norton, 1930.

West, D. J. Boys and sexual abuse: An English opinion. *Archives of Sexual Behavior*, 27:539–59, 1998.

Westermarck, E. *The History of Human Marriage*, Vol. 2. New York: Allerton, 1922.

Wickelgren, I. Discovery of "gay gene" questioned. *Science,* 284:571, 1999.

Wiedeking, C., J. Money, and P. Walker. Follow-up of 11 XYY males with impulsive and/or sex-offending behaviour. *Psychological Medicine*, 9:287–92, 1979.

Wikan, U. Man becomes woman: Transsexualism in Oman as a key to gender roles. *Man*, 12:304–19, 1977.

Wikman, K. R. van. *Die Einleitung der Ehe: Eine vergleichend ethno-soziologische untersuchung uber die vorstufe der ehe in den sitten des schwedischen volkstums*. Acta Academiae Aboensis, Humaniora, XI.1, Abo, Sweden: Abo Akademi, 1937.

Wille, R., and K. M. Beier. Castration in Germany. *Annals of Sex Research*, 2:103–33, 1989.

Williams, W. L. *The Spirit and the Flesh: Sexual Diversity in American Indian Culture*. Boston: Beacon Press, 1986.

Wilson, C. A., I. Gonzalez, and F. Farabollini. Behavioural effects in adulthood of neonatal manipulation of brain serotonin levels in normal and androgenized females. *Pharmacology Biochemistry and Behavior*, 41:91–98, 1992.

Wolpe, J. *The Practice of Behavior Therapy*. New York: Pergamon Press, 1969.

Worth, D., and A. M. Beck. Multiple ownership of animals in New York City. *Transactions and Studies of the College of Physicians of Philadelphia*, 3:280–300, 1981.

Zucker, K. J., S. J. Bradley, G. Oliver, J. Blake, S. Fleming, and J. Hood. Psychosexual development of women with congenital adrenal hyperplasia. *Hormones and Behavior*, 30:300–318, 1996.

Index of Names

Subject Index

mayhem, 75
sadistic procedures, 58
Semen depletion theory
  endangers research, 33
  germ theory, 206
  Hindu culture, 44
  masturbation, 32, 206
  Tissot, 32, 44–45
Semen transfusion theory
  New Guinea and Melanesia, 45, 98
Semenarche
  age of onset, 95, 99
Serial endosymbiosis theory (SET)
  evolution, 127, 171
Serotonin
  BuSpar mimics, 218
  lithium carbonate, 218–19
  male/female neonatal rats, 86
  pharmacology, sex, and yawning,
    164
  SSRIs, 218
Sex chromosome syndromes
  45, X Turner syndrome, 40, 83, 153
  47, XXY Klinefelter syndrome, 42,
    83
  47, XYY supernumerary Y
    syndrome, 83, 151
  46, XX CAH syndrome, 83
Sex education
  abstinence, 108
  aphoristic wisdom, 81
  explicit content tabooed, 81
  good touch/bad touch, 82
  group therapy, 209
  phobia, 226
Sex offenders (offending). *See also*
    Paraphilias
  castration, 75, 210
  CPA and MPA antiandrogenic
    treatment, 213
  demonology and criminology to
    biomedical science, 213
  deviant, 210, 219
  endocrinology explained, 214–16
  libido reducing drugs, 217
  Megan's law, 224
  serotonergic neurochemistry, 218
Sex police
  pornography, 196
  sportive sex research, 231
Sexological history taking
  impostoring, 153–54

Miccio-Fonseca Inventory, 92
  techniques, 65
Sexological pharmacology
  Anafranil, 218
  androgen depletion, 210–16
  BuSpar, 217
  Ismelin, 216–17
  Lithium, 218–19, 228
  Mellaril, 216–17
  nitric oxide (NO), 226
  papaverine hydrochloride, 226
  phentolamine, 226
  prostaglandin E1 (PGE1), 226
  Prozac, 218, 229
  SSRIs, 218, 228
  Viagra, 26, 51, 56, 196, 208,
    226–27
  Xanax, 217
Sexual addiction
  arbitrary norm, 52
  Catch-22 dilemma, 91–92
  fetishistic transvestism, 52–53
  fixation, 52, 54
  lovemap symptoms, 49
  serial infatuation, 48
  Sexoholics Anonymous, 223–24
  sobriety treatment, 109
Sexual apathy and inertia
  hypophilia, 42
  Ismelin, 216–17
  paraphilic tranvestism, 73
Sexual arousal
  eyes vs. nose, 127
  porno pictures failed, 184
Sexual body morphology
  young prison inmate, 64
  visualization of lust, 78–79
Sexual desire. *See also* Nymphomania;
    Satyromania
  apathy and inertia, 42, 73
  insatiable, 52
  lacking, 42
  Viagra, 56
Sexual instinct
  Freudian theory, 117, 119
  Krafft-Ebing, 116
  perversion, 116, 117
Sexual phobia
  flourishes, 226
  presidential impeachment, 226

Of related interest from Continuum

Harriet Evans

Women and Sexuality in China

"Evans is well grounded in both feminist and Chinese studies, which allows her to deepen her analysis with references to China's present-day pop culture and conversations she has had with Chinese colleagues."—*Library Journal*

236 pages

Raymond B. Flannery, Jr., Ph.D.

Preventing Youth Violence
A Guide for Parents, Teachers, and Counselors

"Full of up-to-date scientific references and community resources, this book is essential for those who work with children in any capacity and recommended for all public and academic libraries."—*Library Journal*

160 pages

Robert T. Francoeur, Editor

The International Encyclopedia of Sexuality

Winner of the *Choice* Outstanding Academic Book Award. "An extraordinary, highly valuable synthesis of information not available elsewhere."—*Library Journal*

3 volumes 1,750 pages

Erwin J. Haeberle and
Rolf Gindorf, Editors

Bisexualities
*The Ideology and Practice of Sexual Contact with
both Men and Women*

A scholarly analysis of the whys and wherefores of people
who love people of both sexes. Includes original articles by
Milton Diamond, John Money, Pepper Schwartz, and many
other experts.

288 pages

Dalin Liu, Man Lun Ng, Li Ping Zhou, and others

Sexual Behavior in Modern China
*The Report on the Nationwide Survey of 20,000
Men and Women*

"A groundbreaking study that profile[s] attitudes about everything from premarital sex to extramarital affairs to divorce."
—*Time*

556 pages

John Money

Principles of Developmental Sexology

"Perhaps no one since Freud has provided us with such a blend
of biological and psychological facts, theory, and clinical material intensively integrated into an increasingly coherent picture
of the origins of human experience."—JUNE REINISCH, PH.D.

Charles Moser, Ph.D., M.D., and JJ Madeson

Bound to Be Free
The SM Experience

"Perhaps the first intelligent, fully informed, fact-based discussion of what SM is . . . a perspective that is uniquely accurate, sensitive, and fair in its depiction and interpretation of erotic sadomasochism."—*Library Journal*

216 pages

William E. Prendergast, Ph.D.

Sexual Abuse of Children and Adolescents
A Preventive Guide for Parents, Teachers, and Counselors

A thoughtful and compassionate guide for all those —teachers, students, parents, and others—touched by sexual abuse of themselves and/or those they care for.

336 pages

The Continuum Publishing Company
370 Lexington Avenue
New York, NY 10017
1-800-561-7704
www.continuum-books.com